City Baby

praise for City Baby:

'Unmissable...
an uplifting story of the survival of friendship, principles
and a whole way of life against sometimes overwhelming
odds. Ross Lomas and Steve Pottinger have combined to
produce a fascinating and essential read.'
Louder Than War

'Always compelling'
Record Collector

'Absolutely captivating'
Vive Le Rock

'Fits perfectly on my bookshelf next to *White Line Fever*'
Trust (Germany)

City Baby

Ross Lomas
with
Steve Pottinger

Ignite Books
2013

ISBN: 978-0-9567786-8-0

Typeset by Steve at Ignite.
www.ignitebooks.co.uk

back cover image by Helen Simmonds

Printed and bound in the UK
by Berforts Information Press
Stevenage, Herts.

To Charlotte, Samantha, and Bridget.

This book has been a long time in the making.

I first met Ross when we worked on the Birmingham crew. A little after that, I stage-managed a punk all-dayer. There was Ross, playing bass in GBH. They were brilliant. The crowd loved them. Everyone I knew loved them. No-one had told their story.

So I asked Ross if he'd like to tell his.
He said yes.

The interviews for this book were recorded sitting in the back of my camper van whenever the two of us were both in Brum and had a free day. That was harder to organise than you'd think. But it was worth every minute. It's been a pleasure to work with Ross, he has some great tales to tell, and I hope you enjoy reading the book as much as I enjoyed putting it together.

all the best

Steve Pottinger

If you want to see what else I get up to, you can find more of my work, blogs and short stories, at stevepottinger.co.uk

My original gratitude list was twice the size of an average town's telephone directory. People I know and have met, and thousands that I haven't. Steve suggested I go away and try again. I want you all to know you were on the original list.

Thankyous, apologies, and love to the following:

Nikki Lomas · Barbara Cargill · Barbara Lomas · Donald Lomas · Auntie Pauline · John & Jayne Phipps · Alex Phipps · Daz Barnes · Andrew Simmonds · Helen Simmonds · Kim Lomas · Dan & Jason · 'Auntie' Margaret · Roy Crowton · Tony Quinn · Stephen Fellows · Karen & Ross Johns · 'Big' Graham Bannister · Paul 'Fudge' Rudge · Carol Coombes · Sharon Maher · Sue McCarty · Avril McCarty · Helen Charles · Della Charles · Ybet Molina · John Fletcher · Sharon Fujimoto · Suzi Fujimoto · Linda Aronow · Toscan Elrod · Michel Cook · Juan Jiminez · Kevan Wilkins · 'Big' Mick Hughes · Alan Whitaker · John 'Huggy' Hughes · Harry Davenport · Richard 'Tomo' Thompson · Danny Abrahall · Sally Mason · Hudley Flipside · Frank Visone · Mr & Mrs Visone · Jason Miller · Danny Bianco · Anthony Galetto · Stage Diving Daisy & Steve · Richie & Jesse from Machete · Pete & Sally Wakefield · Pinch Pinching · Matt Graham · Nigel Green · Stuart Simms · Lynn MacKinnon · Adam & Eve's · Lamp Tavern · Market Tavern · the good people of Vlaardingen · Deb Pagell · Rob Jasper · Eddie Tatar · Dave Perkes · Grace Kennelly · Alan Campbell · Tokyo Hiro · Sean 'o' Hill · Chris Fretwell · Cheryl Geary · Lee · Dave Woodard · David Holm · Amy Nicoletto · Satoki Fujita · Moe Holmes · Stagecraft · John 'Pedro' Ennis · John Purcell · Henry Zanoni · Lia Blyth · Thalia Harithas · Jill Bruce, Holly and Lily · Tammy Lees, Jack and George · Sean McCarthy · Andy 'Wilf' Williams · Joe Montanaro · Kai Reder · Karl Morris · Micky Coyle · Drongos For Europe · Colin Abrahall · Jock Blyth · Scott Preece · CJ Union Church of Honolulu · Michele Stanger.

To all Punks, Skins, Rastas and Metalheads, bang on Brothers and Sisters, bang on.

Ross Lomas

snapshot

I knew I was making the biggest mistake of my life.

All day, out on the milk float, doing my rounds, I'd hoped there'd be a message from Jock when I got in, letting me know that he'd got the flu, that the pub had burned down, that aliens had landed in the middle of Birmingham, that *something* had happened, and that the gig was cancelled. Because right now, the idea of getting up on stage was terrifying me.

See, the only times I'd done any performing were all back at school, at Mapledene Juniors. I'd been a knight, I'd danced round the maypole with the other kids, and I'd been one of the three kings - the black one - in the school nativity play. Normal kids stuff. I couldn't see how any of that was going to help, and I really wished I hadn't badgered Jock to let me join his band, because now I was going to get up in front of a room full of punks and play bass, and just thinking about it made me want to throw up, or do a runner.

We were in *the* pub on Birmingham's punk scene, The Crown on Station Street, upstairs in the little gig room which could squeeze in 150 people on a good night - maybe 200 before the floor gave way and you'd find yourself drinking downstairs in the bar - and we were headlining. I think there were eighty people there. Maybe a hundred if you're generous. Most of them were mates, which made it worse, because playing to strangers is a thousand times easier than doing it in front of people you know. I looked out at the audience and recognised Fudge and Mouse and Baby Mark and all the skinheads.

I saw Carol, and Gary Critchley, and my mate Roy Crowton. The Drongos had just finished playing, so they were there, of course, and so were all the old heads, all the Birmingham punks. All paid 80p each to get in, all waiting for us to start our set and finish the night off.

I'd practised, and I knew I could play. If I wasn't the best bass player in the world, at least I could bang out some GBH. That wasn't the problem. But I was quiet and shy, and no way used to being a performer, and I was sure I was going to screw things up. All the way through the first song I was shitting myself, waiting for it all to go wrong. Then I looked across at Colin, and he looked really confident, and that inspired me to think *Come on! What the fuck's the matter with you?* And after that it was fine.

We had ten songs, and we played them all, and threw in a really long version of 'Great Balls Of Fire' and our take on 'Wild Thing' as well, and there was still time for more. So we played some of our songs again, and everyone loved it, even the dodgy characters by the bar. Even me - which was what surprised me most.

I'd been in GBH eight days when I played that gig at The Crown, and by the end of the night I knew I wanted more. I'd loved it. But I never thought it would go anywhere. None of us did.

It's strange how things work out. By 1982 we were touring the UK. The year after that we went to Germany, America, and Canada. Thirty years later, and GBH is still at it. We've never stopped gigging, and we've kept the same line-up, and we're still mates. Still getting up on stage and never quite making a living at it.

This is the story of how we spent thirty years making it up as we go along. It's the story of my life, too. It's about writing songs, travelling the world, and having fun. It's about living without a safety net and - mostly - it's about getting away with it.

All without anything resembling a plan.

city baby

It all started in the *Addams Family* house.

In a street of classic suburban houses, inter-war semis with bay windows and pebble-dashing up the outside walls, ours was the one that wasn't really looked after, the one that let the whole street down. This was where I lived with my dad, who worked for the council as a paver, my mom, who'd been a seamstress when she was younger, then worked at Rover, and ended up as a nursing auxiliary in Solihull maternity hospital, and my sister.

It was out in Sheldon, on the edge of Brum, and to be honest, you wouldn't rush to Sheldon if it wasn't home. I mean, there's not much there – just the Wheatsheaf pub, a few shops, and lots and lots and lots of houses. In 1938, the local paper reported Sheldon had *One cinema in action, fried fish shops, and the various accompaniments of modern civilization!* I guess people got more excited about that back then, but nowadays – well, Sheldon's not a big tourist draw, especially now the cinema's gone.

It was a great place to grow up as a kid. Me and Tony Quinn – my best mate and colleague in crime right through my childhood – played football every hour we could. We climbed trees, scrumped apples, and stole birds' eggs. We lobbed bricks through greenhouses just to hear the glass smash, legged it, and hoped not to get caught. At weekends or in school holidays we'd head over to Sheldon golf-course, and hide out there for the day. We'd nick any golf balls we could lay our hands on, then sell them later. 20p each. A lucrative little side-line which kept us in chocolate, pop, and cigarettes.

4

If the golf-course security came after us, we'd leg it. If they got too close we'd throw golf balls at 'em. And if any of the flashers up there bothered us - every now and then you'd hear a rustle, and a strange man would appear out of the bushes - we'd throw golf balls at them too. All good, clean, healthy fun.

At this point, I still liked school. I was at a tiny little school out on the edge of the city, Mapledene Junior School, which had an eye-catching uniform of green blazer with gold trim, and a gold crest of a maple leaf on the breast pocket. Very *Harry Potter* - except that Mapledene was right next to the runway at Birmingham airport, so the whole building rattled and vibrated each time a plane took off. You'd be halfway through a lesson, and two hundred people would fly over on their way to Alicante. We just thought it was normal.

Discipline was strict. Mr Bates, the teacher, would give you a smack on the back of the legs in the morning, whether you needed it or not, but that was entirely normal. We'd line up, first thing in the morning, before we went in to class, and if we weren't in a straight line - *Slap!* - on the back of the legs. Just to get us ready for the day. That or a cuff round the ear. Nothing malicious in it, just discipline being exercised, a little reminder of where you were. We had it lucky compared to the Catholic schools. Tony's school, Thomas More, was packed with nuns, and the atmosphere was totally different from Mapledene. The nuns smelt of disinfectant, authority, and power, in one unholy trinity, and the kids were really careful not to annoy them in any way at all.

At home, my folks were unbelievably easy-going. There was no racism, no political diatribes, just a good set of values and a Vesta curry on a friday night. My mom would hit me with a frayed old bamboo stick - I think it had been passed down to her from her mom, and her mom in turn, it was practically a family heirloom - if she felt I needed it, but my folks taught me and my sister what was good and what was bad, and left it at that. For the early '70s that was going it some.

My dad loved football. When England got to the World Cup final in '66 he sent me and my mom on a coach trip to Cheddar Gorge for the day so he could watch the game and have some beers with some mates. Which is how I ended up listening to the final on the radio with the world's most miserable coach driver who wanted to be at home watching it on TV as well. England - look away if you don't want to know the score - won, beating Germany 4-2, and now, like every other kid, I wanted to play football every waking minute, to be Geoff Hurst, or Bobby Moore, or Nobby Stiles. So my dad took me along to watch Birmingham City.

My memories are of everyone drinking in the pubs round the ground till the last minute, till five to three, then rushing down to get in. These were the years of *Star Soccer* on ITV, with Hugh Johns. The clock in the corner at the Railway End, advertising Davenports beer. My first pie, my first Bovril. The smell of piss and cigars. The bogs on the Tilton End hidden behind a cloud of steam at half-time as thousands of blokes took a piss on a cold winter's day. Before long, my football heroes were Johnny Vincent, or Trevor Hockey, or any of the Blues players, and Geoff and Bobby and Nobby were last year's news.

My dad didn't just take me down the Blues, he even played football with me, in that kick-it-around-the-back-garden way that dads do. And seeing as I loved football above just about everything else, and played for Mapledene in the school league (started in goal, moved to right wing, very versatile, criminally underrated, best days behind me now) I couldn't have been happier. Right up to the point where he broke his leg.

I was eight. And it was all my fault. That's what I thought, anyway. We'd been playing football in the back garden as usual,

I kicked the ball to my dad, he turned to get it, and his right leg didn't. It stayed where it was, there was an almighty *Crack!* and my dad went down like a sack of spuds. He had a compound fracture of the tibia, he needed six pins and a plate in his leg, he was on the sick for the best part of a year, and I was left riddled by guilt.

So when Mr Bates took me out of class - no-one else, just me - walked me down the corridor to a stock room, and said *Come in here* I thought there was something unpleasant coming, something I probably deserved. He shut the door behind us, pointed at a rack of old school clothes, blazers and the like, and told me *Try one of those on.* My dad was off work, money was tight and was going to be for a while, and my folks couldn't afford a new uniform. The school knew all this, so they sorted everything out, and took me to one side to do it, so the other kids didn't have to know. Again, for the time, that's going it some, I reckon.

It's no surprise my dad never played football with me again - he never quite walked properly from then on - but he did go back to work. And he took me with him. In my school holidays and weekends I helped him build the NEC - the National Exhibition Centre - this brand-new state-of-the-art complex out where the countryside started and the city stopped. It took years. I was only ten when I started, but I'd do a bit of this, a bit of that, a bit of the other. I worked with my dad, landscaping the gardens and the flag mound, I helped mix compo, I fetched people's sandwiches, I made them their teas, and I got a proper wage packet. There were loads of guys working on the job, but I think my presence made all the difference. Take a look at that flag mound if you're not sure - worth £2.50 a week in anybody's money.

That's what the guys clubbed together and paid me: £2.50 a week. Undreamed of riches to a kid. What did I do? I went out and bought an album - and being as Slade's 'Mama Weer

All Crazee Now' was all over the charts, the first one I bought was *Slayed?* Then it was something by Mud, and, later on, Showaddywaddy. Remember them? They had two drummers, and when you're a kid that's really special. So special I went and saw them at the Odeon in 1974, so very special I joined the fan club (Ross Lomas, life member, still owed a few newsletters Mr Bartram, if you're reading).

I also took up smoking.

I was about nine when I started experimenting with cigarettes. Most of the kids I knew smoked, or tried to. Just about every adult we saw had a fag in their hand, and we wanted to be grown-up too. This meant a lot of nine-year-olds in Sheldon smelt strongly of tobacco, and I was one of them. After all, I had ready access - my mom smoked Carltons, and when she was working nights at the hospital, and had left her fags at home, I'd help myself.

At first it was just one or two, but then it got out of hand. You see, Carltons came as two packs of ten in a twenty. So when you finished the first ten you had to rip the silver paper off the other lot to start them. And it got to the stage where my mom'd go out and there'd be fifteen in the packet, then she'd come home and there'd be five or six. So it was pretty obvious what was happening. But she never said anything.

Then one day I must have left one burning in the kitchen, and she came back and said *If you're going to smoke, smoke your own!* and threw a packet of ten Cadets at me. I was a bit older than nine then. Even I wouldn't let a kid smoke at nine. I was thirteen, fourteen, I reckon. And I smoked right up till five years ago, when I stopped in case it stunted my growth.

Football, cigarettes, music, and a bit of manual labour. These early years set the pattern for my life. The odd and the unusual drew me in and intrigued me too. And Sheldon had its fair share of the weird and the wonderful. For starters, there was Vera Caton.

Vera was probably ten years older than me. He always wore an anorak with a purple shirt buttoned up tight, and trousers that were far too short, and he was always walking along in a hurry, leaning forward, rushing along with a brick in his patchwork bag, pretending it was shopping. *Can't stop! Shopping!* and he'd bustle off at speed. Why was he called Vera? I've no idea. He didn't dress as a woman or anything. He was just... Vera. I never thought to ask why.

Now, Vera never went in a shop in his life - why would he when he already had the brick? - but he did run a cinema. For 20p you could go to Vera's garden shed and he'd get his torch, show to your seat on a wooden bench, and sit you down. Then he'd go to his little projection room and get the film ready. Most of the time he got films in before Sheldon cinema did, before they were even released, which meant you got to see them before anyone else. Which was fantastic. And sometimes, if you were short of cash, Vera would let you in if you *pretended* to give him 20p.

But then that was fine, because Vera was only pretending to show films. He showed make-believe films in a make-believe cinema, and when Vera shouted *Interval!* he'd sell you make-believe ice-creams too. It was completely off the wall. It was loads of fun. I went to Vera's right up till I was sixteen, because he had some really good films. I even took a girlfriend once, though I'm not sure she liked the film... There was nothing dodgy about it all. Vera didn't have any 'special' boys, it wasn't as if he got you in the shed to touch you up. He just liked showing films and running a cinema. And shopping. *Can't stop! Shopping! Shopping!*

Vera was wonderful. The loony kid wasn't. You'd be out on the playing fields, having a kickabout, and he'd jump out of the bushes and scare the living daylights out of you, because he was truly odd. He'd stare at you and then he'd ask

Wanna shake my hand?
Wha'?
Come on, shake my hand! Do you love me?
Wha'??!!

Back then, as a kid, I never thought of people doing things with other people in bushes, but a couple of times you'd see someone head into the bushes with him. Grown-ups. Now that I'm older and wiser I know what the crack was. Then, I didn't. He'd disappear, then he'd jump out again a few minutes later.

Wanna shake my hand? D'you love me? Love me in the bushes?
No! I wanna play football! Fuck off!

The boy was my age, and he clearly wasn't all there, and he was being abused, when you come down to it. Well fucked-up. God knows what his mom and dad were thinking.

And then there was the guy on the three-wheeler, on a big old tricycle with a basket on it. He was a midget, he looked like a munchkin, and he wore a bus-conductor's hat. He'd sit at the bus stop in Sheldon all day, on his tricycle, noting down bus numbers, and then he'd pedal off home, and Tony Quinn and me would see who wanted to buy our golf balls.

Looking back, growing up in Sheldon nurtured three talents in me (four if you count my skills down the right wing). I was great at throwing things - golf balls at flashers, or bricks through greenhouses - and I was even better at running away, generally from people I'd thrown golf balls at, or who owned a greenhouse. They were the kind of talents any kid should learn. And on top of that, I'd learned to be curious about life on the fringes, about the Veras of this world.

None of those talents were much use at Mapledene, but I guess I thrived there, as much as any kid who lives for football can. And in the end I passed my 11+, which was pretty good going for someone at a school quite so perilously close to jet engines moving past at speed, and at the end of that summer I turned up at Central Grammar full of enthusiasm for a big adventure. There was a lecture theatre. And a big sports field. Proper teachers with mortar boards and capes. And it was going to be wonderful.

I couldn't have been more wrong. It was a fucking prison.

attacked by rats

I entered Central Grammar full of hope and expectation, and left five years later with no qualifications and an abiding distrust of authority.

What went wrong? Just about everything.

The place was a poisonous mix of the incompetent, the brutal, and the truly fucking bizarre. It had been an all-boys school for over a hundred years, the teachers were all old mortar-board and cape, most of them were gay – not that there's anything wrong with that, but back then they had to keep it under wraps, and we got the brunt of it – and far too many of them had problems and used to take it out on the kids. We'd been brought up to expect a clip behind the ear, or a slap on the legs, but now it all went up a notch or two, or three, because – as teachers – none of them were equipped to deal with teenage boys. Which meant we weren't really taught, just corralled. Kept in one place while our hormones raged, till they sent us out to get a job.

It wasn't education, or anything close. It was a war of attrition, pure and simple. They handed out the beatings, we did our best to make their lives hell, and between us we fought each other to a stalemate.

We had one teacher, who we nicknamed Cag because he had an old Vauxhall which went *cag-cag-cag* as it came up the drive to school. He was Welsh and he taught French and you couldn't understand what he said in English, let alone a foreign language, so he was on a hiding to nothing. Anyway, the slightest little thing and he'd be off. Ranting round the room shouting *I used to fly bombers in the war for cunts like you, you... guttersnipe.* We found this hilarious, so we'd wind him up even more. In return, he'd physically beat us, or throw chairs round the room. He was also the medical officer, so after he'd given you a good beating, he'd say *See you in my medical room at dinnertime.*

You knew what was going to happen when you got there. There'd be a queue of seven or eight kids - usually me, Tony Quinn, David Ashurst, Tony Comerford, Steve Jones and a couple of others - and Cag would open the door. *Come in, Lomas, come in!* all sweetness and light. But as soon as he'd shut the door, it'd be *You fucking bastard!* and he'd chase you round the room and smack the shit out of you. Now the teachers whose staffroom was opposite the medical room knew exactly what was going on - there was no way they could not know - and they never did a thing. You'd open the door, all sweaty and dishevelled, rubbing your arse, and he'd be *Thank you, Lomas. Feel better now, eh? Next! You, Quinn, come in!* And it'd all kick off again with whoever was in there.

If it wasn't Cag, it was someone else. There was this one teacher who kept his slipper in the stockroom. If he was in the mood, it'd be *Come in the stockroom, Lomas!* and you'd go in the stockroom and he'd get *Fang,* his plimsoll. I mean what kind of guy gives his slipper a name? I can't remember his name now, but I do know he was a ju-jitsu expert, and when he got you in that stockroom he'd truly plimsoll the fucking shit out of you.

Or there was Mr Peck the art teacher, Gregory Peck to one and all. He'd come up behind you and start massaging your neck *Oh no, here we go...* because he was another martial arts expert, and he'd massage your neck till he found the spot, and he'd press. And you'd be out cold while Gregory moved along to the next victim, wafting round the art room, round his domain, leaving a trail of unconscious boys behind him.

There was no point in complaining to anyone about all this. Where would you go? The deputy head? Not a chance. He was another weird fish. In fact, I don't think there was a teacher in the school who didn't have something strange about them. Every single one had a quirk. But the deputy head was particularly odd. If you were in detention – and I was in detention a lot – he'd make you do this thing where you had to dance across the floor with your knees together. What that was about, god knows. I dread to think. If you hadn't danced to his satisfaction he'd give you a *Thwack!* with this big long ruler, then get you to do it again. Pain and humiliation, and no escape, until I sussed that even if the detention room was on the second floor, you could jump out of the window and land safely on the grass outside. So I'd dance my way over to the window, open it, tell him *Fuck you!* jump out, and leg it. There was one exception to this: if detention was in the library, you were stuffed. The windows were too high to climb out of, so you were trapped in detention for the full hour, dancing with your knees together.... And *then* you had to deal with the goat.

The walk home from Central Grammar was a mile-and-a-half, through the fields and over the train tracks, and in the fields was the goat. A nasty, old, foul-tempered goat. You'd be on your way back from detention in the winter, in the dark, a group of thirteen-year-old schoolboys, and suddenly one of you would go flying through the air. And you knew. You knew the goat was out there in the darkness, waiting. But you couldn't see a thing, and you'd no idea where he was... And then he'd sneak up behind another one of you, and butt you into the middle of next week. It was terrifying. We knew how to fight back against teachers. Against the goat we didn't stand a hope.

So between the teachers and the goat, we were pretty much screwed. But just in case that wasn't enough, there was sport. In the summer, it wasn't so bad. Mr Weightman, the sports teacher, who was an upstanding bloke, didn't rely on beating the crap out of you to show who was in charge, and I actually looked forward to his lessons. He reckoned I had athletic potential, and so he encouraged me, helped me along. He'd have me doing the 100m, 200m, long jump, triple jump, anything like that. All those years of running away from people whose greenhouses I'd broken gave me a natural advantage over the other kids - I'd had years of training they could only dream of. Summer sports were great. Winter was something else entirely.

Probably every kid in the country can remember playing football or rugby at school in winter, on a playing field that was dogshit and mud, with the rain pouring down or a north wind blowing sleet in your eyes. Crying because it was so fucking miserable and cold and your hands were turning blue. And on the touchline there'd be teachers shouting at you to *Pull your socks up! Get on with it!* even if there was inches of snow on the ground and grown men would have given it up as a bad job and gone home. Nothing but nothing stopped school sports. However bad the weather was, you'd be out there, running around in shorts being yelled at by teachers wrapped up in ten layers of clothing or more, big heavy greatcoats, scarves, hats, the fucking works. All that was normal. We probably built an empire on the back of it - I don't know, I hated history.

But sport at Central Grammar was special. First off, you were supposed to play with no underwear on, and then put your kit on. That's how they did it. The teachers who were taking games - some of whom had no Physical Education qualifications whatsoever, by the way - would check to make sure you took your underwear off when you were getting changed. And if you forgot your shorts, tough. You played without your shorts. No excuses, no exceptions.

The more you think about it, the weirder it is. Did they hate us that much? Did they do it for kicks? We were eleven or twelve years old, and if we forgot our shorts, school policy was we played half-naked, wearing our top, and our boots, with our tackle hanging out for the world to see. Puberty was kicking in, so it was an embarrassing time to be running around in front of anyone with your bits out, but there we were, out on the school playing fields, with a couple of teachers who had nothing to do with sport looking on. There was a teacher who reminded me of Norman Tebbit: pinstripe suit, starched shirt, tie, patent leather shoes, perfectly turned out. He never looked you in the eye, he'd always flick his gaze away. He wasn't even taking the lessons, but he'd be there every week, watching. Just watching.

Is it any wonder I thought school was bullshit?

wagging off*

I've total respect for those kids who knuckled down at Central Grammar, because I think anything they learned and achieved was totally down to them and nothing to do with the teachers. Apart from Mr Weightman I don't remember one single teacher who inspired me to want to learn. The longer I was there, the more I wagged off.

I didn't tell my folks, of course. I'd get up in the morning, put my uniform on, grab some toast, and leave for school. I just never quite got there. Instead I'd hang out in the park with my mates, playing football and baiting the wag-man. The Birmingham City Council Truant Officer, to give him his proper title. We'd wait till he got about ten yards away, then give him the fingers and take off. When it came to sprinting I was one of the best. *You little bastard! Come back here!*

Nope. Ain't never going to happen.

We got to know Les the park keeper, the ex-boxer, and we'd sit with him in his office while he told us his old war stories, or tales of life in the ring. Sometimes we'd have a few cans, and a couple of roll-ups, and if Will Sheehy brought his home-made poteen - his dad had a still in the back garden - we'd get slaughtered. Roll-ups and poteen could get messy, and then Les would open up the dressing rooms for us and let us have a kip. Or if Charlie Wag-man came round looking for us, we'd hide in one of the lock-ups and Les would cover for us. He was a diamond bloke.

Life was slowly taking shape. I loved football - I'd wag school for a kickabout, to go to Blues away games, or even to

* *wag off (v): to play truant, to be absent from school.*

watch their reserve games – and I hated school. It seemed to me like school just got in the way of all the important things in life, like football, like hanging about with my mates, or listening to someone like Les talk about his life. Any of that sure as hell beat the shit out of being leered at by teachers when you'd forgotten your shorts.

I still went along to school about as often as I wagged off, but there was only one day when I actually looked forward to it. And that was the day we amalgamated with Byng Kenrick School, next door.

Byng Kenrick was an all-girls school, the other side of a wire-mesh fence from Central Grammar, and we must have amalgamated when I was about thirteen. Before that, separation was rigorously imposed. You could only have the most fleeting of contact through that wire-mesh fence before the spotlight came on, the tower guards started firing, and the alsatians were unleashed. *Step away from the fence, Lomas!* Watching the girls on the other side was like looking at another species. And then we amalgamated, and the world turned upside-down.

Some of our teachers couldn't handle it. Suddenly they had to be in contact with females, and for a couple of them this was the final straw, and their resolve broke. Our school, being all-boys, had been one of the last sanctuaries for men who really didn't like women or girls at all. And now it was gone, and half of every class was girls. I remember going to school the first day after we'd amalgamated, and it was different. It smelt... fragrant. And it was full of girls we'd never seen or talked to before, other than through the fence. It was like the Berlin Wall coming down. There were boys brim-full of testosterone, and girls in short skirts with shirts unbuttoned down to here, and all of us going *Whoo-hoo!* walking around with a spring in our step and a glint in our eye.

There were new lessons in fraternisation, exploration,

and naughtiness. Tony Quinn didn't waste any time at all. I can't remember the girl's name - and perhaps she should stay nameless - but they were in the Domestic Studies block, and Tony was... performing... with about ten of us looking through the window at him, cheering. Then Mr Hutton turned up, barking *What's going on here? Move, boys! Move!* He pushed his way through us, and suddenly he didn't know where to put himself or what to do. I don't think he'd seen anything like it before. Complete apoplexy. That set the tone from there on in, for Tony at least. He was always one step ahead when it came to girls. Not like me. I was still too shy to talk to girls. One of them came up to me once, and asked if I wanted a shag.

Fuck off! I told her *I'm playing football!*

I mentioned it to Tony, and of course he was in there like a shot. But nothing interfered with my football. Nothing.

It changed the whole atmosphere of school, that amalgamation. Any half-naked sports were entirely extra-curricular now, not on the rugby pitch. And there were a whole raft of new teachers, with a different set of quirks. Mr Jones would bring his girlfriend to sports on fridays in summer, and get her to measure the long jump, wearing a short skirt with no underwear. They obviously knew just what they were doing, the two of them, and they were getting off on it, while we didn't know where to look. At that age, you can't believe she knows what she's doing, exposing herself, but you do find yourself looking forward to summer games....

Is your girlfriend coming today, sir?
No, she's not, Lomas.
Thwack!

I even put myself down for the school trip to Wales. A weekend in the countryside, with a trip to a hydro-electric power plant and an old mine, and the opportunity to broaden our horizons under the supervision of the accompanying teachers. It wasn't that I'd developed an interest in energy-generation, more that this was a mixed group, and Tony Quinn had convinced me I needed to make up for lost time. That had to be worth a few hours trundling up the A5 in an old blue Commer van.

So we got to our base, a couple of cabins next to a hydro-electric dam, and that afternoon the teachers took us down to the local village, with pen and paper, and told us to note down traffic flow and the like. We weren't daft. We knew this was just to keep us out of the way while they went down the pub smoking and drinking, but seeing as it gave us a chance to mingle with the girls, we were fine with that. It gave us time to make plans.

At the end of the day, they segregated us: girls would sleep in the one cabin, we'd sleep in the other. And with that came the obligatory warning: *You're not allowed out of your billet till morning!* Five minutes after the lights were out, Tony and myself - inspired by a childhood spent watching *Escape From Stalag Luft III* - had rolled up our spare clothes and left them heaped under our blankets so it looked like we were still in bed, then sneaked across to the other cabin for a bit of cross-pollination. We'd no sooner got in there and jumped into bed with the girls than 'click!' the lights went on. The teachers were waiting for us. *Quinn! Lomas! 'Raus!* and we trooped back, under guard and in disgrace. Again.

Just because girls had turned up, it didn't mean anything had changed, not for the hard-core of us who thought the whole business of education was bullshit. Being at school was still like being at war. Being beaten over nothing, and forced to play sport half-undressed for teachers' entertainment had turned me into an angry young man who wasn't going to back down for anyone. In every war, there are casualties. You just try and make sure it's not you. Mr O'Shea, the Physics teacher, who had a lovely voice, and would sing with us on Paddy's Day, he had a breakdown. The fifth-formers pushed him, and pushed, and pushed till he cracked, and next thing he was dancing around on the tables in the laboratory, kicking over bunsen burners left right and centre, and doing an Irish jig.

As for Cag, he had a heart attack, right there in the classroom. He broke down crying, slumped into a chair, then he went grey. I remember him saying *You boys don't know what you're doing to me....* Someone went and got another teacher, and they took him away in an ambulance, and all I could think was *Fuck him, I really don't care* because by now I had no interest in learning anything. It was us or them, and by this point I'd rather it was them.

Some teachers got caught in the crossfire. Like the RE teacher, a really shy woman who joined us after the amalgamation. She shouldn't have been teaching kids, not kids like us anyway, because we took advantage. Mercilessly. What cracked her up in the end was teaching us about Judaism. She had to mention circumcision, and that meant using words she'd never normally say, and saying them to a class of smirking teenage boys. The thought terrified her. She tried to get round it by mumbling really quietly.

So they have to cut the ......
What, miss?
They cut the...erm... pe....
Sorry, miss. Can't hear you!
The... the... pe...
The what, miss??
Penis! Penis! FUCKING PENIS!!!!

And she was never the same again.

There was quite a high attrition rate among the teachers. Were we particularly horrid as a school? I really can't say. By the point all this was happening, I'd no interest in learning anything. Maybe it was simply in my nature to give it the Vs. Everyone's got it to a degree haven't they? I had it then, I have it now. But school brought it right to the fore, and left me with no tolerance for authority figures who abuse their position. Even now, if someone tries to order me around, to make out they know a whole bunch and I know nothing, then I won't have it. Looking back, I feel kind of sorry for those kids who did want to learn and get on with it, but I wasn't putting up with that shit. Not then, not now, not ever.

It's no surprise I got expelled. It's just a surprise it took so long. I wasn't at school much, and when I was there I wasn't an attentive pupil. I walked out of the only exam I sat. There were two hundred kids sitting in the sports hall in deathly silence, and I thought *This is bullshit! Why should my whole future hang on how I do in an exam?* So I got up and walked out. The teachers tried to stop me, but they couldn't. And at the end of that year, my fourth year in secondary school, the report I got made it clear the school had given up on me, too.

What a waste of a young man's life. This boy has done nothing, and will achieve nothing.

If I could remember what he looked like I could give this boy a report.

I didn't go back till next term, the autumn of 1977. I was in the fifth-form, and more unbiddable than ever. The end came in November, when I smacked this teacher for trying to confiscate my cigarettes. The bell had gone for the end of the day, and I was on my way home, still on school property but two yards from freedom. I'd got my cigarettes out, though I hadn't actually sparked up, and this teacher grabbed me. So I smacked him, and that was pretty much that.

For the next week I played the old trick, and pretended to my parents I'd gone to school each day while I waited for the postman to come with the inevitable letter, so I could intercept it. Sure enough, a few days later it dropped through the letterbox. I opened it, read it, and was outraged. *...vicious assault... blah blah.... serious breach... unless Ross apologises... blah blah blah... meeting... sort this out or he cannot be a member of this establishment...*

I couldn't believe it. Why hadn't they expelled me on the spot? And as for *a vicious assault on Mr Foster* - yes, I hit him, but he started it. There was only one thing to do. I wasn't going to show my mom and dad the letter, I was going to deal with this myself.

So I marched up to the school in my t-shirt and jeans, and went straight to the headmaster's office. They had this traffic light system on his door. Green, and you could go in; red, and you had to stand behind a line and wait. I pressed the buzzer. The light turned red. *Fuck this!* I thought, and barged in.

There was the headmaster, sitting behind his desk.

Why aren't you in uniform, boy?!
I waved the letter at him. *I ain't fucking apologising!*
Get out!
Fuck you!

And that was it. I never darkened their doors again. Do I regret it? No. Not at all. The sense of freedom I had when I marched into the headmaster's office, with the expulsion letter in my hand, ignoring the traffic-light system, and confronted him.... it was worth it. I know some people don't rebel, however much they'd want to, because they're scared, or need the job or the money and can't tell the boss to go fuck themselves, but I've lived my life so I don't have to. I do it now, and I did it then, and I've no regrets whatsoever.

I was sixteen.
I hadn't a qualification to my name.
I was finished with school.

And now I was going to be a punk.

punk

It was Xmas Eve before I told my mom I was expelled. She was putting up the Xmas decorations at the time, and she fell off the chair. When she'd got back up on her feet she did the usual *Wait till your dad comes home* routine, but her heart wasn't in it, and he didn't do anything. I don't think he was either bothered or surprised. The wag man had been coming round every week for the past few years anyway. Charlie Wagman, we called him. If I was lying in bed and heard a knock at the front door, I knew it was him. He'd always shout *Hello Mr Lomas!* and I'd hear my dad at the door, going *It's this punk rock thing. You know, what can I do?* He'd shrug his shoulders. *He was all right till this punk rock started.*

In a way, my dad was right. But then he could just as easily have laid the blame elsewhere. If Central Grammar hadn't been such an awful place, punk rock could have simply passed me by. It might just have been another musical fashion I listened to in passing, which I liked but didn't love. But five years at that school, being corralled and beaten rather than educated, was more than enough to make sure I'd never, ever toe the line again. Which meant punk, and its in-yer-face rebellion, were going to be right up my street.

At that age, your early teens, with your body changing and your hormones raging, you're working out who you are, what makes you tick, what you want to do and how you want to look. You're experimenting, come what may. When the first curry house opened in Sheldon, me and Tony Quinn and Dave Ashurst would save our pocket money, go down there, buy a vindaloo, head over the park and have a competition to see who could eat the vindaloo. It was torture by spices, and

we all failed miserably (but did build up our tolerance for cur-
ries, and an addiction to cold cans of Tizer).

I digress, but you get the point. Teenage years aren't just
hard to beat, they're all about exploration. And music's an
important part of that. I'd started off listening to the Glam
stuff, like Slade - I'd spent my first week's wages from the
NEC on buying their album, remember - and then one day
I'd been round my mate Roy's house, wagging off school,
or on a weekend, or whatever it was, and he had a couple of
Alex Harvey albums. That was the moment I realised there
was more to music than what you saw on TV. My musical
exploration began right there. And continued at - of all
places - Comet on the Coventry Road.

Comet was an electrical store, somewhere you'd go to buy
a cheap hi-fi, or a tumble dryer, which makes it an unexpected
choice of record shop. But for some reason which I never
understood, Comet used to sell albums as well as washing
machines. They sold them really cheap, and there was nowhere
else in Sheldon to go. So I'd wander down there with Roy -
who ended up doing the GBH artwork, by the way - and
browse through what they had to offer. I bought the Alex
Harvey I'd listened to at Roy's, and then I saw the cover of an
album called *Stupidity*, by Dr Feelgood. *Hmmm,* I thought, *that
looks interesting.* I'd never heard of them before, but I splashed
out and bought it. £2.40 I think it was. I got home, played it,
and it blew my socks off. I loved it. Well before punk, it was
Dr Feelgood, and Wilko's guitar playing, that made me think
Music! I really want to be doing this. Not in any thought-through
kind of way, just that sense of a possibility that this could be
my thing, something I'd enjoy. There was a long way to go yet
before I'd do anything about it.

I was drifting between scenes. Seeing what was around,
listening to what my friends were into, finding out what

worked for me. There was a whole bunch of people in Sheldon, some of whom would later get involved in punk, who were interested in music generally, that I fed into. There was the Northern Soul community - I went up to Blackpool with them once, and it was carnage - and there were loads of skinheads, too. And it was some of them who talked me into shaving all my hair off, just before my sixteenth birthday. I'd already got my mom to cut my hair short, but although she could turn her hands to most things and was a pretty good hairdresser, it wasn't short enough. So these mates dragged me up the barber's in Sheldon, up Comberton Road, and he just scalped me. The fucking lot came off. And because they used to do it with an open cut-throat razor in those days, when he did round the top of the ears he nicked them, so I came back home with my ears dangling off, and our mom had a fucking heart attack.

So I was getting into music. I was listening to Alex Harvey and Doctor Feelgood, buying music papers and stuff like that. And then I saw the Sex Pistols on the TV and it all kicked off.

Punk rock. The bane of parents' lives all over Britain.

The music that was going to bring the country to its knees, if you believed what you read in the papers. Well, that sounded good enough to me. I'd had it up to here with school, and being treated like shit. I was ready to rebel, and punk felt right.

It wasn't just me, either. Up and down the country, kids were doing the same thing, getting into something that felt like it set them free. There was one girl at our school who was a complete inspiration. She was really quiet, and really shy. If you saw her walking along she'd have her head down, eyes on the ground, minding her own business, and you'd probably never even notice her. And then one day, before punk really took off - I mean she was the first punk I ever saw - she turned up at school and she'd dyed her hair black, she had black eye make-up on, black lipstick, and she was wearing black bin-liners covered in safety pins. I nearly fell off my chair. The teachers couldn't deal with it at all. I remember seeing her getting stopped in the corridor by Mr Hutton, and he was ranting and raving at her, and she was just looking at the ground. And you knew that everything he was saying was just going in one ear and straight out the other, and it was driving him mad and there was nothing he could do about it. My rebellion was nothing in comparison - the top button on my shirt was undone, and I'd safety-pinned the school crest onto my blazer - but Diane Teasdale went straight in at the deep end. In the emerging Birmingham punk scene, this was enough to make her a legend. She was still shy, though. And so was I. Fifteen years slipped by before I finally talked to her. Punk did a lot of things for me, but it didn't make me any less nervous around girls, not for years...

So like I say, I'd been a skinhead, and a wannabe hooligan. Now I was slowly but surely becoming a punk, or at least getting drawn into that scene. The first proper punk gig I ever saw was on Paddy's Day, 1977, in the Odeon on New Street. The Damned supported T-Rex, and it was an amazing gig. I'd sneaked out of the house and caught the bus into town for that one. I was there to see The Damned, but I thought *I'll stick around for Marc Bolan to say I've actually seen him*, and he was great too. The Damned, though, I'd never seen anything like them, they were fucking brilliant. They were only on for fifteen or twenty minutes, but I'll never forget it. I was completely captivated. The songs, the image, the intensity - I loved it all. If I hadn't been before, I was hooked now. From then on, punk took over my life.

There was a pub called The Bulls Head up the Coventry Road, in Hay Mills, which started putting on a disco every

Wednesday, rejoicing in the title of *Vic Vomit's Punk Disco at the Psychedelic Horse at the Bulls Head*, and we'd sneak into that whenever we could. That was an eye-opener. It was completely radical - people wearing clothes with zips and chains on tight drainpipe trousers and so on - and you've got to remember, back then no-one had ever seen anything like that. Dress like that, and you might as well come from another planet. I knew it was what I wanted. All my trousers were the normal baggy cut, so I'd tape them up so I wouldn't look out of place, and make them really tight. Punk was about attitude, and in the early days a lot of punk - like the bin-bag outfit - was do-it-yourself. Cheap, if not what most people would call cheerful.

Vic Vomit's sometimes put on bands, too. The main Birmingham punk band at the time was called Model Mania, and we saw them up there, and a student band called The MPs, who were all right, too. That was a big deal, to me. Punk wasn't something done a million miles away by people you'd never see - it was in a pub just down the road, being played by people you'd bump into in town, who you might know to say *Hallo* to. I got more and more into the music. Back home, I rigged up a 250-watt amp to my record-player. I'd worked out how to do it all by myself, and now the music I loved was blaring out full-blast down the whole street, with cracks appearing in the ceiling... I was listening to all sorts of nastiness. The Alex Harvey Band, and Doctor Feelgood, but a lot of the early punk stuff as well. Like 999....

I nearly got to see them when they played Birmingham in November '77, supporting The Runaways. Nearly, but not quite. I was still at school, and they were going to play at the Odeon, where I'd seen The Damned eight months before, so I wagged off with Tony Quinn and we headed into town with this Svengali-figure from Sheldon called Martin Tupper, who was a big T-Rex fan. It was hours till the gig, so we trawled up the Holiday Inn, where the bands were staying. We found out what rooms they were in, and - bold as brass, with me and Tony in our school uniforms - we took the lift up to the floor they were on and got in their rooms. I've no idea how, or why, but we find ourselves in Joan Jett's room. Next thing, Martin's lying on Joan Jett's bed, with a tampon in his hand, sniffing it.

Now, I was sixteen, and painfully, painfully shy. If I had to talk to girls I didn't know, I'd make funny noises, or make them laugh, because I was so nervous. Or I'd wait fifteen years, like I did with Diane. Sometimes if I was walking down the street and saw a girl walking towards me I'd have to cross the road, so I really wasn't comfortable with being in Joan Jett's room, with a mate sniffing one of her tampons. It put me on edge. What if she comes in? What do I do? What do I say? After what seems like an age, Martin's had enough and decides we should go back down to the lobby. So we get in the lift, and Joan Jett's in there, with the rest of The Runaways.

It was too much. I had all my hormones raging, I've just been in Joan Jett's bedroom, and now there she is, right in front of me. Tight trousers, wonderful arse. I could reach out and touch her if I dared... which was all way, way, waaaaay too much. We got downstairs, and there's 999 who we'd originally gone to see, and Martin's chatting to The Runaways, and we're going to be hanging out with them all. It was perfect, and I couldn't handle it. I just fucked off. Tony hooked up with the bands all day and only came back to Sheldon at the end of the night, getting off the bus waving a pair of drumsticks he'd blagged. Me? I didn't even go to the gig.

He was all right till this punk rock started.

Yeah, dad. That's right.
But Joan Jett's bum was too much for me.

tin soldier

It was The Damned gig that changed everything. After that, I was off. I'd always been wagging school, but through 1977 I was hardly there. There was a small but growing punk scene in Brum, and being part of that was more important to me than anything else. Being expelled from school just sealed the deal, it didn't make any real difference to my life, because by then school had become completely irrelevant to everything I did. The August Bank Holiday gig that year had just confirmed it, because after that - as I remember it - punk in Birmingham really took off.

The gig was at Barbarella's in Birmingham, and it was the first big punk gig I ever went to. I'd heard the Rezillos on John Peel and when I found out they were playing I thought *Yes! I'll have some of that!* So I walked all the way into town from Sheldon with John Phillips, who was one of the first punks in Brum and who used to wear a punk pinstripe suit, and Diane, the bin-bag girl I still hadn't found the courage to talk to. We'd got no cash, which we knew meant getting into the gig could be tricky, but we just reckoned - as you do when you're young and you're skint - that something would turn up.

We were wandering through the city centre when this van pulled up. A punky-looking guy hopped out and said *Take us to Barbarella's, Broad Street.* We didn't give him a chance to change his mind, we just piled in the van. OK, so we weren't exactly sure where Barbarella's was, or how to get there, but he didn't know that. We reckoned we could blag it. And when we guided the van up Broad Street, found Barbarella's, and jumped out of the van with our new friends, The Drones from Manchester, everyone there assumed we were with them. In we all walked, bold as brass. Result! We hadn't just got in the gig for free, we were sitting in the dressing room! With a real band! Chatting to them! It was cramped and tiny, and a bit like having a party in a cupboard, but none of that mattered. This knocked spots off Joan Jett's bum.

How could I not love punk? It was the best and most exciting thing that had ever happened to me. And yet it was around this time that life so nearly took a very different turn. Because that year, after I'd expelled myself from school, and even though I loved being a punk, I applied to join the army.

Remember the day I went back to school to tell the headmaster to go screw himself? Well, I bumped into Mr Bardsley, one of the teachers. *So what are you going to do now, then?* he sneered. Of course, I hadn't a clue. But I wasn't going to tell him that. My mate Steve Jones had been talking about joining up, so quick as a flash I shot back *I'm going to join the army!* Then, just to prove a point, I went down the army recruiting office at The Swan and got an interview. I walked in and the guy asked me *What do you want to do?*

I'd thought about this. I reckoned I knew exactly what I wanted. So I told him *I want to join the band.*

You could see the guy think *Oh god, here we go again.* And he sighed, and put his pen down, and asked *Why?*

Well, I want to play the drums, or something.

My preferred choice was electric guitar, but I was pretty sure that wasn't going to cut it.

He shook his head.

Can't I do that? What's wrong with that?

No, you can't just join the band, you've got to have something you want to do.

Can't I just be a soldier?

No, it doesn't work like that, son, you've got to have something in the army that you're going to do.

This was news to me. I thought you just joined the army, polished your boots, and your gun, and went out and... I don't know... did stuff. I didn't know you had to have some specific skill. But apparently you did. You couldn't just sit around on your helmet waiting for something to happen.... which was what I'd been banking on.

Anyway, by the end of the interview we'd managed to find something we both thought I could do - I can't remember what it was, but it wasn't being in the band - and he booked me a second interview up in Harrogate. Steve Jones was going up the same weekend, but when his mom heard about this, she put a stop to it. As far as she was concerned, I was a bad influence and nothing but trouble and she didn't want me ruining her son's chances of enlisting, so she asked the recruiting guy to send us up at different times, on different days. If she could have made sure we applied to different armies, she'd have done that too.

So Mrs Jones wasn't keen. And nor was my dad. He'd done National Service, of course, and seen active service in Cyprus. Photos of him from that time show him in uniform, smiling, so I'd guessed he enjoyed it. He had two medals, which he'd show me on special occasions.

This one's for seeing active service.
Wow! And what's that one for, dad?
For saving five thousand lives.
Really?!!
Yes, son. I shot the cook.
A good old army joke.... which I was young enough to take at face value.

He didn't like the idea of me joining up though. Everything I suggested, he had a reason I shouldn't do it.

What if I do this?
Oooh, they're the first to get shot.
What about driving trucks?
Ooooh, you don't want to do that.

By my dad's reckoning, it was all too dangerous. Just about everything was likely to get you shot. And if I even thought about being a cook, then he'd shoot me. After all, he had previous.

So I ended up going to Harrogate on my own on the train, which was a bit of an adventure, and I was billeted there for the weekend, while they put us all through our paces. Physical tests, written tests, assault courses, and so on. A little taste of army discipline. They didn't mess around. At one point an NCO marched in and barked at us *Right, if anyone's got a problem with going to Northern Ireland, fuck off NOW!*

Silence. No-one moved. Not even me.

All through my childhood, a lot of the kids I hung round with had been Irish. My best mate, Tony Quinn, was Irish. It wasn't something that mattered, in any way. But the Birmingham pub bombings had happened a couple of years earlier, in 1974, and twenty-one people had been killed. A girl from our school was down one of the pubs, drinking under-age, and she'd died. I remember going past on the bus in the days after and it was all just smithereens. Wilko Johnson, my guitar hero, he said he was on stage at Bogarts that night, just round the corner from The Tavern In The Town, when the bomb went off. He said they came out to see what was happening, and it was just fucking madness....

34

As a result, things in the city were pretty raw. And very confusing. In the days after the bombings, one lad, who'd been a mate, came in to school spouting off about it, repeating what he'd heard off his mom and dad, about how the British shouldn't be in Ireland, and – even though he was a mate – I sparked him. I wasn't ready to hear someone tell me how 'right' it was to blow people up. I don't think I ever will be.

But I never had to find out what it would have been like to be a soldier. In Northern Ireland or anywhere else.

I passed all the tests, but they told me I'd have to go back and finish my schooling before they'd have me. And I went *Nah, that ain't happening.* My mindset was such that there was absolutely no way I was going to go back to school. Not for anyone. And whether they knew this, and it was a handy excuse to fob me off, or whether it was true, I've no idea. My dad was pretty chuffed, though. And so was Mrs Jones.

She got Steve away from my bad influence. He joined up for eleven years.

I'd have to find something else to do.

pinball wizard

Before I got myself expelled from school, before I tried to join the army, I'd had an interview with the careers officer at school. Just the one. I was fifteen, and I loved music and football, so when he asked me if I'd any ideas of what I wanted to do, I told him I wanted to be a roadie. *Don't be so stupid!* he said. *Go away and think about it. What about being a milkman?*

It was typical of Central Grammar. There was no incentive, and no encouragement to do anything that wasn't utterly, crushingly dull. How many other kids got told to think about it, to be realistic, to pass up their dreams at the first hurdle? What sort of people was the school supposed to turn out? Factory fodder? With all those car factories on the doorstep, were we just supposed to know our place? Was that it?

Thanks, but no thanks.

Now, though, my mom was on my case, asking me what I was going to do. So to get her off my back I told her *I'll get a job!* After all, I was sixteen, without a qualification to my name, and a rebellious streak a mile wide. This would be easy. I decided I'd start my search for a job at the Co-op dairy at Garrets Green. They had a reputation for taking on pretty much anyone, so I wandered up there, they looked me up and down, asked me a few questions, and told me *Yes, you can be a milkman.*

I hadn't expected that. At all. I could see my dreams of rebellion going up in smoke, but the good news - so far as I was concerned - was that I couldn't start work until April '78, which meant I had a good few months to dedicate to hanging out, getting by, and doing exactly what I wanted.

Which was being a full-time punk.

Mainly, this involved walking into town because I was skint, and spending the day in the Riviera cafe. This was a proper old cafe on Hurst Street, with lino on the floors and formica tables, an old-fashioned jukebox which blasted out Toots and Maytals every five minutes, and an ancient black guy called Cedric who was part of the fixtures and fittings. He was a great character, always in there, always sitting at the same table, watching the world go by. He'd talk to us, but he had a Jamaican accent so broad I couldn't understand a word he said, so I'd just nod and smile and head over to the pinball machines where I'd hang out with the other young reprobates: Jock, Fudge, Baby Mark, and Teddy Boy Tex. Because the pinball machines at the Riviera - and the ones at Ivan's chip shop in Sheldon - were our lifeline.

They cost 2p to play, but they paid out, too. Not all the time, obviously, but if you got five balls lined up in the right combination there'd be the welcome sound of 2p pieces dropping back into the slot. On a good day you might make enough to spend all day in the Riviera, feeding the machine and nursing a mug of tea or a bottle of Tizer. On a really good day you might make up to £2.00. When a bag of chips cost 5p, 6p, and a pint was maybe 25-30p, this was more than enough to get by, and we'd head out into Brum with our pockets bulging with change, ready to spend it on chips, beer, and records.

Those were our priorities, and would be for years. I'd walk everywhere so that I had more money to spend on records. I'd walk into town from Sheldon, play some pinball, and if my luck was in and the machine paid out I'd head on to the record shop and buy something new. 'She's A Wind-Up', say, by Dr Feelgoood (their first record after Wilko left, cover picture of a woman's breast with a clockwork winder where the nipple should be), or maybe something by the Ramones or The Damned or The Jam. I'd hand over £1.95, all in 2p pieces, and then I'd walk back to Sheldon and play my new purchase to death.

I had lots of time, and no money to speak of. If I didn't win anything on the pinball, I was reliant on begging some pocket money off my folks, or occasionally helping my dad when he and his mate Alan Dyer were doing some painting and decorating on the side. They turned a very blind eye to health and safety, so I'd be called in to help, generally by holding onto Alan's legs three floors up as he was hanging over the side of a building so he could paint it. No-one batted an eye at that. But when we did Handsworth Community School on a Sunday, the Lord's Day, the black religious community were furious. Especially with Alan. He managed a remarkable impression of a stone-deaf black man who'll take eternal damnation on the chin, and then have his cheese and mustard sandwiches, and his tea with Carnation cream, thank you very much. Top bloke.

So for the five or six months before I started work at the dairy, that was how I got by. I was one of the hard-core of half-a-dozen punks who'd come into town in the day, hang out at the Riviera, learn how to work the machines, and hopefully make a couple of quid. If we did, we'd hit the pubs down Hurst Street. If we didn't, we found ways to amuse ourselves that cost us nothing. We got very good at just trolling round town, killing time, and making sure we knew about everything that was going on.

There was a little route we followed. It started at the Riviera, obviously. Then we might nip over the road to Patti Bell's fashion shop. Patti was Birmingham's answer to Vivienne Westwood, and her shop was full of stuff we'd look at but never buy. Everything we wore was strictly DIY. Then we'd wander up to The Crown, see who was hanging out there, and maybe have a pint. In the evening there might be a gig up at Barbarella's, or Rebecca's, or we'd take a walk past Rum Runner, which was the main place the New Romantics hung out, all frilly clothing and make-up. There was quite a bit of cross-pollination with them, the Duran Duran lot, although it wasn't my cup of tea at all. By now, I'd got my mom to use her seamstress skills to take my trouser legs really tight, that proper drainpipe look, and I was wearing home-made t-shirts with *FUCK OFF* sprayed on them. I got pretty handy with a stencil and aerosol paint, and my mom - good as gold - would wash them for me, but turn them inside out before she hung them on the line so as not to offend the neighbours. I even got the idea my t-shirt designs made me some kind of fashion guru, and I took one or two of them in to show Patti Bell. *What do you think? Can I sell any of these?* She took a look. *Yeah… Bring 'em in - we'll see what we can do.* Which I knew was a polite way of telling me *No.* I wasn't going to get rich that way. Back to the pinball.

You see, the pinball suited me down to the ground. It was nice and innocent, and I was good at it. I wasn't into crime at all, but everyone I knew was looking for some way or other to make a bit of cash. There weren't many options, and most of them were somewhere on the dodgy side of legal. There was petty theft. There was mugging people. And there was Bagshot.

The Crown wasn't just a punk pub, it was one of the only 'alternative' pubs in Brum, and it attracted all sorts of people. Gay, straight, indifferent. Miscreants and misfits. Deviants and oddballs. You'd go in there at night and you might be standing next to someone out of ELO, or Steve Gibbons would be in there, hanging out with punks, or Nobby Nobbs, who was hard as nails and had his boxing class upstairs, would be drinking at the bar. Or Colonel Bagshot might be looking for trade.

That wasn't his real name, of course. But it was what everyone called him. He wore jodhpurs and riding boots, and carried a crop, and he'd pop into The Crown looking for someone he could pay to come back to his flat and slap him about a bit. Birmingham's gay scene wasn't really out in the open – Hurst Street was nothing like it is now – but The Crown was near enough to whatever scene there was for him to feel safe. And there were some public toilets outside beneath the little traffic island that had... more activity than you might expect. So if you wanted to make a few bob, and you were that way inclined, Bagshot was an option.

I never went there, but I knew people who did. One mate – a skinhead who's dead now, bless him – had to be restrained once when he got a bit carried away. He kicked the shit out of Bagshot and halfway killed him. OK, the guy liked getting a beating, but it was a hell of a way to earn some cash, even if you were helping him out.

If violence really wasn't your bag but you needed 10p, Bagshot would pay you to ride up the escalator in front of him in the Bullring. You'd fart, he'd inhale. Again, it wasn't something I ever did, though I know plenty of people who did.

What can I say? 10p was 10p. A bag of chips and change. For a lot of people on the punk scene – the ones who were no good at pinball – that was easy money, and a regular income. And better than being skint.

There was always this element of sleaziness and sex on the punk scene. Punks and gays hung out together to an extent, because there were so many other places we couldn't go, where we wouldn't be welcome. And some punks were gay, of course, and some gays liked punk. But it wasn't always sweetness and light. We weren't all gathered together in some rainbow coalition. The truth was more complicated.

Another of the places on the punk scene was a cafe called the Lorica, down by Digbeth Civic Hall, where Cheesy Mick hung out. It was right opposite the coach station and so it got a lot of transient people passing through, which made it the perfect place for Cheesy Mick and his partner to prey on young boys. Or find young boys, anyway. Maybe they were up for it, how would I know? The story goes that if you walked in the Lorica and Mick had left his false teeth in a glass jar on the counter, that meant he'd gone out back with someone and he'd be back in five minutes. But for now he was servicing someone. Or being serviced. Whichever it was. Give him five minutes and he'd be back to do your sandwich, or your cup of tea....

Now Cheesy Mick was harmless enough, and right up till the time when they rebuilt the Bullring you'd bump into him, trawling round the back streets in his old Ford Anglia, looking for young lads. If he saw me and Jock walking along, he'd slow down and wind down the window and peer out

Oh it's you two! No good asking you!
No, Mick, it isn't, See ya!

But his cafe attracted a range of predatory older men, which is why I never went there. A friend of mine had been coerced by one of them into giving him a blow-job. This guy was an intimidating bloke, a good bit older than we were, and he was a bully who used his power to get what he wanted. My mate wasn't gay. What happened left him suicidal.

I don't give a monkey's who you sleep with, or what you do in bed. If you and whoever you're doing it with are happy, that's fine. It's none of my business. But when you force some-one into sex, then - gay or straight - what you're doing is wrong.

What happened to my mate made me more streetwise. If we were somewhere I felt uncomfortable I'd always make sure I was sitting next to someone like Jock, someone I could trust. And one time, when we were sitting in another greasy spoon, Gino's in the Bullring, and a known predator sat next to me, I got up and pushed him away and onto the floor.

Sometimes you had to make a scene. That way everyone knew you weren't fair game.

milk and alcohol

After six months of doing whatever I fancied, getting up at five in the morning for a six o'clock start came as a bit of a shock. But after six months of living hand-to-mouth, a regular wage made it worth it. At the end of my first week as a milkman I picked up my wage packet, my first wage packet since I helped build the NEC, and it was £24.50. *Fucking hell!* I was living at home with my parents, and once I gave them £5.00 for bed and board, that would leave me with loads more money than I could ever hope to win at pinball. And I was paying my way. And I got to drive a little electric milk float too. Jesus, life was good.

One thing I was clear on, though. I would never become a weekender. Being a weekender meant you weren't really being a punk. You were just playing at it, spiking your hair at the weekend. The rest of the week it was straight and so were you. Fuck that. My hair was spiked whether I was out on the town or out on my round. And spiking your hair wasn't easy. Now you just nip down the shops and buy some gel - back then we had to work out what would spike our hair in the first place. Brylcreem? No. Milk? No. Didn't work and smelt bad. Soap? Better than nothing. But if it rained - and in Brum it rained a lot - you'd go to work with spiky hair and end up covered in soap. Luckily the regulars on my round in Kingshurst weren't worried.

I was their punk milkman, and they got used to it. Not all of them liked it, though. One day I went to work with a hole in my jumper, and one miserable old boot took me to task. The world was going to hell in a handcart and it was all my fault. I had a whole string of stock responses for situations like these, but none of them cut any ice with her. First line of defence, offered with a cheeky grin: *It's punk rock, love.*

Nope. She wasn't having that. So I tried the old *I snagged it on a nail* excuse, with a shrug of the shoulders. Life, eh? What can you do?

She wasn't falling for that either. Time for the injured innocence of *Look, I didn't do it on purpose!* But that fell on deaf ears. She was well into her stride now, ranting and raving and pointing her finger. There was only option left.

Bab, I told her, *who gives a fuck?!* I stormed back to my milk float, and roared away, at five miles-per-hour. That showed her.

Life was good. Most afternoons, when I'd finished my round, I'd hang out in Sheldon with my mates, drinking. By early evening I'd be pissed, and wobble home to bed ready for an early start the next morning. If it was the weekend, or there was a gig on, I'd head straight into town from work. There were two or three punk rock milkmen, and you'd see us all at Barbarella's, still in our Co-op tops, giving it large. Because suddenly, after never being sure of where the next penny was coming from, I had money to burn. I could go out as much as I wanted. I could buy people drinks. Beer was 30p or 40p a pint, and £19.50 seemed to last forever.

I met girls, too. I was still pretty nervous round them, and they needed to take an interest in me first, else I'd never do anything, but I was, you know, learning. At the end of October '78 I met a girl with bright pink hair when I was at a gig by a band called Pure Hell, from New York. This was Karen. She'd be my first serious girlfriend, the mother of my daughter Charlotte, and part of my life for many many years.

Even with so much money going on beer, I still had cash to spare. I bought a leather flying jacket, which immediately became my favourite article of clothing. I lived in it. If I was going into town I'd be wearing that, tight jeans and a stripy top, and - naturally - I'd have my hair spiked up. I'm pretty confident that was exactly what I was wearing when I was doing the relief round one week for a milkman who was off sick. Friday came, and I had to collect the money for the week's milk from all the houses on his round. I pulled up outside someone's house in the float and she refused to pay me. Who was I? What had I done with her regular milkman? She got straight on the phone to the dairy to tell them he'd been attacked. Some impostor was trying to steal her money! I could almost hear the sigh come back down the line. *No, that's Mr Lomas. Yes, he is a milkman....*

I had my flying jacket. Next I splashed out on an electric guitar.

It wasn't the first guitar I'd ever owned. Not at all. When I was nine or ten, Mrs Hendricks from down the road fell downstairs in her house, went straight through a plate-glass window, got as far as the phone, and then bled to death before she could ring for help. The silver lining in this cheery little story is that I got her acoustic guitar.

It was a half-size guitar, a little Bert Weedon affair. Perfect for a kid. I learned how to tune it up, and I taught myself a few chords from the Bert Weedon songbook that came with it. I also got Mrs Hendricks' harmonica, but I never played that - every time I looked at it I imagined it full of a dead woman's spit. I concentrated on the guitar. No-one in the family was musical, so progress was slow, but I plodded on. Then Alan Dyer's son Everton bought himself an electric guitar, and I started going round his house and practising with him. I learnt new chords and tunes, and then I bought my own electric guitar. And the world opened up.

Everyone knew everyone in the punk scene in Brum, so finding someone else into music wasn't difficult. There was a punk house down in Stechford I used to visit with Karen, and sometimes Big Graham from there would come round my folks' house and the two of us would sit up in the box room and jam for hours. I'd play guitar and he'd shout the lyrics to 'Wild Thing' or 'Pretty Vacant' while everyone in the street covered their ears. Graham was by far the biggest bloke any of us knew - he's about 6'6" and I don't think he's stopped growing yet - but he had the smallest room in the Stechford house. The broom cupboard under the stairs. He slept in this little wedge-shaped room he barely had room to stretch out in. But he had a heart of gold. If Karen and me went round there at the weekend, and needed to crash, Graham would let us have his cupboard and he'd sleep on the floor of the living room. I guess it made a change. And the wide open spaces of the living room savannah meant he had - for once - a bit of a view.

Loads of people were forming bands. Most of the time it was nothing more than a couple of mates jamming in someone's bedroom, like me and Everton, or me and Graham. After a couple of months it'd mostly peter out, but every now and then something more dynamic came along. Everton had started playing in a band, and he wanted me to join them, but I had my eyes on getting in another band entirely.

When I was growing up in Sheldon I'd played football for Mapledene. I'd got to know this lad Colin who played down the left wing for Lyndon Green, and was like a streak of lightning. Later we both played for Sheldon Boys, and now, seven or eight years on, we'd both got into punk. Which meant we both ended up drinking at The Crown.

Colin had got together with Jock, and Wilf, and a guy called Sean, and they'd started a band. It sounded like a lot of fun. They called it GBH.

I wanted in.

the importance of a pram

The great thing about punk was that it said *Anyone can do this.* It stripped away a lot of the mystique about making music. If you wanted to be in a band, you got yourself a cheap guitar, or a knackered old drum-kit, and you gave it a go. Groups sprang up everywhere, and split up just as fast. Sometimes it seemed like half the punks in Birmingham were in a band. There were the Drongos. There was CID, Silly Rob's band. There were The Dung Beetles, who supported The Damned once in Digbeth, and who I thought were brilliant. And there was GBH.

I'd seen them just once, at a gig round the back of Digbeth Civic. I'd only got there for the last two songs, but they sounded really good, in a raw punk kind of way. It was good to see mates getting up on stage and doing songs, and it made me determined to do it too.

I was already jamming with Big Graham in the box-room, banging out old punk songs on guitar. But now I was also playing with Jock. The two of us would head over to Washwood Heath on the bus, to Phil Denny's house - Phil was in The Dung Beetles I thought so much of - and practise in his garden shed. That was how I got into playing bass, partly because Jock was a guitarist, and partly because it seemed to me that everyone needed bass players. They were in demand, and I was shrewd enough to recognise it.

I was also clear that, if I was going to join GBH, then Jock was my way in. I was good friends with him. I was on nodding terms with Wilf, enough to make idle chat in the pub, and while I knew Colin from the football as a kid, he wasn't a close mate at that time. Sean, I hardly knew. Jock was the one I spent time with, so Jock was the one I hassled. On the bus over to Phil's, or between songs in the garden shed, I'd mention to him that if ever GBH found themselves looking for someone to join their band, if ever they needed a bass player, well, then I'd be up for it. You know. If ever they were. And then we'd bash away at another tune or two, or have a fag.

It's a difficult balance, seeming keen without looking desperate. Reminding people you're there without getting on their tits. And I guess I must have got it about right, because after a few months, when Sean left, Jock phoned me up and asked me if I fancied joining the band. *You up for that, Ross?* They needed a new bassist.

I was in.

I went straight into town and bought myself a bass guitar. My first one ever. A Hondo bass which was a goldy-brown colour, kind of like bronzed shit. It cost me £65. And it did the job for a good while. It got me through that first gig in The Crown, where I got over my nervousness about being on stage – in my enthusiasm for being in a band I'd blocked out the fact this meant performing in front of an audience – and a good number of gigs after that. Because I'd joined a band that loved to play. GBH were always gigging. Their first gig had been a prostitutes' benefit with Poison Girls at Digbeth Civic, and before I'd joined they'd been all the way over to Nuneaton to support UK Subs at the '77 Club there, so they'd already started to make their mark. Some bands talk a great gig but never get past jamming in a cellar. GBH did the gigs, and practised wherever they could.

When I first joined, we practised at a place called Struggles, up in Erdington. We'd meet up at Jock's house, chat with his dad, Robert, who was a bit of a character – think Fraser out of *Dad's Army* and you're there – pile our gear into an old pram, and wheel it round to Struggles. Ours was the very first punk rock pram, and it gave rise to a catch phrase which has dogged us ever since. *I bet The Clash never had to do this.* Even now, if something goes tits up, one of us'll sigh and go *I bet The Clash never....* and we're right back there, trudging down one of Birmingham's busiest roads, with a drum kit in a battered old pram, on our way to Struggles in the rain.

It was an archetypal, dirty, musty-smelling, damp-carpet, rocknroll rehearsal studio over a shop, down the road from a painters and decorators with a painting of a man on a ladder. Very glamorous.

We practised there right up to the moment we finished rebuilding the stage at The Crown, and then we moved. That was a typical bit of DIY punk activity - The Crown got a new stage, we got a place to practice for free - where everybody won. We saved time and money, cut our umbilical cord with the pram, and got our very own rehearsal space, with our favourite bar downstairs. Which meant we didn't save money, come to think of it, because we practically lived there. Most nights we were in The Crown practising, or getting pissed. We'd learn how we worked together as a band, so that everything we did on stage felt natural and right. Then we'd nip down to the bar and watch Bagshot touting for trade, or Nobby Nobbs sitting at the bar with the lads from his boxing club. And at weekends, we'd have a gig.

It might be upstairs in The Crown, or we could be at the Golden Eagle, or the Star Club, or the Festival Suite over the old Co-op on the High Street, where I saw Crass for the first time. Every week, we'd be playing somewhere on the Birmingham circuit. If we'd written a new song, we'd lob it straight in the set, give it a run out, see whether it worked. It's the way we've always done things. Then we'd settle back and watch whoever else was on the bill. One or other of the Birmingham bands. The Drongos, The Partizans (the Birmingham ones, with a z), TV Eye, or The Big Inch. We'd watch and listen, and learn from each other.

At this stage, all of us were playing to people we knew, to our mates from the Birmingham punk scene, with a few punks who'd come over from the Black Country, or Coventry, or Leicester. It was all just a laugh, a bit of fun as far as I could see, something that made spending all week on the milk float worthwhile. We never thought we'd get anywhere. We never even talked about it. We were just writing songs and gigging, and drinking beer, and not thinking about anything more than that. We were young, and full of ourselves. And then, on Friday 13th March 1981, we supported Discharge at the Cedar Club in Birmingham, and everything changed.

We'd played the Cedar Club before. It was a 500 capacity club, up Constitution Hill in Birmingham, and it had become the big punk gig once Barbarella's closed. Like just about all the clubs in Brum, it was run by the Fewtrells, who'd started out as barrow boys and built their way up, and who have something of a reputation in the city, though they were always good to us. They'd run Rebecca's, Barbarella's, and XLs, and the Cedar Club was another one of their ventures, a little sweat-box, with Fewtrell's security on the door, which meant you weren't ever going to fuck around. Old style security. No nonsense, and good with the fists. Big Black Tex, and Jimmy The Con. You might expect these big hard blokes to hate punks, but - to a certain extent - they looked after us. Certainly Jimmy did. We played the Cedar Club a lot over the years, and if ever anyone was fucking around with us, Jimmy would give them a slap. Even if they were a mate of ours. He was from Dudley, and that was how he did things.

No, Jimmy! He's all right!

Slap.

Oi ay 'avin 'im fookin' around, lads.

So we played the Cedar Club with Discharge. It was the first big gig I did, and it was rammed. Maybe just thirty or so of the people in there were there to see us, but it was still packed when we were on. There were kids from my school down the front, going mental. I remember thinking *This is what it's all about!* The nerves I'd felt during that first gig at The Crown were a thing of the past, and I was enjoying myself. Nothing in life was as good as being on stage. And supporting Discharge was a bit of a dream come true.

I'd been mooching about in Inferno Records with Jock and Colin a year or so earlier, and I'd found this record by a band I hadn't heard of at the time. It had an iconic design, a picture of a leather jacket with studs in the back. I bought it, took it home and played it, and what I heard gave me goose pimples. I'd never heard anything like it before. It was just noise, pure noise. But good noise! I'd played it again and again and again, and now here we were, actually supporting the band that made that noise. Discharge.

By now, they were one of the biggest bands on the scene. Exploited were the other, and we'd already become mates with them when they'd played the Cedar Club, just by hanging out with them. With Discharge, it was different. We were actually *playing* with them. On the same stage, on the same bill.

We weren't daft enough to think this meant we'd cracked it, though. We'd seen what happened to The Dung Beetles. At the end of their gig with The Damned in Digbeth, they thought – we all thought – they'd made it. They were drunk and exuberant, and on their way to bigger things. Only they weren't. They'd just done a support slot, a local support slot, for another band who *had* made it. Which wasn't the same at all. Not long after that, they split up.

So we had no illusions about what this gig meant. It was fun, and we loved it, but we never thought for a moment it would lead anywhere. We never even talked about it. Someone asked Jock if we thought we'd ever be big, and I remember him saying maybe we could be as big as Discharge some day, if we were lucky. I thought *Yep. That's something to aspire to.* But we knew this gig at the Cedar Club was just a local support slot to a band that had made it. That was all.

Then Discharge asked us if we'd like to do more gigs with them. And everything changed again.

The next gig we supported them at was Retford Porterhouse. Just like the Cedar Club, it was packed to the rafters. Discharge gigs always were, which was great, and we always went down well, which was even better. We went on to support them all over the country: Letchworth, Stevenage, Northampton Roadmenders, the 100 Club in London, even Gillingham, when Colin's dad drove us down in his Commer van, and we weren't allowed to smoke, or swear. All the way to Gillingham and back at 45 mph, minding our language. Very punk rock. There was a bad case of Tourette's when we spilled out of the van in Gillingham. And the cast-iron certainty that this was definitely a one-off - Colin's dad wouldn't be driving us again.

But all these gigs with Discharge were an amazing stroke of luck. Even though we didn't think about it much, we knew we'd fallen on our feet in a big way. Discharge were great, and being on the road with them taught us a lot. We started to think about how we looked on stage, for example. Colin started wearing black instead of just turning up in a pair of jeans and whatever t-shirt he had on. We all took a bit more interest in our image. And playing to new audiences each night really honed our set.

By the time we played Victoria Hall in Stoke, we were really tight, and putting on a better show than ever. Which was just as well, because this was Discharge's hometown gig, and the biggest one on the tour. Which meant it was the going to be the biggest gig we'd ever done.

It turned out to be a memorable one, too.

The joker in the pack for this gig - and with GBH, there's almost always a joker in the pack - was that I was still working the milk. Up at 5am for a 7am start. Most days that wasn't a problem, but the Stoke gig was on a Friday, and on Fridays I had to collect the week's money off all my customers, which meant my round took longer. So we agreed that the rest of the band would head to Stoke early in the afternoon, and I'd make my way up by train as soon as I could.

Everything took forever. Maybe longer. Everyone wanted to chat, or change their order for next week, and no-one - apart from me - was in any kind of hurry. By the time I finished and got to New Street it was half past six and I was running way, way late. I got the first train I could to Wolverhampton and on to Stoke, and took a taxi to the gig. There's a guy there, waiting.

You're the bass player, ain't ya?
I was amazed. How did he know?

I'm nodding and saying *Er... yeah* and he grabs me - *Come on!* - and drags me into the venue and up some stairs. He opens a door, pushes me through it, and there I am, on stage. There's 2000 people going crazy, going absolutely batshit loopy while the rest of GBH give it their best. There's no doubt about it, I really am late. I walk over to where my bass is leant against my amp, and pick it up just as the song finishes. Colin waves an arm in my direction and announces to the audience *And here's Ross!*

I just have time to join in and belt out the last song in the set. And it's all over. We're packing up our gear and walking off stage. It's been our biggest gig ever, maybe the biggest gig we'll ever do, and I've missed it. Why? Because I was busy doing a milk round in Kingshurst.

And I'll bet *that* never happened to The Clash.

all change

The rest of the band were pretty pissed off with me for turning up late to the gig. There was a chorus of *Where the fuck have you been?* when we got off stage. What could I say? Nothing, except *Work, lads. Sorry.* And I was. It should have been the biggest gig of my life, and I'd missed it because I'd been stuck on a poxy milk-float, trundling round north-east Birmingham. Work was turning into a proper pain - I liked the money, and I didn't particularly mind the job, but the hours were really starting to clash with being in a band.

Still, this wasn't something I had to worry about much longer. A couple of weeks after the Stoke gig, I got the sack.

It wasn't really a surprise the Co-op wanted rid of me. I'd had eight months off with glandular fever not long after I'd started with them - I'd go out and collect bottles which had been lying around for months, with green mould all round the neck, and then grab a bite to eat without ever washing my hands, so with all the bugs I was exposing myself to I was bound to catch something - and once I'd recovered from that I'd joined a band and was spending all my time rehearsing, or at gigs, and turning up to my round late and hungover.

It didn't make me a model employee. So the Co-op, in their wisdom, decided it was time to give me the shove. I was called into the office, and there were three decrepit old blokes, covered in cobwebs, from the firm. Alan Ball, the shop steward, was there to look after my interests. And they called him *Mr Ball*, with all due respect, and they called me *Sonny*. I wasn't having that.

Hang on! You've got to afford me the same civility you're giving to him!

55

Alan Ball was next to me, going *Shhhh....* but I was having none of it. I knew I wasn't leaving that room with a job. And I couldn't really complain about that. But they weren't straight with me. If they'd said *Look, we've got to let you go* and left it at that, well, that would have been one thing. If they'd called me on my timekeeping I'd have told them *Yeah. But look, I'm eighteen, nineteen. I'm doing all the stuff they told me at school I couldn't ever do. No offence, but doing the milk just isn't the most important thing in my life....* and we'd have gone our separate ways with no hard feelings.

Instead, they claimed I was stealing money from them, and that was like a red rag to a bull. I've never stolen off anybody, so I wasn't having it. I lost my temper, tore my overalls off, and told them *Fuck the lot of you!* And then I threatened to hit them, which kind of sealed things, I guess. Even Alan Ball wasn't going to be able to sort that one out. I stormed out, went back to the depot, and everyone asked me *How'd it go?*

I'm not sure, lads, I said, *but I think I've got the sack.....*

The good news was, this meant I was free. The bad news was, it meant I was going to be skint. I'd been getting a good wage while I was on the milk, which paid my way, because I wasn't really making anything from being in the band. Now I was on the dole. With a girlfriend and a baby daughter.

Karen, my girlfriend, had been living at my parents' house for about a year and a half. In fact, she'd moved in not long after we met. She'd been living with her mom her sisters and her brothers, and she wanted a change and I said *Come and live with us.* I didn't even ask my mom and dad, just mumbled something to them about Karen being there *for a bit,* and trusted they'd be fine about it. Which they were. My sister had buggered off to join the Navy, so Karen just slotted right in.

There was an easy routine. Every morning I'd get up first thing to go and do the milk, then mom and dad would head off to work, and Karen would go to her clerical job in Shard End. Most days, I'd finish in the early afternoon. Then I'd build my alcohol tolerance with the old skins, or nip into town to the record shops and The Crown, or jam with Graham or Jock, or - later - I'd rehearse with GBH. Then at the end of the day I'd get the bus over to Karen's work and meet her when she finished.

So although we were living in the same house, we weren't living in each others' pockets. And we didn't get a lot of time to ourselves. But one weekend my folks went away, and the two of us made the most of it, and that sexual faux pas resulted in Karen falling pregnant. On June 9th, 1981, my daughter Charlotte was born. One week later, I got the sack.

I signed on, of course. I had to. Karen wasn't working because she'd just had a baby, and so she got child benefit, and I signed on. I can't think how I got the fact I was in a band past the dole, but I was always straight with them about what I was doing.

I'm playing a few gigs.
What about the money?
What money?

They said as long as I had less than a couple of thousand in the bank - which wasn't ever going to be a problem - then that was all right. Because most of our gigs just about covered our expenses. For those gigs supporting Discharge, for example, we were getting £30 or £40, and out of that we had to pay for a van to get us there, and the petrol and some beers and a bag of chips each, and then divide what was left between us. Which wasn't much.

So signing on was fine.

Every fortnight I'd lope down to the dole and make my mark. But it was the other piece of paper I signed that month which was the really exciting one.

When we'd done the Stoke gig, Mike Stone from Clay Records had walked into the dressing-room after the show and introduced himself. He'd loved the attitude that Jock, Colin and Wilf had shown, that they'd gone on and done the set even though they were missing the bass player. And he also loved the way I'd just ambled on stage like being late was nothing, picked up my bass, banged out the last song, said *Bye!* to the audience, and then settled down with the others to watch Discharge put the cat out.

Mike hadn't ever seen anything like it. And he wanted to sign us to Clay Records.

clay

Signing to Clay more than made up for missing the gig. In less than a month I'd lost my job, become a dad, and now - to cap it all - I was in a band which was about to sign a record contract. As the Co-op door shut, another far more exciting one was opening.

It felt wonderful. It felt like - well, it was - the beginning of something new.

For a pivotal moment, it was pretty low-key. We went back up to Stoke by National Express, got off at Hanley coach station, and wandered down the road to Hope Street. It was just your average terraced street, but in between the newsagents and the chip shop - notable for our first encounter with the chips and gravy that would be such a major part of our diet for so many years - was Mike Stone's record shop. Your archetypal dingy record shop, with banks of records on each wall, and a counter at the top of the shop, and full of that lovely smell of vinyl. The smell of new music. Exquisite.

Mike was tall and skinny, about ten years older than us, and not in the slightest punk rock. But if you were a punk band from the provinces looking to get a record deal, then there were two labels out there, signing bands up. Clay, and a label from Worcester called No Future. Was there much to choose between them? I don't know. We did know that Mike already had Discharge on his books, and they seemed happy enough, so it was a very big deal for us that he'd shown an interest in us when he'd turned up at their Hanley gig. If he wanted to sign us, it was well worth coming back up to Stoke on the bus.

Anyway, Clay Records, like everything Mike did, was based in the shop. And that meant this very important meeting to sign our first ever record contract was interrupted by people coming up to buy the latest Human League platter, or ask if Mike had anything by ABC. (He did. Business is business.) But in the end, it was done, and we celebrated with our own take on the traditional music biz photo op. Instead of champagne across the bonnet of a Bentley, we had a can of Breaker over the front of a Mini in the street outside, and then went for a session down the pub with our mates from Discharge. Typical GBH.

Once again, we'd landed on our feet. Because Mike was a good man. (If we'd ever been in any doubt about that, some of the other people we'd deal with over the years would hammer the point home by not sharing his values.) He didn't rip you off, and he paid you, and I haven't got a bad word to say about him. We signed to Clay and we never regretted it. In all the time we dealt with Mike, he was never anything less than trustworthy. Whenever we went to visit, we'd come back with shitloads of records, whether we liked it or not. He was generous to a fault and we always came back with something. And if one of us was short of cash, we'd get on the phone to Mike and he'd sort us out. If Karen told me we needed money, and I asked Mike for £100, we *all* got £100. He always made sure we all got equal amounts, he always looked after us and did right by us, and as far as I'm concerned he's a top bloke and I really respect him.

He did have some rubbish ideas, though. In among Mike's good ideas, there were some corkers - like signing us, obviously - and there were some others which were borderline crazy, and which we point blank refused to go anywhere near. It took us a while to learn this, because Mike spent every waking minute coming up with ideas, and his enthusiasm could be infectious. Fortunately, we'd grown up in Birmingham, and that more or less inoculated us from being led astray by enthusiasm. Otherwise things could have got messy.

Not long after we'd signed to Clay, Mike told us he had a plan, and we were all ears, because GBH never planned anything. So this was going to be good.

Summer's coming up.
Yes, Mike.
It's going to be hot.
Uh-huh.
The kids are going to be wanting something new.
Yep.
So I think -
Go on...
I think we should be doing a cover of 'School's Out' by Alice Cooper.
Noooooooooooooo! That ain't going to be happening any time soon, Mike.

Getting a knock-back never discouraged him, though. You soon learned that. Another one of his brainwaves was to do a song for Sefton. Remember Sefton? He was one of the horses that got blown up by the IRA in London in 1982, when they bombed Hyde Park. Good old Sefton became a kind of icon for innocence maimed, and Mike thought it would be a great idea, bless him, to write a song for Sefton. And we went, well we won't be doing it. So he got one of his other bands - Demon, who often went along and did the stuff we refused to - to do a song for Sefton.

He gets a picture of the horse to stick on the cover, prints maybe a couple of thousand, and goes down to London where the barracks is, convinced that this is going to be the making of Clay Records. And they tell him to bugger off, say the horse has had enough of all the publicity. So there's Mike with thousands of copies of this single dedicated to a wounded horse who's decided to retire from the public gaze, and there's nothing he can do but take them back up to Stoke and hide them in a cupboard for a while before throwing the whole job lot on a fire, chalking it up to experience, and coming up with another idea by morning.

Occasionally, just to mix things up a little, *we'd* have ideas that *he* wasn't into. Like in '84 when we wanted a 12" version of 'Do What You Do'. Mike assumed we just wanted a longer version of the same track, that it just needed splicing to make it last eight minutes instead of three. So that's what he did. He brought this 12" to us and we went *No no no. We mean a proper dub track.* You see, we fancied a bit of punk-dub, because no-one had done anything like that - apart from The Ruts, of course. We knew full well it wasn't what people would expect from us, and Mike didn't really get what we were after either, but when we went *Take it back. We'd like some proper dub, if you don't mind* that's exactly what he did, bless him.

But I'm getting ahead of myself here. When we signed to Clay, the big deal so far as we were concerned was that we'd get in a studio and make some records. We'd been in a studio down in Leamington already, and done a demo tape, and at the time I remember listening to it and thinking we were the best band in the world ever. *Listen to this, mom!* I don't know if we sent Mike a copy, or if he ever heard it, but if he'd listened to it he'd never have believed it was us. It was very punk-pop, and nothing like what he'd seen us do on stage at Hanley, even if that was minus a bass player.

So, Mike sent us up to a studio in Rochdale called Cargo. This was run by a guy called Colin Richardson who'd go on to produce lots of death metal bands, but for now he had this rickety old place in Rochdale where the equipment was hanging on by the skin of its teeth. He'd be fixing various buttons and faders on the desk while we were going along, cleaning them and oiling them, keeping the whole thing running on a wing and a prayer, and doing a good job of it for the most part. But even he couldn't do anything about the taxi firm.

If you listen to the tracks we recorded there, about halfway through 'Knife Edge' you'll hear the controller for the taxi firm next door to Cargo, talking to his cabs. A lot of people thought it was meant to be there, that we were being really smart and clever, but the truth is you hear the taxi firm because their radio signal was coming through the speakers in the studio and we had no choice. And when Colin Richardson suggested a re-take, we went *Nah, fuck it. We'll leave it* because that's just the way we are. So the taxi firm stayed.

We came out of Cargo with our first ever record: *Leather, Bristles, Studs and Acne*. A title inspired by the way we'd ended up dressing. We had this punk-biker look - leather jackets with denim over the top, covered with studs - and when we went and got some passport photos taken, all you could see was... leather, bristles, studs, and acne. Not that I had the acne, of course. That was probably Colin. Or Jock.

It was a 12" with eight real songs and a novelty track, 'Alcohol', which marked the start of a GBH tradition of fucking around in the studio. I loved it. I wasn't the only one, either. *LBSA* sold well, it got great reviews, and people actually liked it.

Things were definitely on the up.

the damned

You might think, what with us being signed to a record company, having a 12" single out, and it selling well, that GBH had suddenly turned into some slick, professional outfit. Nothing could be further from the truth. We were just making it up as we went along, like everyone else, and we were still extremely rough and ready.

Looking back, it's easy to see how we were getting bigger and more well-known. At the time, we were just enjoying each gig as it came along. We had no expectations, so pretty much everything was a bonus. The Discharge gigs had been great, and opened a lot of doors for us, but - for different reasons - supporting The Damned when they played in Birmingham later that year was every bit as memorable.

They were the first punk band I'd seen, back at the Odeon in March '77, so to be on the same bill as them was a bit hard to get my head round. These were people whose gig had helped set my life off in a new direction, and now we'd be sharing a stage.... It's something I've never got used to. When Joey Ramone came to our first ever gig in New York in '83, all I could think was how I'd bought my first ever Ramones single in Sheldon, at the corner shop by The Wheatsheaf pub. When the Dickies played with us at big gigs in LA, I remembered buying the *Incredible Shrinking Dickies* in the same shop. Sometimes you find yourself rubbing shoulders with your musical heroes, people you've looked up to, and I don't think it ever stops feeling slightly strange to be there. I'm always waiting for someone to tap me on the shoulder and say *I'm sorry, there seems to have been a mistake....*

Anyway, The Damned gig. It was at the Locarno, at the

top of Hurst Street. Us, them, and the Anti-Nowhere League. We got paid £50, most of which we ended up paying to The Damned's sound engineer to mix our sound, but the highlight for me was when Captain Sensible popped his head in our dressing-room after our set. *You guys are playing too sharp,* he said. *You should use a guitar tuner.*

Jock and I looked at each other.

A tuner? we asked.

Up until that point, we'd tuned by ear. I certainly don't think we'd ever changed our strings. How often did you need to do that, anyway? Every year? Every two? I knew it affected the sound, but I didn't know how, and I'd given the whole thing up as a bad deal after the incident with the pan. I'd read how this old blues guitarist - Little Walter, or someone - used to take his strings off and boil them to get them to sound right, and I thought I'd try it too. I put them on the boil, and promptly forgot about them. Two hours later I found the strings welded to the bottom of one of Karen's best pans, which ended up in the back of my head, for obvious reasons.

After that I went back to tuning up by listening to a record at home. That didn't always work, either. I'd tune the bass, walk out of the house into the cold, sit on the bus, leave the bass in a pub while I had a pint, do a rehearsal, go home, get up next morning and head to a hot sweaty venue where I'd get on stage, play a note, and it would sound... wrong.

How did that happen? It was in tune yesterday!

So Captain Sensible showed Jock how to tune his guitar, explained about guitar tuners, and politely suggested we might find them helpful. It was thanks to him that we learned how to play in tune, but we were more excited about getting to talk to him than about learning how to tune up properly, if I'm honest. Actually getting a tuner was just an ambition, an impossible luxury we'd get round to some day when we weren't spending all our money on chips and beer. For now, we carried on doing things the old way - Jock would come over to my side of the stage, I'd pluck a note, he'd twist the tuning peg till he thought it was about right, and that was it. As long as we were in tune with each other, that was fine.

We must have got a tuner between us eventually, but I don't know when. I've tapes of some of our early gigs, and you can hear us tuning up on stage, so we clearly didn't have one then, but as for when that changed - and it must have been a big deal at the time - I've no idea. All I do know is that when we did the show with The Damned we were still rough and ready, and wet behind the musical ears. But then that was the spirit of the times, wasn't it? I remember people taking the piss when we did start using tuners, same as they did when we started getting our records produced.

Whaddya need to do that for? Why'd ya have to get it mixed?

There were some people who saw anything like that as the first step to becoming some mainstream sell-out primadonna who was going to demand a dressing-room draped in white, who'd need all the blue M&Ms removing from the rider, or who'd only drink some expensive organic beer imported from god knows where. It was all some slippery slope as far as they were concerned - one moment you were just buying a tuner, next you'd be throwing a hissy fit if you didn't have a private jet of your very own.

Well, rest easy, folks. GBH seem to have avoided that particular pitfall.

on the road

All through the rest of '81, we carried on gigging. With or without tuners. We were still playing Birmingham all the time, but now we started getting gigs of our own - rather than support slots - outside Brum as well, and we thought we'd hit the big time. The first one was in Preston, and I remember Colin going *You'll never guess what! We're getting sixty-five fucking quid!!* We nearly choked on our pints. £65 seemed like an incredible amount of money, even after you'd taken out the cost of the van, the petrol, the chips and the beer.

Most of our gigs till then had just about covered expenses. Now that was starting to change. We got paid £65 for the Preston gig, £120 for one in Telford. We were doing a headline gig every week, going to London regularly, playing the Fulham Greyhound, or Angel Islington, or the 100 Club. We were putting in the miles, playing anywhere that paid, soaking it all up, and learning from it all. It's the nature of being in a band - you watch how a group look and act on stage, or you listen to the rhythms they use, or a particular chord change hits you smack between the eyes, and it all adds to your knowledge of how music, and live performance, can work. And then we'd head back to Brum, to our new rehearsal space behind a chip shop in Dale End, and all that experience would get added to the GBH mix, one way or another.

We were living to go gigging, and meeting other bands was half of the fun of it. We bumped into Peter And The Test Tube Babies for the first time on our way to a big festival on the Isle of Wight. They were behind us in the queue for the ferry, mouthing off, and we thought *Southern wankers! Here we go...* But we got on the ferry and they were great, just a bunch of piss-taking fuckers, and we've been best friends ever since. Peter gets very emotional when he's had a drink *I love you. You don't know what you mean to me...* but he's a great laugh. And I remember Wilf chatting with Gene October of Chelsea when we played together once. He asked him *Are you going to be one of these bands who's here for five minutes, or are you still going to be doing it in ten years?*

To me, it was obvious. We'd keep on doing it. And thirty years later, here we are. Still playing. Still waiting for the fucking payday! Yes, the money had got better by the time Gene and Wilf had a natter and a beer, but we were nowhere near worrying about where to park the private jet. We got to our gigs courtesy of a lass called Tina, from Stoke.

Tina was a big northern lass with dyed red curly hair, and - and this was the important bit - *her own van.* This alone was enough to make her a more than able replacement for Colin's dad. And as long as she got paid, she didn't mind if we took Colin's settee out of his front room, stuck it in the back of the van so we'd be comfortable, and sat there smoking and drinking all the way to the gig. Naturally, her wage and the petrol costs came out of our fee; our hangers-on had to fend for themselves.

There were three of them. Joey, Softy, and Stan. They called themselves our roadies; we called them the Gannet Brothers. They were like a plague of Brummie locusts who'd walk off with anything that wasn't nailed down. At the gig in Telford they raided the freezer in the venue, and robbed a shitload of frozen pies and pasties, just because they could. And then they sat there, sucking on frozen pasties, pleased as punch with themselves. Sometimes, when we did a gig, we'd crash on people's floors rather than drive back to Brum, and if we did, and they were with us, then nine times out ten we'd be trundling down the motorway the next morning and they'd suddenly produce a bundle or records out of nowhere.

Where d'ya get those, Joey?
That house we stayed at.
Oh, come on!
Nah. Fuck 'em.

When they left a place they were invariably better off than when they arrived. Why did we let them come with us, when we knew what they were like? After all, I wouldn't let them within a country mile of *my* record collection. I guess the only answer I can give is that they were our mates, our lovable little rogues, and so we just shut our eyes to what they were doing. *We* weren't nicking anything, so it was nothing to do with us, that's how we thought about it – if we thought about it at all.

In December '81, we played the *Christmas On Earth* festival at Leeds Queen's Hall. Everyone was there: Black Flag, The Damned, Exploited, English Dogs, Anti-Nowhere League, and so on. The same as nowadays, to be honest, but a hell of a gig at the time.

We'd done a gig in Manchester the night before, and wherever it was we crashed out – someone's flat, or house, or whatever – they had cats. Now Jock's allergic to cats, and in the morning he has a massive asthma attack and needs to go to hospital. So we take him there, he gets put in some kind of oxygen tent, and we head on to Leeds. I remember there was really heavy snow and the journey was awful, and I couldn't help thinking Jock was getting the better deal, catching the train across later, even if he had got asthma. But we get to the gig, and it's rammed. A proper stomping good punk rock day out, if a bit on the cold side.

Our three lovable rogues got stuck into whatever food and drink was in the dressing-room. They'd been travelling round with us, and as far as they were concerned they were part of the unit, which meant they had as much right to the food as anyone. We got stuck into the beer. Whether everyone thought the Gannet Brothers had a right to the food, I can't say, but we were all lean and hungry, and if you were relying on a rider to keep body and soul together, then you were fucked whether the Gannet Brothers dropped by or not.

Anyway, Jock arrived, we watched some bands and drank some beers. Then we played our set, drank some beers, talked some shit, drank a last few beers, climbed in the van with a couple of beers for the road, and headed off through the snow.

We ran out of petrol on the way home. But seeing as we coasted downhill and into a petrol station, we got away with it. The Gannet Brothers had been too busy eating to think about acquiring anything they shouldn't, Jock's asthma had eased, and none of us had frozen to death, so all in all *Christmas On Earth* went well. We were doing what we enjoyed so much - gigging and being less than sober - and we were happy enough with that. And it kept on getting better.

Six months later we did our first gig abroad. In Holland. In the summer of '82.

It took us weeks to recover.

drugs party in 526

None of us had been abroad before, so this was going to be an adventure. Before we left Brum we'd each picked up those one-year British Visitor's Passports you used to be able to get at your local post office, just a folded bit of cardboard with your photo on which was enough to get you round all of western Europe, and with those tucked safely in our pockets, and carrying our instruments with us, we took the train out of New Street, down to London, and on to Harwich.

We caught the overnight ferry to the Hook of Holland. And being a group of lads, and being all excited about going abroad, and seeing as we had time on our hands and the ship had a bar and a duty-free shop, we spent the whole time drinking. Our mate Lumberjack, who'd come along with us for the *craic*, fell asleep out on deck with his trousers round his ankles, so naturally we gathered round, laughing and shouting and taking the piss. The wind was whipping in off the North Sea, and even though it was June, it was cold enough to freeze your nuts off, so Lumberjack's dress code was doing him no favours at all. Eventually, one of the ship's officers came out to get us all to calm down and shut up, and I've this really clear memory of him gently tucking Lumberjack's tiny little blue pecker back into his pants before he pulled his trousers up and dragged him back inside where it was warm.

So we weren't at our sparky best by the time we got to the Hook. Taking the piss out of Lumberjack for having a cock half the size of nothing was about the only thing that brightened our day. The kids who'd invited us over - Simon, Leanne, Martin, and Bill, who'd never seen us play but loved what they'd heard and invited us over on the strength of that alone – met us with a minibus and drove us to Vlaardingen, this little village about ten miles outside Rotterdam, where we were going to do our first ever european gig in the Sommerstraat youth centre. Not one of the more established venues on the european circuit, I grant you, but a landmark for GBH.

We'd spent all night drinking, and we needed a little pick-me-up. Luckily for us, someone was at hand to help us out. An English lad called Toby turned up out of nowhere, chopped out a massive line of speed as long as your forearm, and invited us to help ourselves.

This was proper Dutch speed. The result? We didn't get a wink of sleep the whole time we were there. By the time the gig started we were flying, and this ordinary little youth club in sleepy Vlaardingen was packed to the gills. Rammed with what looked like five or six hundred people. We were going for it, they were going for it, everyone was having the time of their lives. It was a great gig. We really rocked it.

I have no idea how the riot started.

All day, everyone had been really lovely. Then the show finished and it all went a bit tits up. Suddenly, loads of Dutch punks were running amok in sleepy little Vlaardingen. Shop windows were getting smashed and people were just taking stuff they wanted, and as I stand and watch, right in the middle of it all I see Lumberjack, getting stuck in and smashing stuff with the best of them.

The local police turn up, but they haven't got the numbers, so they call in the riot police from Rotterdam. By the time they arrive, it's like armageddon. With added riot shields and tear gas and dogs. And Lumberjack, standing chatting with a copper, stroking the guy's dog, shaking his head and telling him *This is fucking disgusting, ain't it?* Like butter wouldn't melt in his mouth. I watched him, thinking *You're one of the main protagonists! You're one of the ones causing this carnage! You're petting his dog, and a lot of this is down to you!* But that was Lumberjack for you. An absolute master at winding it all up and then slinking away.

Once things had quietened down a bit, we headed back to the hotel. It was called Villa Park. As a Blues fan, I wasn't too happy about this. As a Blues fan full of speed, I let everyone know - when I could get a word in edgeways. Because we were all still raging, and all of us had lots to say. All the time. To just about anyone. Sleep was utterly impossible. Next day dawns, and we're still wired, and we haven't slept, so we decide to go into Rotterdam for the day before we catch the ferry home.

We spend the day shopping and drinking. We visit a coffee shop, as you do, and buy some hash, and then we find a shop that sells flick-knives, and decide they'll be great souvenirs. So we buy some of them. Then we drink some more. We stumble onto the ferry back to Harwich still trolleyed, full of booze and speed, primed to behave even worse than we did on the way across, and find, to our amazement and delight, that it's full of Scottish schoolgirls. Sweet sixteen and never been kissed, and all on their way back from some field trip or other.

Anyway, we're in cabin 526. And Lumberjack decides it's going to be a great idea to write notes saying DRUGS PARTY! CABIN 526!! post them under the schoolgirls' doors, and just sit back and wait for them to rush our cabin to get at a bunch of blokes who haven't washed or slept for two days. Of course that didn't happen - we ended up smoking our dope on our own in the cabin and filling the sink with roaches. Some party.

We arrive into Harwich in the morning without so much as a smile off the schoolgirls, and catch the train to London.

As we pull into Liverpool Street there's coppers everywhere, all down the platform, with dogs, and I think to myself

Something must be kicking off! Something big's going down!

The train pulls up, we get off, and they just pounce on us. *What the fuck??!! We haven't done anything!!* But they take us up to the police station there in Liverpool Street, split us up, and tell us we're getting searched. Clearly Lumberjack's DRUGS PARTY! notes and our sink full of roaches were having some repercussions....

Like all the others, I got strip-searched, the full works. Now bear in mind that all I'd taken with me for my trip into Europe was a toothbrush, a tube of toothpaste, and my bass guitar. No clean clothes. I'd been partying for three days straight, I stank of speed and beer, I hadn't washed in any way, and the clothes I was wearing were the same ones I'd had on when I walked out the door in Brum. They're minging. So I'm standing there, butt naked, offering the copper my clothes so he can search through them, shake 'em down, and he's going *No, no. That's fine. You just give them a shake for me, turn the pockets out... yep, that's right... Now the underpants....* Because when all's said and done, he doesn't want to go any nearer them than he has to. Fine, mate. I'll do your job for you. You take it easy.

I had no drugs, But I did have the flick-knife I'd bought in Rotterdam. Mine was actually spring-loaded, for what it matters, which meant the blade shot out of the front rather than round the side, but that's by the by. It was still illegal in the UK. So the copper sees this, and tells me he's going to have to charge me with possession of an offensive weapon. And yes, I can put my clothes back on now.

Me, Jock, and Colin all had knives, and we all got done for them. Lumberjack and Wilf had a tiny bit of dope, but the copper who was dealing with them just took it off them and threw it in the bin, and let them go. So the irony was that the people *with* drugs - which was why we got stopped in the first place - got let off and got a coach back to Birmingham, while Jock and Colin and myself spent all day in the cells till they chucked us out and told us we had to be in court next morning.

We couldn't go home. We were stuck in London with just £5.00 between us, which Jock - being an archetypal Scotsman - had managed to hang onto while the rest of us were spending every penny we had on the party. We'd no money left from the gig. That had all been spent on having a good time. We were skint, we were coming down hard, we were trapped in London. And we had nowhere to stay.

The only option I could think of was a kid I knew in Leytonstone, whose name I thought was John, who might let us stay with him. The only way we could get there was to use Jock's money to catch the Tube. Jock wasn't happy about that. Oh no. He didn't like that at all. He liked it even less when we got to Leytonstone and John wasn't in, because we had to use the rest of his money to get the Tube back into London. By now it was late, we hadn't two pennies to scratch our arse with, and we still had nowhere to go. We tried sleeping in Liverpool Street station, but we got kicked out. In the end, we dossed down in the Bank of Nigeria doorway, with our guitars, and tried to get some kip there. Next morning we were making our way to Mansion House, on next to no sleep, with our guitars over our shoulders, and we get surrounded by cops. Again. They tell us they think the guitars are guns. *For fuck's sake! Just leave us alone!!*

Before we even go up in front of the judge, the copper's already told us *This is how it's going to go. I think you were carrying knives 'cause you were scared of skinheads. So you had the knives for protection and you were carrying them with intent to use them.* I thought *You know that's not true!* But he wants to make it look good for the judge, and there's no point in arguing about it because that'll just make things worse. I'm tired and speedy and edgy, and I've never been in trouble with the police before, and it's the first time I've been arrested, and certainly the first time I've been in court, and I don't know what's going to happen. What will my mom say? What do I tell my mom and dad? Will they come and visit me in prison??

I got a £25 fine for possession of an offensive weapon. So did Colin. Jock got fined £30. Partly because he'd been in trouble before, but mainly – I suspect – because he was Scottish.

So now we all had criminal records (or a longer one, in Jock's case), no cash, and were still stuck in London. Nowadays, in a situation like this, you'd sort it by calling a mate on their mobile, or paying on plastic. Not in 1982 you didn't. The only option we had was to ring people on their landline, and hope they were at home and didn't ignore it. It was a lottery, with our chances of winning drastically reduced by the fact that most of our mates didn't even have a landline we could ring for them to choose to ignore. After half a lifetime of ringing the handful of numbers we knew, Colin got through to someone. Now we had to wait while they took the cash for our coach fare to their local police station, their local station could be bothered to let the station we were nearest know they'd been given the money, and that station scratched around in the petty cash box to give us the exact same amount. Then we could drag our sorry arses to the coach station to buy a ticket to get home.

Two days after arriving in Harwich, hallucinating with exhaustion brought on by high-quality Dutch speed and the ensuing lack of sleep, we finally made it back into Birmingham. By then, the rumours doing the rounds were incredible.

What's this I hear about you in some drugs bust in London, son?
Sounds good, but that ain't what happened, dad.
What are you going to tell your mom?
It ain't what happened.
How much money did you make?
We didn't make a penny.
Spent it all on drugs, more like.
It ain't what happened.
Then why did you get busted?
It ain't what....

Our first gig abroad, and we spent two days full of speed and beer, and came back without any money. In fact, I was a £25 fine and a criminal conviction down. It was prophetic.

Because as far as GBH was concerned, that was the next few years in a nutshell.

And Lumberjack, who'd caused all the trouble by writing the notes in the first place, didn't even get nicked.

There's a song about it all on our second album. 'Drugs Party in 526.'

It's pretty self-explanatory.

the charts

It wasn't as if we'd done nothing in the six months between the Leeds gig and the Dutch gig with the riot. Far from it. All through that time we'd been busy gigging anywhere and everywhere, and when we hadn't been doing that we'd been beavering away in the rehearsal rooms, writing songs. By now we were rehearsing in a place called Diamond Sound Studios, just off Dale End in Brum, and we'd got our hands on a wheelbarrow to cart our gear around in rather than a pram, which we all felt was a step in the right direction. And the studios were up by Inferno Records and had a chip shop across the road – so it was just about ideal.

We also bumped back into the guy who wanted to play keyboards in GBH.

A few months earlier, we'd been drinking in The Crown when this bloke came up, told us he played keys, and added that he really wanted to play keys for us. How he saw keys fitting into a four-piece thrash punk band, I don't know, but he was keen. We looked at each other. *Nah,* we said. *Thanks but no thanks.* And off he went. Then one day we rolled up at Diamond Sound, and there he was, playing keyboards in a new band Kevin Rowland had put together: Dexy's Midnight Runners. Being turned down by GBH clearly didn't harm his career any, because by joining up with them he'd landed squarely on his feet. Still, in idle moments I wonder whether we should have taken him up on his offer, and explored an entirely different musical direction. GBH could have written 'Come on Eileen', and the world would have got to see Colin in dungarees. But there again, no. Maybe not. Nobody's ready for that.

Anyway, fuelled on chips, beer, and the smell of fresh vinyl in the morning, we wrote a lot of songs in Diamond Sound. Which was good news, because Mike Stone wanted us to put out an album to follow up on the success of *Leather, Bristles, Studs and Acne*. It had been selling really well - I don't have figures, but I do remember that the first royalty cheque Mike ever gave us was for £500. Each. It felt like an impossibly large amount of money. It was certainly more than I'd ever seen in one go. Unbelievably, we were making some kind of living playing our music, which meant we were being paid to do exactly what we wanted to do anyway. What could be better than that? Now Mike wanted an album, and we had songs to spare, so back we went, into the recording studios.

This time, we didn't go to Cargo. Mike had found us a studio closer to home, FSR Studios in Bagot Street, Aston, by the fire station. We fully expected to be in and out of there in a day, because we don't fuck about in the studio. We go in, play a song live, and as long as the bass and drums are OK, as long as they've got the spine of the song, then we make sure the guitar's fine, maybe add another guitar on top, Colin does the vocals, we all do the backing vocals, and that's it. Done. Now for the next track! It's proficient, it's cheap, it's what we'd done at Cargo, and it's what GBH has done on just about every album since.

We hadn't reckoned with Mike.

Mike had ideas. Lots of ideas. Mike was mad for ideas.

The snare drum, guys.

Yes, Mike?

How about we leave the door of the drum booth open...

Yeah...

...and put the microphone down the hallway...

Really?

...by the front door...

Why the fuck would we want to do that, Mike?

... so we pick up the ambient qualities of the snare sound, fellas.
Uh-huh.
It'll sound really special, trust me.
Hmmmm. Right.

We were in FSR for five days, which was an eternity for us. But in the end we had an album. With a very special snare sound I'm sure blew your socks off the first time you heard it. Now all we needed was a title.

One evening we finished practising in Diamond Sound, walked out onto Dale End, and there was the bloke selling the *Evening Mail* from his little kiosk on the street corner, as always. Under the metal grille at the front of the kiosk was the day's headline, blown up huge on a sheet of thin paper.

It said *City Baby Attacked By Rats.*

We thought *That's a fucking good title for an album!*

So Colin lifted up the grille and took the sheet. He's still got it.

And the rest, as they say, is history.

We'd recorded the album that would become *City Baby* before we went to Holland, but it came out after, once we'd extricated ourselves from the whole flick-knife-drugs-party fiasco. The week it came out was unforgettable. That sunday evening I was sitting at home in the flat in Chelmsley Wood, listening to the chart show on the radio, like you did, with Karen and Charlotte there, and my mom and Karen's nan and granddad over to visit, and suddenly the DJ went *Straight in this week at number seventeen! It's GBH!*

What the fuck??!!! Whoo hoo!!

And he played *City Baby Attacked By Rats.*

This was the mainstream charts, not some indie or alternative equivalent. We went in at number seventeen, and the highest new entry was Jimi Hendrix at number sixteen, which made us the second highest new entry that week! I can't tell you how hard that was to believe. We were in the charts, in the *Top Twenty*, and from here on, everything kicked in. Suddenly we were in the position of the bands we used to idolise, like our mates in Discharge, or The Damned. I'd always thought *they* were massive, and now we were. In other people's eyes, anyway. On another level, for us, nothing had changed.

We were still doing the same old thing: living the way we wanted, and making our music. That was it. After the initial euphoria, we never really got excited about it all, which is probably why we never built on our success in the way we could have done. We just don't work like that. We never have done. We didn't go *Right! Let's seize the opportunity! We're big, let's get bigger!* Did we miss our chance, when it was staring us in the face? I guess you'd have to say we probably did. But that's GBH. That's just how we are. And I doubt it'll ever change. Old dogs, new tricks, and all that.

How did I celebrate our chart success? I went out and bought the Jimi Hendrix album that pipped us for highest entry. A double live one, as I remember. The first time we went down the pub there were a few comments - you know, *Oooh, it's the pop stars!* that kind of thing - but it was just banter, a bit of piss-taking among mates. After a week or so, life carried on much as it had before.

The thing I remember most is that sitting in your own living-room listening to yourself on the radio while some DJ who'd never heard of you the week before and who's probably more famous than you'll ever be is telling the nation about you, well, it's a bit fucking hard to get your head around. Ever so slightly surreal. Karen was excited, though.

And I think that the moment when the DJ said *Straight in at number seventeen! It's GBH!* was the moment my mom finally forgave me for getting expelled.

police

Because we'd been to Holland just before *City Baby* came out, we'd decided we wanted to put *Thanks to the Dutch punks* on the sleeve, and while we were at it we'd have *No thanks to the Gannet Brothers* on it too. The printers - who had no idea that the first lot had shown us a great time, while the second just liberated other people's belongings - put *No thanks* to them both.

The Dutch punks went mad.

What the fuck have we done? We looked after you, we got pissed with you, we had a riot with you!
Sorry, guys, it's just a mistake.

Far from publicly thanking them, we'd royally pissed them off, which was never our intention. But then GBH have always been able to get ourselves into trouble without meaning to. And although we were finally able to clear things up with the Dutch punks, there were some other people we were never able to square things with. Never in a million years. Because early on in our existence, GBH fell foul of the punk police.

You see, punk had split. Apparently someone had built a fence and you had to choose which side of it you came down on. On the one side were the self-declared political punks, the anarchos, who decided they didn't like people like us; and on the other side were people like us, who simply didn't give a fuck. People got really worked up about it, and I never understood why. It seemed so stupid to spend all your time fighting to get out from under the rules imposed on you, and then immediately turn round and make some new rules yourselves. It was divide and rule gone mad.

You had to declare yourself for vegetarianism, or world peace, or animal rights. And god help you if you didn't. Jump through the right hoops and you could be a *good* punk. Fuck it up, and the fingers would point and the tongues would wag, because you were a *bad* punk, and nothing was worse than that.

In the early days, we'd all rubbed along. Back when we'd supported Discharge, they'd shown *Protect And Survive* before their gigs. This was an infamous government propaganda film which told you that – in the event of a nuclear blast – whitewashing your windows and crouching under the kitchen table would keep you safe from harm (while the government would, naturally, be hiding in the biggest deepest bunker you could find). I think showing it was mainly Cal's kick, but anyway, it meant both sides of the punk divide came along – the vegetarians and vegans in the all-black uniforms, and everyone else. There'd be heated debates about anything and everything. But that window soon closed.

I've never been a fan of rules and regulations. When Crass had arrived on the scene I went out and bought their first album, and I'd never heard anything like it, either musically (who had?) or lyrically, with all the politics. But I was intrigued, so I went and saw them when they played the Festival Suite in Brum. And it was more like a production than a gig, with the film show and everything. But I was left feeling there were rules and regulations that went with it all, a prescribed way of life, and that put me right off. I remember thinking *What do these people do for fun? Do they have fun?* Don't get me wrong, it didn't stop me liking them, but I wasn't a fan of the rules.

At that stage, though, you could still bridge the divide. As time went on, positions hardened. By the time GBH were up and running and putting records out, the self-righteous box tickers – the ones who decided whether you were a good or bad punk – were in their pomp. One of my favourite bands at the time was Rudimentary Peni, and if ever we were writing to a fanzine answering the questions they'd sent us, you could guarantee they'd ask *Who are your favourite bands?* and I'd always include Rudimentary Peni. Then I heard that one of the guys in the band said it made him physically sick that someone from GBH could like his band. *You what? You don't even know me, you wanker.*

As far as we were concerned, we were out to make music and have a laugh. So what had we done to be so reviled? Simple. On the B-side of our first single was a track called 'Big Women'. It got us banned from every student union in the country.

big women I love their size
big women flabby thighs
big women big women they fill my eyes

here they come walking down the street
big and bouncy they look so neat
can't wait to get between the sheets
big women give me a treat

Half the girls in The Crown helped write that song. Now it's not Shakespeare, I grant you, but – really – what is there to get excited about? You don't have to *like* it, but to ban the band that wrote it? That's a little over the top.

But GBH had wandered into a minefield. The political punks were trying to undo thousands of years of patriarchy and still get home for tea, and 'Big Women' was waaaaay beyond the pale. Patriarchy was bad, so sex had to be bad as well. You certainly couldn't say you fancied someone, not if you

Boxing Day, 1955.
My folks get married...

1961. I arrive.
They put me in
a dress

with my sister...

both of us with mom

the Addams Family house...

coal-faced city baby

model pupil

rugby, with our shorts on for once.
me: dead centre
Tony Quinn: front row, white boots

GBH and Peter Test-Tube

Karen and Boring John

the glamour of life on the road...

...but Wilf gets a proper bed

in San Francisco with Big Mick and Peter Test-Tube

boring Wilko senseless in Japan

playing asteroids with Tomo in the tunnels

Geoff, and his dreads

were a bloke, not if she was a woman. People were trying to make a better world, which is fine, but they were throwing the baby out with the bathwater, and making problems that weren't there. 'Big Women' demeaned womankind as far as they were concerned, and that was that. The punk police were swinging the pendulum of power away from blokes, and by writing a song that simply said *Phwooooar!* we were playing the patriarchal game. GBH was sexist. Absolute rubbish, but there you go.

The fact we had a song on *City Baby* called 'Slut' didn't help our cause at all, mind. Looking back, that was a bit naive. Rough Trade decided they wouldn't handle our records because these two songs were *derogatory to women*. When we went to Germany in '83, some kick-boxing lesbians turned up at the gig in Freiburg, blaming us for thousands of years of female oppression and wanting to kick the living shit out of us. Now *that* took some calming down.... but it shows you how much anger was around, how black and white some people thought the issues were. To my mind, it was all a massive over-reaction to anything we might have done, but then those were the times. In the mid-80s you couldn't *look* at a woman without being called sexist by some muppet. And whatever hoops you leapt through, it would never be enough for some people. Even Crass ended up unable to breathe because of it, so we had no chance.

In all this time, however, no-one we knew got the hump about it. None of our mates turned round and said *Those songs are out of order.* But we still ended up not playing 'Big Women' or 'Slut'. It just wasn't worth the aggro we got from the punk police. Women would come up and ask us to play it. *It's my favourite song!* And we'd say *Well apparently we're demeaning you by playing it.* And when we did start playing it again, we'd suddenly have a stage full of women, and some of them would want to get their tits out.

What's going on? Are we hypnotising you?
No.
OK. Just checking...

See, some women want to do that, they like getting their tits out. You might not like it, but they do. You think it's demeaning, they think it's having a laugh. Are you saying they're wrong? Are you saying I should stop them? That I should tell them I know what's best for them, and they should put their clothes back on? No. It ain't ever going to happen. Why? Because we're all adults, all making our own choices.

That's the GBH philosophy. Live and let live. Col's veggie. Jock's trying to be vegan. I eat meat. But none of this causes any ructions within the band. There's no political ramifications about the fact we've made different choices and do different things. So we don't always agree? Big deal. We're in a band together, and we make music. The rest is just window dressing.

Back in the day, I remember one guy in a band we played with said you shouldn't be making music unless you were being political, or wanted to change something. You couldn't just be in a band to have fun, or to sound off when you were wound up. But for the four of us, GBH has always been about being creative, about making music, about having a space to bounce around and have a good time. Isn't that enough? Do you have to be preaching about everything that's wrong with the world all the time?

Don't get me wrong. The first GBH gig was a prostitutes' benefit, and some people would say that's political. We've been in the Gary Critchley campaign - though I don't think it's our songs that got him out - and that's political. We write about everyday stuff and how it affects us and the people round us, and you could argue that's political. If we believe in something, like Gary's release, we'll get involved and offer our support, but that's not why we've spent all these years getting in a van and firing off up the motorway to go somewhere. We do that for the music, and the lifestyle. We do that for love.

We have *never* had a political dogma. Colin will write about *anything* - his views, his experiences, big women, something poignant, whatever's on his mind. I read a review of *Punk Junkies* and it said they'd never heard such a heartfelt impassioned vehement outburst about having your car clamped. Why had Col written a song about having your car clamped? Because he'd had his car clamped, obviously.

See what I mean? We write what we write, and we do what we do. And we're good at it. And we don't need to prove to *you* that our hearts are in the right place. Our mates know that. And we do too.

tour

Despite the best efforts of the punk police, everything in the GBH world seemed to be coming up roses. We'd got royalties coming in from Clay. John Curd in London was giving us regular gigs on the punk circuit down there, at the Klubfoot or the Lyceum or the like, which were always packed and which paid well. We were headlining our own gigs. We weren't awash with money, but - as long as there were chip shops - we weren't going to starve.

At this point, the biggest gig we'd done had been Leeds Queen's Hall - the *Christmas On Earth* show where we'd first crossed paths with Henry Rollins - where we'd been third or fourth on the bill. This was all about to change. Our own gigs were about to get a lot, lot bigger.

Two promoters turned up. They wanted to put together an *Attacked By Rats* tour. There'd be four bands on it: The Blitz (an Oi band from No Future records); Abrasive Wheels; The Destructors from Peterborough; and GBH, who'd headline the whole shebang. They set up a string of dates, starting in Birmingham Bingley Hall on October 22nd 1982, and running through to the start of December. There were something like twenty dates, in big venues. There'd be a truck full of PA and lights, there'd be catering, there'd be all sorts of shit. It would be a really big deal. What did we think?

We thought it sounded like fun.

And that's exactly what it was. Every night I watched the show, and I enjoyed it all, because it was a good strong bill. First up were Destructors, who were thrash; then there was

Abrasive Wheels, who were down the line punk; Blitz were singalong Oi. And then you had us, doing our thing. All of us performed in front of this 'set', a backstreet scene of dustbins and graffiti, which we knew nothing about till we turned up for the first date and there it was, set up on the stage, looking – well, looking like dustbins and graffiti on a stage. A bit fucking weird. But hey, we went with it.

The audiences loved it, because they had four acts one after the other, *bang bang bang bang*. Birmingham was a hometown gig, and it was rammed. 1500 people. 800 in Manchester Apollo. Cardiff Top Rank, packed to fuck. Newcastle Top Rank, packed to fuck. It was like that everywhere. Did any of them sell out? I really don't know. To be honest, that wasn't something we were bothered about. We weren't racing up to the promoters each day asking *How's ticket sales?* We were heading to catering, going *Wa-hey! Chips again!!* We were doing the biggest gigs of our lives, but we weren't really thinking about that, or about the money. In the GBH world, the really big deal was that we got fed. Ask me about the *Attacked By Rats* tour and I remember free food, a proper minibus with seats to travel round in, not having to head to the chip shop every day, and getting £10 a day pocket money to spend on beer and fags. Whichever way you cut it, things were looking good. Not that long before, GBH were being driven to Gillingham at five miles an hour by Colin's dad, watching our language. Now we were the headline act on a national tour. It was almost too good to be true.

The way the tour was set up, it was split into two halves. The first half finished at the start of November, and then there was a break for a couple of weeks before we'd start the second half. I think the last gig we actually did was Oxford Apollo, which turned out to be one of the livelier nights on the tour. The Oxford Mental Mob, who used to follow us, were there, and right from the start the audience were really going for it. Then suddenly, for whatever reason, it all kicked off. Big Graham was out in the audience swinging his fists around in the general madness, and I could see the security getting really twitchy.

Now the Oxford Apollo's a proper theatre, so it has a fire safety curtain at the front of the stage they can drop down if there's a fire. Or trouble. And this curtain was coming down and going back up like a bride's wedding dress, because the kids were going mad, and security didn't know how to handle it. So every couple of minutes one of them would have a panic and press the button to drop the curtain. We'd be limbo-ing underneath it as it dropped, carrying on playing, then it'd hit the deck in front of us. There'd be a pause, then it would start rising back up into the heavens. *Hi everyone! We're back!!* No sooner had it made it to the top than some muppet would press the button again, the curtain was on its way down, and we'd be giving the limbo our best shot once more. We've done some bizarre gigs over the years, but that Oxford gig was definitely up there.

In many ways, that fire curtain was kind of symbolic. Up till now, GBH had just danced from one stroke of luck to another. Everything we'd done, from supporting Discharge, to signing to Clay, had worked out brilliantly. It couldn't last, and it didn't.

The second half of the tour never happened.

All the dates – Plymouth, Hitchin, Brighton, Glasgow and half a dozen others – were cancelled. Our two promoters had run off with all the money. The deal had been that we'd get £10 a day each during the tour, and get properly paid when it ended. But it never ended, so guess what?

We never got paid.

I hope that wasn't the same for everyone - Concert Lighting had provided the lights and the PA, and if they got stiffed I guess it was a lot of money - but for GBH it was a bit of a setback. We set out on this big, high-profile tour, did just seven or eight of the dates we expected, and never saw a bean.

It was the first time something had gone badly wrong. We'd been looked after by Mike Stone, and we'd done well out of being on Clay, and now we'd been ripped off. How did we feel? Even now, all these years on, I don't know. Obviously there was a lot of gossip, a lot of chewing over what little we knew, but strangely there was almost something like kudos, too. We weren't fixated on money anyway, and since we had no idea how much we'd lost, it was easy to shrug our shoulders about it all. *We've been ripped off! How punk is that?!* In a way, it enhanced our relationships within the band, and made us stronger, because we were all in the same boat together.

It turned out that one of the promoters had run off to join the Red Cross - I don't know if this was some kind of penance, or whether it had always been his aspiration - and the other had bought himself a black cab, so we'd wonder what the chances were of jumping in his cab on the way to donate to the Red Cross. *Wouldn't that be ironic, eh?* I'm not sure if that was us dealing with it, or just burying our heads in the sand. I know I didn't lose any sleep over it.

It was the speed that was stopping me sleeping.

speed

Growing up in Sheldon, drugs had never been part of the scene. There was only Sheldon crack: a pack of ten B&H, or ten Cadets. When I was sixteen, Tony Quinn and myself had tried smoking dope - we went to the Rasta pub and bought some grass, and then went back to his - but since neither of us could roll joints, it wasn't a success. Like a lot of kids, we gave banana skins a go as well, and we even smoked orange peel once, but neither of them was much cop, so we went back to fags and booze.

And yet all around me there were people taking all kinds of shit. There was Artane, which was for Parkinson's disease and was only good - so far as I could see - for giving you the raging horrors. Do-Dos were for asthma, but would keep you awake, and were a staple, and then there were the various pre-scription speeds: lemons and limes, purple hearts, dexys and the like. But I didn't dabble, not in the early days.

That changed after *Christmas On Earth*, the big festival in Leeds Queens Hall. I remember watching this guy - his mouth was all over the place, he was chewing the inside off his face - thinking to myself *What's up with him?* I was completely naive about it. Jock went *He's speeding his tits off, ain't he?* And I think it was in the back of the van that night, on the way back down to Brum, that I first tried speed. I'd seen everybody else doing it, and they seemed to be having fun, and I went *Go on then. I'll have a go.*

It was just a little experiment. Just a bit of sulphate. Ten minutes later I was talking complete bollocks, and I haven't stopped since. You see, the thing about speed was it was always there. It never ran out because pretty much everyone had it -

if you wanted a little top up, you only had to ask, because someone was bound to have some, and they were happy to share. I think the *Attacked By Rats* tour was entirely fuelled by amphetamine. We'd finish the gig, I'd have a few beers and a couple of dabs, stay up talking and drinking and speeding, go to bed late and catch an hour or so of half-sleep, then get up and have another little dab to give myself a lift when I started flagging because I hadn't slept because I was full of the speed I'd taken to give me a lift because I was so tired.

Maybe that's why we weren't really too bothered about the promoters running off, not because we'd raised ourselves to some zen-like plateau of understanding, where we were above worrying about money, but because we were too busy grinding our teeth, smoking tabs and talking shit. We didn't just talk cobblers to each other, either. I'd walk in the venue and chew the ear off anyone I found. Thinking about it now, I'm amazed nobody punched the shit out of me.

It was our first big tour and it was one big party, and there were always people milling about, chopping out lines of this that and the other. Sometimes, if it was too long a drive back, we'd stay in some dodgy hotel, but a lot of times we'd get back to Birmingham in the middle of the night and sit up at Colin's place in Edgbaston, smoking and drinking. And then we'd get up next day and do it all over again.

Sounds fantastic, doesn't it?
It wasn't.

I was a nightmare to live with. I was living out in Chelmsley Wood with Karen and Charlotte, and I'd arrive back at the flat in the small hours of the morning, completely wired, and sit up till seven or eight in the morning, listening to 'I live off you' by X-Ray Spex over and over again, thinking it was the greatest song ever. Then I'd come down and feel like shit for the rest of the day, go and sit in my room and not want anything to do with anyone. I think it's fair to say I wasn't much of a dad, and it upsets me to think about how I was and how I behaved. There were things I did, but shouldn't have done; things I didn't do, which needed doing.

One time I got back to the flat and my mom was there. I'd just walked all the way home from Colin's place in Edgbaston, and I was so full of speed, so wired, that even after a nine-mile walk I couldn't keep still, I couldn't sit down. I was raging. My mom knew I was on something. She must have done. She came up with this story about a woman she knew at work whose son was taking drugs, and how he and his mom needed to sit down and have a chat about it and sort him out. I stood there, grinding my jaws, thinking *Does she mean me? I can't handle this!* And I did a runner. Just scarpered down the road and left her to it.

God knows what that looked like to my mom. But I was off in my own little world. I was either full of speed and false confidence, or I was coming down to earth with a bump, locking myself away, struggling with bouts of depression. I think I'd been like that before I ever started taking speed, but it certainly didn't help. There were days when I was really on my arse. The band was one of the best things in my life, and Karen was the other.

Now, there was speed, too. And the more that speed and the band filled my time, the less I had left for Karen.

deutschland über alles

We'd been robbed blind, and my personal life was less than perfect, but life in the GBH camp was generally pretty positive. We just got on with doing what we did best: making music and going out and gigging. And Mike Stone was still looking after us, coming up with a million ideas a minute, and throwing the occasional curveball in to the mix to keep us on our toes.

Lads, I've got a surprise for you.

And he had. Our new single was 'Give Me Fire', and Mike had got it pressed as a picture disc. The picture was of the four of us - Colin, Jock, Wilf, and me, with my head popping over Wilf's shoulder - outside the studios in Bagot Street, all dressed in denim and leather, as always. And seeing as a picture disc was quite unusual in those days, Mike achieved the result he was after, which was to make sure people sat up and took notice, and talked about it, about Clay, and about GBH. Not all the talk was positive, mind. The Newcastle punks who'd been following us saw this as selling out, and they didn't like it. The picture disc would be just the start. Next the slippery slope would lead to private jets, stadium gigs, and Hollywood mansions, and they didn't approve at all.

So it's no surprise that GBH appearing on *The Tube* didn't go down too well with them either. It was a cold, sunny day just after the *Attacked By Rats* tour when Jools Holland came up to Brum with a production company, and filmed us playing 'Give Me Fire' on the roof of the studios in Bagot St. We had a load of friends with us at the time, people who were up in

95

Brum from all over the country, and so we made sure they got in the video too. If you watch it, you'll see them, and you'll see Jools Holland in his camelhair coat, trying to hide the fact he really doesn't like our music at all, but you won't see any of the Newcastle punks, because they weren't there. Once that picture disc came out, we never saw them again. But hey, each to their own. We didn't take it personally. And anyway, we were off to Germany.

There were seven of us going. Roxy - who'd been working for us since before the *Attacked By Rats* tour - was the driver, some bloke called Ian had blagged his way in as tour manager, there was an old mate of Wilf's, and the four of us. We packed the gear, drove to Harwich, and headed off for two weeks in Germany in a van.

I don't know about the others, but for me this was a really big deal. Like every other kid in the country, I'd been brought up on *Dambusters, 633 Squadron,* and *Guns Of Navarone.* If I wasn't watching war films I was having some old bloke chew my ear off about living through The Blitz. The Hun were bad news, and now I was going over there to spend two weeks amongst them. As we drove down from the Hook and crossed the border into Germany, I was looking up at the sky and thinking how when my dad was a boy there'd been warplanes flying overhead, dropping bombs. History suddenly didn't seem so long ago.

It may seem daft, in the age of the internet and the world wide web, when all the information you could possibly want is there at your fingertips and we're far too busy down-loading porn to worry about history, but going to Germany and meeting Germans - and discovering they were just the same as us - was a very very big deal. For me, anyway. Up till then I'd been half-convinced they were all nazis, but now I learned they weren't. They were just like us, except they had crisps which they called chips, and chips which they called fries. So yes, they were a little weird, but at least they didn't goose-step everywhere. And they did have great beer. When the barmaid who served us our first *Erdinger weiss* showed us how pouring it was an art form, how you had to roll the glass, and when we tasted it... well, so far as I was concerned, that was the moment punk truly became international.

Our first gig was a squat in Dachau. We had a road atlas, a vague idea of how to get there, and a monumental language barrier. Ian claimed he'd been everywhere in Europe, driving trucks, but as Roxy drove us down the Autobahn and every junction we passed said *Ausfahrt*, he looked more and more puzzled. Eventually he piped up.

Tell you what, lads, this Ausfahrt's a fucking big place...

We weren't stupid. We weren't about to tell him it meant *exit*. It was far more fun watching him pretend he knew more than he did, because this wasn't a one-off. Above the toilets in the squat gig it said *Scheisshausen,* and Ian - who claimed he could speak German, just like he knew Europe like the back of his hand - decided this meant *toilet*. Which it does, sort of. You might ask your mate, *Col, where's the shitter?* but you probably wouldn't use the same phrase when you're talking to your mom. But everywhere we went in Germany - restaurants, service stations, pubs, and bars - Ian would ask where the *Scheisshausen* were, remain completely oblivious to the looks people gave him, and believe we thought he was doing a grand job of guiding us around.

But I'm getting ahead of myself. We got to the Dachau squat, and there they were: punks. Just the same as us. With pretty much the same priorities. There was one tiny bedroom where we all slept - with five or six other people in there snoring their tits off, or shagging, or whatever – and there was a bar. We were doing the tour with a band called Napalm, and that night in Dachau their drummer Kai decided a good way for us to get to know each other would be a night on the piss.

You like snakebite, ja?
Er, yes, Kai.
I show you German snakebite.

I've no idea if German snakebites exist, or whether this was purely an invention of Kai's, but what he had in mind was cider mixed with absolutely everything else you could get your hands on from behind the bar, all thrown together in a massive Stein about two feet high. It did the job, it broke the ice. That was my first session on the piss with Kai. There'd be plenty more in the years to come.

The gig, by the way, was fantastic. And next day, before we left Dachau, we decided we'd visit the camp. We couldn't be that close to part of the machinery of genocide without taking a look, even if driving round town asking the locals *Do you know where the camp is?* feels ghoulish in the extreme. We got there, and what can I say? It was a sobering experience. I stood in the camp, and tried to imagine what had gone on there within my dad's lifetime, just a long day's drive into Europe. And I couldn't. It was impossible, just impossible to get my head round it, and while I'll never forget going there, I was very glad to leave.

After Dachau, we played in Braunschweig, Stuttgart, Freiburg, Bonn, Hamburg and Berlin. Some of the gigs were in squats, some weren't. Some were huge, some less huge. Most of them were memorable, one way or another.

First up, for no good reason, there was the battle of Bonn. I can't remember where it was we played, but the Hell's Angels had come along, there were fights kicking off everywhere, and we were all completely pissed. I was probably more pissed than anyone, and when Wilf started moaning about hating this shit and wanting to go home, my head went, and I glassed him. Then I pushed my way through some of the Angels, smashed a chair, and grabbed one of the broken legs. I don't know if I was going to use it on Wilf or have a go at some of the Angels. Maybe I was just at war with the world. Luckily, we never found out. Before I got my hide tanned, Kai and the guys from Napalm bundled me out of there, threw me in their car, and drove me away.

I woke up the next morning knowing I'd never done anything in my life that I regretted as much as I regretted glassing Wilf. The gig that night was in West Berlin, so I spent all day with Napalm in their car as they drove from Bonn to Berlin - which is a fucking long way - knowing I'd made a fool of myself and behaved like a complete cunt, and worrying about how things would be when I saw Wilf again. Even driving through East Germany and seeing the little wooden Trabants they drove around in didn't cheer me up. I was an idiot. What on earth had I gone and done? What was going to happen now?

Finally, we got to the venue, SO36 in Kreuzberg, and there Wilf was. I took a deep breath, went straight over to him, we gave each other a huge hug and said *Fuck this bullshit,* and then we got on with being in a band again. I can't say how relieved I was. Wilf's a big bloke and a hard man, and if he'd wanted he could probably have panned me from pillar to post and back again without drawing breath. But fortunately there was no lasting damage, to him or to our friendship. I think the glass I'd hit him with just bounced off his head and smashed against the wall, and he carried on drinking. It speaks volumes about GBH that we shrugged it off, put it all behind us and got on with life, but I knew it wasn't my proudest moment.

It's not as if I was the only person going slightly crazy, though that wasn't much consolation. Ian had already blotted his copybook. He'd been banging on about how he'd driven everywhere in Europe, and how we should let him drive. So one day we let him, and what did he do? He panicked. Where were we? On a bridge over the river Rhine. He was about to drive us into the side of the bridge when Roxy jumped on him and brought the van to a halt. We were furious.

Can you drive, Ian?
Er, well…
Can you actually fucking drive?
No.
You nearly fucking killed us, you prick.

Don't get me wrong, I've met Ian since and had a drink with him, and he's a nice enough bloke, but this tour was his first time abroad and he didn't know his arse from his elbow and was making out he'd done it all. On top of that, he and Roxy were on a wage, while we weren't, so some days paying them ate up just about all of the cash we'd made. It was the final nail in the coffin as far as having paid roadies and crew went - our take was *We're all in this together* and we should all get the same money, whereas his was that he should be earning a living and hiring out his expertise. You can see it both ways, I guess. But when he'd nearly driven us off a bridge, and then went out and bought a leather jacket with the money he was earning, while we were sometimes scratching around for the money for a beer, it was hard to feel generous about it. I made him take the jacket off, because wearing it felt like rubbing our noses in it, and reminding us how skint we were. And when we went to Checkpoint Charlie in West Berlin - where you could climb up to a platform and look over the wall across no-man's land to the East German border guards with their machine guns - Ian went running up the steps and started screaming at them.

Fuck you!
Er.. Ian...
Come on, then!
Ian, that's not a good idea.
Shoot me, you bastards!
Ian! Get the fuck down!

Crazy.

But then we were in a crazy place. I'd never been anywhere like West Berlin. It felt dangerous, on the edge - people here were living the cold war, they were right on the front line in this outpost of Western Europe, surrounded by a communist state. Half a city, stuck behind a wall, looking out on border guards with guns. A lot of the young people came to Berlin to avoid doing military service. Some of them were really political. Some of them were just slightly deranged.

We were in the venue in Kreuzberg, and I was chatting to a lady called Rat Jenny - so called because she always had a couple of rats with her, sitting on her shoulders. This big skinhead came up, grabbed one of the rats, bit its head off, and handed the headless body back to Jenny. Unsurprisingly, she was in shock. I was pretty staggered myself. I remember she just took the headless body and painted the blood all over her face, using it like a lipstick. Then I turned round and there was some German bird pulling down her trousers and having a piss in the sink in front of me, bold as you like.

Blimey, I thought, *they really don't give a fuck over here, do they?*

It was a tour of intense gigs. But Freiburg was the real eye-opener, the gig that stood out. It's a beautiful little place, a university town nestled in the corner of Germany, tight up against France. The gig - the AZ, a classic punk gig - was in a big old factory which went deep underground. It was solid, industrial, constructed out of concrete and steel, and looked like it was just made for punk. It wasn't, obviously. God knows what it was built for. Some nights the local punks would set up a cinema there and show films, and other nights - like when we played - they'd put on gigs. So in the afternoon we set up our gear and had a quick soundcheck, and then we went into town, having a look around and drinking the odd beer or three. Or nine.

When we got back in the evening to play the gig, the place was rammed. It seemed like there were thousands of people there, and we hadn't the tiniest hope of getting in through the doors. Not a chance. One of the Freiburg punks showed us the alternative. Round the side of the building there were chutes - just about wide enough for a person to fit in - which led down into the basement. With so many people already in the building, this was our only way in. So that's what we did. The one and only time I can think of that GBH arrived at a gig by sliding their way down. It was worth it, though. Berlin might have been bigger, but Freiburg was mental. Absolute carnage. Totally brilliant.

We stayed in Freiburg a few days, and got to make a lot of friends. There were German punks, French punks, and Swiss punks, all hanging out together, and none of them took any shit off anyone. We called them the Freiburg Peace-keeping Force. They seemed to have some kind of ongoing battle with the local farmer types, and they clearly weren't losing. We were drinking in a bar with a French guy called Arnaud, and some farmer started taking the piss. Arnaud didn't pause, he didn't stop drinking, he just dropped him. You could see the birds twittering round the farmer's head even before he hit the floor. Everyone carried on as if nothing had happened.

Slowly, the beefy farmer types twigged that it was best to give the punks a wide berth. If the farmers took the piss, the punks would stand up for themselves, and they'd just get a kicking. It wasn't worth the hassle. So when we were out in a restaurant in Freiburg one evening, the group of farmers at another table left us well alone. But there was a Chinese bloke sitting on his own, so they picked on him instead, and made him the object of their ridicule.

I watched.

He was sitting there, not batting an eyelid, drinking his beer, not giving a shit, while they took the piss and called him names. Then, nonchalant as you like, he stood up, wandered over to their table, looked them all in the eye - and pulled a gun out of the waistband of his trousers.

Everything went quiet. The farmers froze. Then they legged it out of the restaurant. The Chinese guy put his gun back in his trousers, went back to his table, sat down, and carried on drinking his pint. He caught my eye.

I nodded at him.
He nodded back.
And we each carried on drinking.

america

The tour of Germany had been a typical GBH production. A smattering of madness, a lot of beer, and a host of wonderful people. It was the trip to Holland and *Attacked By Rats* writ large. 1983 brought more of the same, in more new places we'd never dared to dream we'd see.

Up till now, Mike Stone hadn't had anything to do with sorting out our tours and gigs. I guess he'd had enough on his plate with Clay, with getting us into a studio from time to time, and with trying to sell us his great ideas. But in March '83 he branched out, and got us on the bill at some huge festival in Copenhagen. Birthday Party were headlining.

So we got to chat to them, and hang out with Nick Cave – a very mysterious chap, even back then – and we did our set, and then we got pissed. Somewhere in the lost weekend that was the GBH trip to Copenhagen there was a visit to a porn cinema where Big Mick's seat collapsed underneath him the moment he sat down, took out the back two rows of seats, and we proved that a bunch of pissed English blokes can find their way out of a dark room in a foreign country at a speed top athletes would sell their nan to better. Yes, we wanted to watch some porn, but we wanted not to cop the blame even more.

By the end of that night, we were back at the hotel, raging drunk. We're in Mike's room, and he wants to go to bed, so he just gets undressed, makes a half-assed attempt to get under the sheets, and passes out. On the one hand, I couldn't believe he'd just stripped off in a room full of men – I have enough trouble getting naked in front of my wife – on the other hand, falling asleep with us around, especially when we've had a skinful, was simply asking for it. We wrapped him in toilet paper so he looked like a big cocoon, and ceremonially burnt his underpants. I guess you had to be there to understand just how much fun that was, and how long it took us. From then on, those underpants became the Immortal Underpants Of Stone. You'll see Jock wearing them on the *Hanley Victoria Hall* video, and I keep them safe in my box of GBH memorabilia at home. They shall never leave, and I shall have them forever.

But my main memory of that trip to Copenhagen is that I learned just how much I hate flying. I took one look at the ropey old plane that was going to ferry us over, and I was terrified. It was like the first time I went on stage, thinking *I don't want to do this!* but a thousand million times worse. Because every time I get in a plane I genuinely think I'm going to die. Or at least that it's possible. I imagine all sorts of things... A crash at take-off. Fighting to get out of a plane on fire. Another plane hitting us in mid-air. What then? Will I be vapourised? Will I be plummeting to the ground, strapped in my seat, air temperature -50, watching the ground rushing up to meet me? It's incredible what your mind can throw up to torture you. And even when none of it happens, the terror never dies, it just creeps away into the shadows till next time you step on a plane.

Before Copenhagen, none of that mattered. Now it did. We'd be flying again, and soon. Because we were off to the States, and we weren't doing that without getting on a plane.

Crescent Moon Productions had rung from New York, wanting us to tour America. Were we up for it? Of course we were. It meant getting full passports instead of the cardboard Visitors' Passports we'd had till then, and it meant getting visas to visit the US, which meant a trip down to the embassy in London. At this point, things got more difficult. The repercussions of our trip to Holland and the criminal convictions we'd got for possession of an offensive weapon meant that we had to answer questions and jump through hoops and make solemn promises about our future behaviour. All to get a visa waiver which meant I could get back on a plane so I could spend eight hours being terrified because I was convinced we'd die horribly in some mid-air horrorshow before we ever landed in New York.

We didn't. Despite my worst fears, the four of us and Big Mick - who'd come along as sound man again - landed safely at JFK, made it through Immigration, and walked out of the airport. And life suddenly went all Spinal Tap. Waiting for us was a guy in a suit and a cap and a big white limousine.

Fucking hell! Whooo!!

We didn't know whether to embrace it, or get in a huddle and have a quick discussion of whether riding in a limo was what we were all about. So before he could change his mind, or realise he should have been picking up someone else entirely, we leapt in. Just as well we did. That limo ride was where the frills for the tour started and ended.

We got dumped at a hotel in mid-town Manhattan. The Iroquois Hotel, 44th Street, between 5th and 6th Avenue. Outside was New York City, in all its wonder, with the skyscrapers and the yellow cabs and all the things we'd only ever seen on TV. But we weren't going out there. No way.

You see, everything we knew about America, we'd learned from the TV. And on TV, the cabs and the skyscrapers had always been the exotic backdrop to detective series about people getting stabbed or shot or mugged or murdered. Just as our view of Germany had been coloured by the war, our expectation of the States - and of New York in particular - was that the mean streets were a jungle filled with mobsters, muggers, and guns. As soon as we stepped outside the hotel, we'd be fair game for the miscreants and deviants who'd be waiting just for us.

So we stayed where we were. Five of us gathered together in one hotel room, jet-lagged, hungry, and thirsty. And scared. Eventually Big Mick got up and headed for the door.

Where are you going?
I'm off out for some food.
Don't do it!
But I'm starving.
Stop him, guys! They'll kill him!

But he left, and we genuinely thought we'd never see him again. Twenty minutes later he walks back into the room with the world's biggest sub. By then I didn't care if I did get mugged - my stomach thought my throat had been cut anyway. It was time to take my chances on the mean streets of NYC. I left the hotel, crossed the road, walked about twenty yards - that was all I was prepared to risk on a first trip out of the hotel - and found a deli. The sign on the wall said "We don't make sandwiches, we *construct* them", and you'd have to say they had a point. I got the biggest sandwich I'd seen in my life. If anyone tried to mug me, I could wield it like a bat. Things were looking up.

The guys running the place were from El Salvador, and once again I was reminded of something I should probably have known anyway, that national boundaries mean absolutely nothing. People are the same wherever you go. Germany, the States, Chelmsley Wood. It's all the same. There's good people and there's bad people, and sometimes - if you're lucky, or if you're in New York - the good people make sandwiches which'll feed a family of four for a week.

Next day, the guy who was going to drive us round the States for the next six weeks turned up. He was an English guy. He looked familiar. It was John Greenhalgh, who'd been the sound man for The Damned when we'd supported them on Hurst Street back in Birmingham. *Hi! Remember us!* There was a good bit of banter about the fact he'd charged us £30 to do the sound for our set then, and now he'd moved to the States and was trying to get his foot in the door touring with bands on this side of the pond.

It didn't matter what we said, we weren't getting the £30 back, but to be fair John deserved every penny he got, because he was a proper trooper who ended up driving us round North America for the first two tours we did there, and some of those drives would be utterly monumental. One time we had to get from a gig in LA to another in Chicago. Whoever had drawn up the tour schedule must have been having a laugh, but a schedule's a schedule, and has to be stuck to. John drove for thirty-six hours straight to get us there. I'm not condoning whatever... er.. assistance he may or may not have had in order to keep driving and get us to the show on time, kids, I'm just explaining how it happened. And once again, I'm getting ahead of myself. Let's get back to New York.

Now we'd got over our fear of becoming a crime statistic the moment we left the hotel, we'd started enjoying ourselves. We hooked up with Al Pike, the bass player from Reagan Youth, who'd been one of the first people to write to us from the States, and he showed us round. It was amazing to look out over the city from the top of the Empire State, to watch steam rising out of manhole covers, to soak up the sounds and smells, to sit in a deli while the world walked by, and to feast on hot dogs and bagels and coffee. We even went and stayed with him out in Brooklyn. And we did all of that without ever getting raped or stabbed or mugged, not once, which was a definite bonus.

Our gig, our first ever gig in the whole of North America, was on the Lower East Side, across the road from CBGBs, in a place called Great Gildersleeves. We never got to play CBGBs, which was a great shame, but the GG gig was an interesting one. It was packed out, and it was right next door to the Angels' clubhouse. We were standing outside and some kid knocked over one of their bikes, and they came out and stabbed him. If that had happened on our first night in New York, we'd have run back to the hotel and barricaded ourselves in. Now - once it was clear the kid wasn't going to die or anything - we just saw it like everyone else did, as a bit of a kerfuffle. The Anti-Nowhere League were in New York too, so they turned up and hung out with us, and we met a guy called Harley Flanagan, who's a proper New York character, an original New York street punk, a drummer named after a motorbike with a life-story you wouldn't believe. Oh, and the gig got reviewed. I got slagged off for stage-diving, and as for GBH, as far as the reviewer was concerned: *Their exuberance makes up for lack of ability.*

He should have seen us on a bad day.

Next day we set off. And if there's one thing you're going to learn on a tour of the States, it's just how big it is, and how long it takes to drive from one place to another. Just in case we were feeling short-changed on road miles, the organisers threw in a little bit of Canada too. A self-drive tour in North America means a lot of time spent staring out of a window at scenery that never seems to change. After hour upon hour and day after day sitting in a van going mad with boredom, gigs are even more of a relief than normal.

And the gigs were great. We went from one side of the country to the other, from top to bottom. We met loads of good bands and loads of good people. We played in front of 80 people, and we played to 3000. In Richmond, Virginia, we played Benny's Cafe, a tiny place on a street corner, about 100 feet long, with a bar down the right-hand side. It's a bit of a legend in punk circles, but it held about eighty people if you packed them in shoulder to shoulder. So it was a tiny gig we can't possibly have made money on, but a great night even so. Then a few days later we were on the west coast, playing Santa Monica Civic Hall, where Golden Voice Promotions had gone out on a limb to put on the first ever punk gig there, with us, Circle Jerks, and a couple of other bands, and it was packed to the rafters. 3000 people. One extreme to the other.

We played all along the west coast. Adam's Avenue in San Diego, La Casa in Santa Barbara, Cafe La Grande in Hollywood. And then we got to San Francisco and played on Broadway, and while we were doing our set this spotty little punk rocker - eleven years old, escaped from home, sneaked into the gig - climbed up on stage and sang all the words to 'Big Women'. Pretty fucking cool. That was our first meeting with Lars Frederiksen and his mate Tim Armstrong, who'd sneaked in with him. They were two very cool kids who are still friends now. They loved being on stage that night in SF, and later they started a band of their own. They called it Rancid.

And then, in one of those my-god-it's-a-small-world moments, we step outside the venue at the end of the night and there, leaning against the wall, is Kai from Napalm.

What are you doing here?
Oh, you know. Hanging out.
Fancy a few days in the van?
Ja, why not?

And that's what he did.

Meeting Kai again was pretty weird, but it wasn't the strangest thing that happened on that tour.

Not by a very long chalk.

forbidden zone

We were in Chicago. We'd come back to the hotel after a bite to eat and a couple of drinks, and some guy was having an argument with his wife through the door of their room. You know the scene.

Honey, let me in!
No fucking way!
Come on… please.
Go fuck yourself, asshole!

So we come walking down the corridor, someone says something, we start chatting, and next thing you know he's back in our room with us, telling us his life story and having a few beers. I guess that eventually he left, and his wife let him back in to their room, because when we woke up in the morning he'd gone. There was an envelope posted under our door. We opened it.

As a thankyou, our mystery man had left us a whole sheet of acid.

A whole sheet.

A whole fucking sheet.

I can't begin to think how many trips that was, but it was a lot. The design on all of them was a white background with a purple triangle and a gold crucifix on top. We looked at each other. We knew our weakness, and our weakness was that we could resist anything.

Anything except temptation.

Those trips burnt a hole in our pockets all the way to Iowa. And then we'd checked into a hotel and there was nothing whatever to do, and somebody mentioned the trips. Well, it was a day off. What else was there to do? In for a penny, in for a pound. We necked one each.

The exception was Big Mick. He'd drink his own weight in beer, but he wouldn't do drugs. So he sloped off into the room next door, and the rest of us waited for the acid to kick in. I guess it did, because five minutes or half an hour or three days later there was a banging on the door. Big Mick had come over to complain about all the noise we were making, and ask us to keep it down. John answered the door. We all hid, because by now Big Mick was a big angry bear, rampaging through the woods, and we were tripping, and if the bear found us, he'd probably kill us. So we hid behind the door. The bear would never find us there.

John did what seemed like a fine job of placating Big Mick, and off he went. We were cheering and congratulating John on his good work, and someone knocked on the door again. Fuck's sake. Was Big Mick back already?

He wasn't.

John opened the door, and it was the police.

By now, I'm coming up strong, and the others are too. And that means John must be. He's tripping his tits off, and he's got to answer the questions and defuse the interest of a couple of Iowa's finest, who never have anything resembling a sense of humour at the best of times, and are unlikely to share our enlightened attitude to the ingestion of LSD. If the bear was scary, this is off the scale. But John is doing a sterling job, holding it together, answering the coppers' questions, and remembering to call them both 'sir'. He must have the constitution of an ox.

Two oxen. Whatever. It's fucking impressive. If I'd been in his shoes, I'd have been running down the road screaming.

Finally, when they feel they've sufficiently asserted their authority and put John in his place, the coppers leave. John shuts the door, and collapses in a heap like a puppet whose strings have been cut. I watched him deflating like a punctured balloon, poor bastard.

It was pretty intense, so I wandered into the bathroom to get away from it. The bathtub spoke to me. *Climb in for a ride!* it said. Well it seemed like it could be fun, so that's exactly what I did. I climbed in, the bathtub took off, and away we went, travelling round the universe for a couple of hours. I'm out on the edge of the universe in this bathtub, watching stars and planets and comets, marvelling at it all, and then I look at the glowing end of my cigarette, and it's the Earth. Me and the bathtub take a closer look, and we see it's total rubble. The Earth is just glowing ash and embers. But there's one thing that's survived – sticking up out of the rubble is a McDonalds sign. And when we saw that, me and the bathtub laughed our tits off, because we'd been all the way round the universe and come back to find the whole world destroyed and just a fucking McDonalds sign to show what there'd once been.

And suddenly, in all the laughter, I hear the voice of God. There's this loud repeating thud, and this big echoing voice. *Are you OK in there?*

Fuck me, bathtub! It's God!!

Well, it's Jock. Banging on the bathroom door, checking I haven't died. And I climbed out of the bathtub, opened the door, and there's a whole other world I'd forgotten ever existed, with Jock and Colin watching the TV, and John giggling in the corner. He looked a lot happier than when I'd seen him last. When he fell to the floor after the coppers had gone, he'd looked up at us, pale and sweaty and on the edge of complete panic. You could see him trying to find the words to explain what had just happened.

Finally, he found them.

Lads.... Lads.... I was talking to him... I was talking to the copper. And then... then his head turned into a snake.....

Sweet jesus.

And we had a whole fucking sheet of this stuff.

neil sedaka

You might think that by now GBH were coining it in. We weren't. We finished that six-week tour of the States with just $120 each. About £50. What did we do? We blew it all in New York, wandering round Greenwich Village, getting pissed and buying whatever caught our eye. And that tells you everything you need to know about GBH, right there. It's always been as much about having a good time as making money.

I could have hung onto that cash so I went home with something to show for my time away from Karen and Charlotte. Instead I ended up trying to board the plane home with a Louisville slugger and several miniature metal hoovers I'd bought from head-shops, which – I'm told – people used if they were snorting powder, whatever that is. I just thought they looked cute. What happened at boarding? I got strip-searched and given the third-degree. They don't like you getting on transatlantic flights with a baseball bat.

Or drug paraphernalia either, apparently.

I got back to Brum without a penny to my name. But the way I saw it, I'd spent six weeks seeing the world with a bunch of mates, hanging out with interesting people, and playing music. Oh, and I'd heard the voice of God in a bathtub in Iowa. How good was that?

All of us were busy enjoying the ride. It never occurred to us for a minute that if we wanted to build on the lucky breaks we'd had when we supported Discharge and signed with Clay, then maybe we should stop, take stock of what was happening, and take some kind of control. The GBH plane was taking off, and there we were, sitting at the back, having

115

a drink and a laugh, and enjoying what came our way. If we weren't gigging, we were rehearsing, or in the studio. Or we were at the bar, meeting new people who'd become our friends, who we could get pissed with. We were too busy living in the moment to worry about something as conventional and dull as plans.

It's our absolute strength. And it would turn out to be our weakness too. But we'll come to that later. For now, everything was good. We got back from the States, dusted ourselves down, popped down the pub for a couple of beers, caught up with our mates, and went back in the studio to record another album.

This time Mike had found a new studio for us: Strawberry Studios up in Stockport, which was owned by 10cc. For ten days or so we stayed in a B&B nearby, and – in between visits to the local pub and the chip shop – we recorded *City Baby's Revenge*. It went really well, but then it always does. And because we'd been in studios quite a bit now, and found our feet, and felt comfortable being in one, we started taking an interest in how it all worked, what this process of recording involved, how getting the racket we made down on tape was done. The first time we'd seen a mixing desk, we'd wondered how on earth anyone ever made any sense of it. Now we wanted to know everything, and we wanted to know it now.

For the engineers it must have been hell, like dealing with a bunch of manic kids in a sweet shop, but by the time we'd finished badgering them, we'd got our heads round the fact that each column of knobs was for a different channel, and each knob in that column did different things to the sound. Want more bottom end on the bass sound? Twiddle this knob. Want a bit less floor tom? Tweak that one. There may have been some chemical enhancement, for some people, and we may have got in the way a little bit, and the engineers might just have come close to a nervous breakdown, but by the time we'd finished, we were confident we knew everything about everything. There was nothing we weren't experts on.

So when Steve Gibbons came up to Stockport to add a touch of harmonica to the track 'Vietnamese Blues' for us, I decided I'd explain to him how to play the harmonica. He's been playing it for the best part of two hundred years, and I've been in the game five minutes, and here I am trying to musically direct him. I think it pissed him off. He didn't actually tell me to my face I was a wanker, but I think he'd have liked to, bless him.

But we were full of ourselves, and full of mischief, and always up for a bit of larking about. The devil finds work for idle hands, and when we weren't actually recording, or playing pool with Mike while we waited to record, our hands were definitely idle. And there, on the desk in the studio, was a directory with all 10cc's contacts. Well, 10cc had to know some famous people, didn't they? When no-one else was around, I went through it. There were some right nuggets.

We got on the phone.

Hallo?
Hi. Is that Neil Sedaka?
Er... who is this?
Hi Neil, we're fans of yours from England.
Look... I'm... Neil isn't here right now.
You're Neil!
No...
You are!
Who IS this?
Sing us 'Breaking Up Is Hard', Neil! Go on!

click.

Jonathan King, we rang him too. And Suzi Quatro might well have been in the mix, but I'd have been to shy to speak to her. There were too many teenage fantasies of her in the catsuit singing '48 Crash'. I couldn't actually *talk* to her, never mind take the piss.

So GBH were in the studio, having fun. Out in the real world, our old mate Spooner had died. He was a Birmingham punk we'd known since '78, since the days down The Crown, who'd always had a liking for heroin. Even back then, if me and Jock and Spooner were out on the piss, there'd be some point in the evening where Spooner would go missing. He'd have sidled off to shoot up, and we'd search the toilets, knowing we'd find him passed out in one of them, with the needle sticking out of his leg.

Every now and then he'd clean up, but he always went back to it. After a while, his reputation preceded him, and by the end, when he was living over a chemists near East Birmingham hospital, they'd have nothing to do with him. He even went in there dressed as a woman to try and con them into giving him some meds, but - if nothing else did - his monkey boots gave him away, and they threw him out of the shop.

He wasn't the first person from that punk circle to die. Chucky the skinhead had got there a few years before when he was caught shoplifting in M&S. Security chased him out of the building, and Chucky decided he'd scramble up a drainpipe to get away. When it gave way, he'd climbed high enough for the fall to kill him. Spooner's death was, maybe, less unexpected. It's hard to say. If you ask me how I felt when I heard he'd died, I can tell you that I felt nothing. I don't get upset by people dying - you won't see me sobbing over the loss of them - I get upset by my lack of response, if you see what I mean. It's always the same. When I was fifteen and my dad told me my granddad had died, I remember thinking *What should I feel?* And that's how it was with Spooner, too.

But it must have been playing on my mind in some way. The acid trip showed me that.

This lad we knew turned up at the studios one day with a bunch of big thick cardboard blotters, black with a red star. He was already tripping, and he seemed really happy on it, and my first trip back in Iowa had been a complete laugh, and I fancied another great time. So I was *Hey ho! Let's go! Let's have some of this!*

I dropped one. Colin dropped one. Ten or fifteen minutes later I felt myself melting. On top of that, it felt like I was crying, like tears were running down my face, which meant I couldn't really see what was happening on the space invaders machine I was playing. Not that it mattered, because the aliens weren't just on the screen, they were everywhere I looked.

Col looked fine. As far as I could tell, he wasn't melting. And when I asked him if I was crying, he told me I wasn't. *Come on*, he said, *let's go down the pub!*

There was no way I was going out for a drink and sitting in a pub when I was melting and crying and seeing aliens. So the others got me a taxi to go back to the B&B, and off they went. The taxi turns up, I get in the back, and we head for home. And then I see the driver's face in the mirror, and his eyebrows start arching and I see these horns are growing out of his forehead, and right there and then I realise I've been kidnapped by the devil. I'm in the back of a black cab, and the devil's driving.

Stop the fucking cab!

And the devil hits the brakes. Somehow this happens when we're right outside the B&B, so I throw all the money I have at the driver and scream at him to fuck off, leg it up the steps and into the B&B, and slam the door behind me. I've made it.

I'm out of the devil cab and I'm safe. Thank fuck for that. I creep up the stairs to my room, and sneak in. The window is open! Who could have done that? The devil, obviously. The bastard wants me to throw myself out of the window. He wants me to kill myself, but I'm not going to. Instead I drop to my knees, crawl across the floor, reach up, shut the window, bolt it, and draw the curtains. Now I'm safe.

Which means it's time for a cup of tea. Because there's nothing a cup of tea can't put right.

So I put the kettle on, and lie down on the bed. And I hear this noise, this high-pitched whine. It's exactly like the noise of the 2" tape running backwards at the studio when we're rewinding it to listen to a track again, but now it's the sound of an alien spaceship hovering over the hotel, sending me messages. They're bad messages, and I'd really like it to stop. Luckily, the steam coming out of the kettle is Jimi Hendrix, coming out of the kettle like a genie coming out of a lamp. And the noise of the kettle is Jimi playing guitar, which is a very good thing, because Jimi's a force for good against the spaceship and the devil taxi driver. I'm lying on my bed, I'm listening to the Jimi kettle, and I can relax. I shut my eyes, and I'm seeing vivid colours, and semi-naked women, and Jimi Hendrix playing his kettle guitar. This is good. This is more like it.

Suddenly - just as I'm thinking I really am safe - everything turns black and white, Jimi and the women disappear, and these huge rats appear and start biting chunks out of me. There's blood spurting everywhere. *Fucking Hell!* In my top pocket I find a crucifix which I picked up in Dachau a couple of years before, and which shouldn't be there but is, and I pull it out and I'm waving it at the rats and the devil shouting *Fuck off!* and I look up at the television and there's this woman

Anne Carpenter who was a nun who left the Catholic church and *who turned the TV on anyway?* and she's telling me I can get my life back together and get it back on track, which sounds like pretty unlikely right now, thanks Anne, and she's not having any of that, so she comes out of the TV and into my room, and then she turns into God, and I get smaller and smaller and smaller. I shrink right down, down, down to the size of a molecule. Possibly something smaller than that. What else are you going to do when you're face to face with the supreme deity?

This went on for hours. More and more of the same. It was incredibly intense. God and Jimi and Anne Carpenter and the devil and the fucking taxi driver, fighting over my soul right up to the point I passed out in exhaustion.

Col and the others? I asked them. They had a great time.

I really should have gone to the pub.

management

With *City Baby's Revenge* in the bag, we headed back to Brum, and life settled back into its regular routine. There were no devil taxi-drivers, and no aliens. We were either hopping in a van to head off to a gig - and there were plenty of those - or we were down at Concert Lighting, rehearsing and writing songs.

We treated it like a job. We'd turn up about midday, and be there for six or seven hours, six days a week. First we'd go for a pint in the pub over the road - you need a drink before you start rehearsing, after all - then once we'd got ourselves in the mood, we'd nip to the chip shop. From there we'd head straight for the rehearsal room. In there, we'd maybe roll up a pair of socks into a ball and have a game of cricket, or have a go on the asteroids machine which you could play for free, then we'd bang out a few songs, and head back to the pub.

That was a typical GBH day. Spent stumbling between the Hen and Chickens, and the tunnel under Concert Lighting which was our second home. There were four tunnels being used as rehearsal rooms, and one of them was ours. Alvin Stardust practised in another. Edwin Starr came in once and practised in a third. We were playing sock cricket and then we heard someone singing *War! What is it good for?* and there he was, the legendary Edwin Starr. American, and living in Tamworth, poor bastard. Still, at least he got to practice in a tunnel next to GBH, so his life wasn't all bad.

Karen hardly saw me. I'd get up, have a wash, get the bus into town, and spend my days with the band. And every now and then, I'd get up, have a wash, and head off on tour. In March '84, just nine months after we'd first toured there, we

122

went back to the US. It was another self-drive tour, on the same circuit, and John Greenhalgh was driving us round and looking after us again, and everything was a little less unfamiliar. The big difference was that Big Mick wasn't there.

He'd hooked up with Metallica. They'd been playing the same circuit the last time we'd been over, and we'd walk into a venue and find they'd left us messages saying *Hi* and wanting to meet up. We'd ignored them. We were young, belligerent, snotty-nosed punks and we weren't going to have anything to do with a bunch of long-haired hippies, and although we were persuaded to talk to a couple of people from their record company when we were in New York on that first tour, when we did meet up with them we just took the piss. They were wearing denim, for fuck's sake.

So even though they really liked us, and wanted us to tour with them and join their label, and for us all to be the next big thing together, we turned them down. Big Mick was smarter. He joined up as their sound man, and he's still with them now, thirty years down the line. There was an opportunity, and he saw it and he took it. We didn't. That's typical GBH. I guess we could beat ourselves up about our ability to do that time after time, but instead we have a drink and try and forget about it, else it'd drive us all mad.

Instead of Big Mick, we had Boring John. He was an old mate from The Crown who'd been a roadie for Sham 69, and Motörhead - they'd boarded his bunk up on the tour bus with him in it, and left him there for a day because he was the new kid on the tour - and he'd got the job by badgering us endlessly when we came back from America the first time. I remember him cornering me in the toilets in The Crown and telling me *Next time you go to the States, you're fucking taking me.* And that's what we did.

We were over there for about six weeks, and this time round, we were meeting up with people we already knew from our first tour, who felt like old mates already. There was Harley in NYC, there were Kraut and Toxic Reasons, who'd been our tour buddies last time, there were the Fujimoto sisters in Santa Monica, these two Japanese-American girls we'd met when we'd been drinking Guinness in the Mucky Duck pub round the back of the Civic Hall, who'd walked in wanting autographs and photos and became friends for the next thirty years, and there were Al and Hudley from Flipside magazine who we'd hooked up with in LA.

The tour was like an endless party, full of enjoyment and good times, fuelled on Guinness, JD, and marching powder. Even crossing the border into Canada, which was always a ball-ache because of those flick-knife convictions, wasn't so bad. And that could take up to six hours. We'd turn up at the border, show the guard the paperwork for the gigs, then he'd suck his teeth and shuffle off to the office so he could phone through to the governor's representative of the provinces the gigs were in to see if they had any objection to these convicted criminals turning up in their patch, then we'd all wait for the governor's representative to scratch their arse and think it over and ring the border guard back so he could wave us through and we could go and do our thing in Vancouver, Edmonton, Saskatoon, Toronto, or Montreal.

It was all worth it. We had a great tour. Did we make any money? None of us knew. None of us cared. The good times were rolling along, and that was all that mattered. And then, for some reason, we decided that what we really needed was management.

We were playing our first gig at the Tin Can Club in Birmingham, which was the new place to play. It was an old strip bar down in Digbeth, with dodgy old accommodating strippers, and one room done up as a Spanish galleon. The place had character. It was run by Jimmy and Nigel, who'd been managers of Duran Duran, and owned the Rum Runner – the biggest club on the New Romantic scene outside London – who'd been round the block and knew what was what. They were big noises, in Brum at least.

I can't remember what we got paid for the gig. Knowing Jimmy and Nigel, it wasn't a lot. But we did get a guest list. And seeing as this was Birmingham, and the world and its dog were our mates, the only piece of paper we could find, long enough to write out all the names, was a toilet roll. So we sat down, scribbled down maybe 300 names, and handed it over to see what they would do.

They chuckled. They liked our cheek, and they liked our style, and they took the toilet roll, and they let all those people in. We liked that. And a little while later we went to them and asked them if they wanted to manage us, and they said yes.

The first gig we did through them was up in Manchester, at The Gallery. We'd been doing fairly well up to this point. We'd come away from a gig like that with, say, £100 each. This time we got just £20. And instead of each of us getting dropped off where we lived when we got back to Brum, we got dropped off in town at silly o'clock in the morning, and left to make our own way home. What was this all about?

Amazingly, none of us questioned what was happening. None of us were happy about it, but these guys were our managers. We trusted them, and we guessed they knew what they were doing. They did. They saw a potential for making money that we didn't see.

The question was, who'd be making that money?

japan

By the time we went back to the States for the third time, in May the next year, we'd already lost one manager. Nigel had jumped ship. We'd had a little two-week tour of Germany and Holland in the spring, which was the first time he and Jimmy had spent more than an evening in our company, and that was when Nigel realised he wasn't cut out for life with a band like GBH, with our love of excess, our fondness for drink, our appreciation of drugs, and our enthusiasm for misbehaviour.

So when we landed in America, the role of responsible adult was Jimmy's alone. Which could have been a thankless task, except that Jimmy was quite ready to share in our misdemeanours. This meant the tour - which was another self-drive, because they always were - was one endless party. If alcohol was there, and we could get our hands on it, we drank it, although there was one year - and it might have been this one - where Colin got hepatitis and couldn't touch a drop. Instead, he had to shit in a box each day and leave it on his doorstep to get collected by the Ministry of Health. Really. I'm not making this up.

At least he didn't have to take the box on tour.

We were veterans of self-drive tours round North America by now. We knew what was what, and nothing surprised us. We'd seen it all. And then we got to California. Punk here had really taken off - it was massive, like nothing we'd ever experienced - and we were playing at the Olympic in LA, which is a famous old boxing arena with a capacity of 5500, maybe 6000 people. The biggest gig we'd ever played. And we weren't just playing it one night, we were playing it two.

And we weren't just playing it, MTV were coming along and recording it. And they weren't just recording one night, they were recording them both.

I stood there on stage that first night, looking out at a sea of faces, looking up into the gods where the ropes of the boxing ring and the microphone for the MC were waiting to be lowered in next time there was a fight, and I could scarcely believe where I was, or how far we'd come. Six years ago, we'd been nothing. Now we were headlining this huge show, and my musical heroes The Dickies - whose album I'd bought on a whim when I was a wet behind the ears punk in Sheldon - were on the bill too. It was too much to take in. I barely moved all night. I just stood there and played. I think someone gave me an award for *world's most inactive bass player* after the show, but I'm sure they meant it nicely.

They were two absolutely memorable nights. Our biggest gigs, and on MTV as well. Everything was looking really good. Our trajectory was in one direction: upward. That's what everyone was telling us, that we were made.

Guys, you've been on the circuit for a couple of years now, you've done your time, MTV have got hold of you, you're going places!

We heard it over and over from everyone we talked to. But they hadn't reckoned with the GBH factor. A lot of bands would have made the most of it, they'd have looked at what was in front of them and they'd have smelt the promise of success, and they'd have played the game. Jock, Colin and myself didn't. I just don't think it was in us. So on the second night, when the MTV director wanted us to wear a little bit of make-up so it looked better under the lights, we told him *No*. When he asked us to wear the same t-shirts for continuity, so they could use the best camera shots from each night and make the whole thing look seamless, we said *Fuck that*. I'd wear the same t-shirt for a week normally, but as soon as someone wanted me to, I deliberately didn't. Who was he to tell me what to do?

It was stupid. It was childish. It was typical GBH. People wanted to work with us and we didn't even see it. It went straight over our heads as we headed for the bar.

Chasing success just wasn't our thing. Doing what we wanted came first, however stupid it might seem to other people, however much the situations that led us into might come as a surprise to ourselves. One night in LA, just after the Olympic shows, Colin and I nip out with the Fujimotos, while Jock and Wilf head down the Rainbow for a drink. We drop by later in the van to pick them up, and Jock's nowhere to be seen. Then we trip over something. It's two people sucking the face off each other so hard they're almost surgically attached. They've morphed into one being down on the Rainbow floor. One of the people is Jock, the other...? We're not sure. So we pick them up, carry them to the van, and drive to the hotel. Normally, I share a room with Jock. Tonight, it's pretty clear I'll be sleeping on Colin's floor.

Two days later, when Jock finally comes up for air, he tells me *Ross, this is Lia. I'm going to marry her.* I still hadn't seen her face, because Jock's was always locked on, and I did wonder about the little matter of the girlfriend back home, and how he was going to deal with that, and I was kind of pissed off about sleeping on the floor. But Jock was madly in love with Lia, and Lia was madly in love with Jock, and nothing else mattered. So a week or so later, when we went through Vegas, the two of them got married in a little white chapel and became Mrs Jock and Mr Lia. Punk rock man and wife. With Boring John as best man.

We were already operating at the outer reaches of chaos, and having Lia on board just added to it. A few days after the wedding, we were back in LA again, waiting to fly to Japan for our first ever gigs there. We get up early in the morning to head to the airport, and - where's Jock? He's gone off to stay at the house Lia shares with her friend DeeDee. OK, it's a nice house, it's Rudolf Valentino's old pad, but he really shouldn't be there. We drive over there as fast as we can, and start banging on the door. No answer. We shout. No answer. Jimmy's pissed off. We're all pissed off. This could screw up our trip, big style. Next thing you know, Jimmy's picked up a brick and heaved it through the window at the front door of the house. It works. It gets them out of bed.

But it was all too late. By the time we got to the airport, the flight had gone. Jimmy storms off to try and get us on another flight that'll take us to anywhere vaguely near Japan, possibly with the option of throwing us out of the plane over it, and we hang about looking lost and needing something to do. Lia nudges me. *Look!* she says. I look round, but there's nothing to see. What is she on about? She hisses it again *Look!!* and this time, she points. Standing right next to me, dressed in some Inspector Gadget raincoat, and barely coming up past my knees - which is why I didn't see him the first time, because I looked straight over the top of his head - is Prince.

Whoo! We've got something to do!

Sad to report, he wasn't receptive to our attempts at conversation. And believe me, we tried.

Luckily for the little man, Jimmy came back having worked some kind of minor miracle, which distracted us long enough for him to make his escape. Or hide under a chair. As for us, we spent twelve hours in LA on standby, and then we flew - first class, and I've no idea how Jimmy pulled that off -

to Seoul, via Alaska, on Korean Air. We get off the plane in Seoul, and there's this nice long red carpet. For us? Really? Are the Koreans that into punk rock?

So we start walking down the carpet, waving to everyone, only to get ushered off it double quick. It's for the President of South Korea. The only interest anyone has in us is getting us out of their country and on a flight to Tokyo as soon as possible. We're straight on another plane, and finally we arrive in Japan, the country we'd have been in twenty-four hours earlier if Jock had managed to peel himself away from Lia, and we're starving hungry, and jet-lagged, and the city is like a scene from *Bladerunner*, and it's a complete culture shock.

There isn't a chip shop in sight.

Don't get me wrong, this isn't the end of the world, and over the next week or so we're going to really enjoy being in Japan, but that first night, when I'm dog-tired and desperate for some kind of comfort food, the traditional Japanese restaurant we end up in isn't the ideal choice. There's a lot of raw fish. Sushi and sashimi. Food that isn't cooked, and which could be dolphin. There's no way I'm eating Flipper. I play safe. My first meal in Japan is a bowl of peas. The promoter takes me to a McDonalds later.

That was one of the things about Japan. People were so helpful, so polite. I'd turned my nose up at his country's food, but the promoter didn't get the hump, he just helped me out. And yet the overriding memory of Japan is how utterly different it was from anything we were used to. The food was different, the people were different, the entire culture was different. Take one small, ordinary, commonplace thing: vending machines. In Japan, you could buy just about anything from a street vending machine. Cigarettes? Sure. Drinks? Of course. Food? Yep.

Fireworks?

Not a problem.

We'd played six or seven club shows round the country, and the crowds had been great. Very enthusiastic, very Japanese. They'd go mad for a couple of minutes, then they'd stop. They'd applaud. Then they'd go mad again. Then they'd stop. Then applaud. It wasn't quite what we were used to. And now we had five days off in Tokyo before one final gig, and the promoter had moved us out of the nice hotel we'd been in, and put us in a version of a Japanese B&B in a place called Azabu City. There was a park across the road, and primary schools all down the street, and nothing to do except drink, or play football in the park, or watch TV. We were bored out of our minds.

The hotel rooms were pretty drab, too. Jock and me had done our best to brighten ours up by buying two budgerigars and a couple of crabs from a pet shop, and sneaking them up past reception. We'd filled the bath, and built a rockery in it so the crabs would feel at home, and Jock had bought himself a bicycle, just because he could, and the budgies were happy flying round the room and fending for themselves, but we still ended up watching tennis on the sport channel with a beer in our hands. Then we found the fireworks.

It's a close call who was more delighted about this, the local kids or us. They'd come out of school at the end of the day, and we'd be playing football in the park, we'd be drunk, and we'd be letting fireworks off left, right, and centre. As far as we were concerned, being in Japan was pretty surreal in the first place, so throwing fireworks in the mix seemed absolutely fine. Especially when we were bored. I'm not sure the kids' moms were so impressed, but the kids loved it. They wanted football, and they wanted fireworks. And we supplied them with both.

Then one day Jock stayed in while I went out drinking with Colin. When I came back there was a note on the door of my room with the lyrics to 'Sympathy for the Devil', and *Ha! Ha!* scrawled underneath. I opened the door, went in, and discovered one of the crabs was dead, the budgerigars had been kidnapped, and Jock had gone missing.

Someone's grassed us up for having the budgies. And they've killed our crab.

What on earth have they done with Jock?

questions

He wasn't anywhere in the hotel. He wasn't with Boring John, or with Jimmy. He wasn't in the park. And he wasn't even at the vending machine that sold fireworks. He was gone, and none of us knew where.

Hours passed. We were wondering how we were ever going to find him in this huge sprawling city which looked like it belonged in a sci-fi film, where we couldn't speak or read the language, and where we knew no-one apart from some primary school kids who were our firework friends. We were wondering who'd play guitar for us in the gig we were here to do, when Jock suddenly re-appeared at the top of the hill, hot and sweaty and knackered, and on his bike.

It turned out he'd been pining for his wife. He'd been missing Lia ever since we'd left her at the airport in LA, and neither the fireworks, nor the crabs, nor the drinking had distracted him from that. Then somehow he'd got it into his head that she was about to turn up in Tokyo.

Quite how he'd worked that out was a mystery. Lia hadn't phoned, she hadn't been in contact in any way. As far as we knew she was still in LA. But Jock had convinced himself she was here, and so he'd pedalled off into Tokyo on his bike, looking for a wife who wasn't even in the country. Normally, when any of us did something this stupid, we were pissed. Jock was just lovestruck. Away he cycled, following his nose and the blind conviction that Lia was nearby. Twenty minutes later, he was hopelessly lost.

He had no idea where he was, or which direction he needed to take to get home to the budgies and the B&B. So how had he found his way back? Jock swears blind he didn't do it on his own. According to him, as he cycled up to one intersection in a part of Tokyo he didn't know from a hole in the ground, the Japanese traffic policeman who was standing in his sentry box directing traffic pointed at him, then pointed down one of the roads. Jock took it. At the next intersection, the next copper did the same. At each and every junction there was a cop in a sentry box who'd point Jock down the road he needed to take to get back to the hotel. They pointed, and Jock took it on trust, and turned left, or right, or whatever.

And it worked. Jock got back to the B&B just in time, because we were all on our way out to go and see Wilko Johnson play. He was in town, and we were going to see him, and I was made up, because Wilko was one of my heroes. When I first got into music, when I first picked up Mrs Hendricks' guitar, Wilko was someone I looked up to.

We go to the club, and we go backstage, and Norman Watt-Roy from The Blockheads is there, and I look over and there's Wilko's iconic Telecaster on a chair, and then I turn round and there's the great man himself. And we watch the show and it's brilliant, and we all go for something to eat afterwards, and I spend the whole meal asking Wilko the most banal questions you can imagine, because he's one of my heroes and I just want to hear him talk. And he humoured me, bless him. I think he realised just how much it meant to me to be talking with him, and he answered every one of my questions without ever looking bored. What a gent.

The next night, our last night in Tokyo, we do our final gig of the tour, the one we've spent five days waiting to play. And Wilko turns up to watch. We finish a song, and I'm tuning my bass before we start the next one, and then I hear Colin shout *Wilko! Get up on stage!* And I look up, and there's Wilko Johnson, on stage with us. Jock's giving him his guitar, and this is an incredible moment, and all I can think is

Then Wilko starts up with the riff to 'Cellblock No.9' and I'm doing my best to jam along and not fuck it up, and my heart's beating so fast I can barely breathe, and then Wilko does his speeded-up walk move across the stage, lays his head on my shoulder, and there I am, playing in a band with the biggest of my heroes. Can it ever get better than this? It does. After the show, some girl comes up to chat, and gives me a tape of the gig. I've met my hero, I've chatted with my hero, I've chewed his ear off and bored him stupid, I've played on stage with him and had him put his head on my shoulder, and now someone's given me a tape of the gig to treasure forever. Being a punk has taken me to some fantastic places and there's been some wonderful times, but that night stands out above them all. It's pretty much perfect.

So being GBH, we have a food fight to round it all off. I'm sure that really impressed him.

Next day, we flew back to England. With no cash, naturally. We got dropped off in Brum, I scraped together the pennies to get a bus to Chelmsley Wood, and let myself in, full of adventures and tales to tell. And there was no-one there. Why would there be? There were no phones, no mobiles, no way of telling Karen just when I'd be home. And for the first time in my life I wanted someone to talk to, because I came back from Japan with questions I needed answers to.

How did the Japanese police know who Jock was?
How did they know where he lived?
And who on earth killed my crab?

new faces

I never did get any answers. Not that I had time to worry about that. We came back from Japan and were back into the old routine of rehearsals down Concert Lighting, gigs wherever anyone would pay us, and recording another album, *Midnight Madness,* at Strawberry Studios.

That album heralded the start of a period of change. When we came back to Birmingham, we found Big Mick there with Metallica. In New York, we'd blanked them and their record company. Now they were on our patch. They were even rehearsing at Concert Lighting. Normally, when we were in there, a whole bunch of friends and hangers-on would take advantage of our open door policy to come and watch us rehearse. Now they dropped us like a hot brick. They abandoned us and started watching Metallica instead, the fickle bastards. There was only one thing to do.

We took Metallica out and introduced them to snakebites. It was the start of a beautiful friendship. And it led directly to us leaving Clay.

Mike Stone had been having a few problems anyway, so when Martin Hooker from Metallica's label Rough Justice had asked us if we wanted to be with them, we were really tempted. We were up front with Mike about it too. After all he'd done for us over the years, we weren't about to go behind his back, so we talked it over with him. He agreed with us: a move was for the best. So that's what we did.

A new record label. And with it, a new drummer. I think, looking back, we were all going through a bit of a wobbly time. After all, we'd had four years of constant travelling, of gigging, drinking, and taking drugs. At some point you have to burn out, and Wilf got their before the rest of us. There was no big rift, no arguments, he'd just had enough. And when Jock had met Lia, Wilf met her friend Dee Dee, and he wanted to be with her more than he wanted to be in the band, so off he went to America, where he and Dee Dee got married and moved to Texas. Which meant GBH needed someone to take his place.

There was one obvious man for the job. We contacted Kai. I can't remember how we did it - I think we may have sent a pigeon, or a telegram.

War over. Stop. Come join GBH. Stop.

Luckily for us, Kai did. He came over from Hamburg with a kitbag and some sticks, stopped with me and Karen for a while, then moved into a place of his own, briefly got married - possibly to save him from having to go back to Germany and do his military service - and generally fitted in to GBH so perfectly it was hard to believe he hadn't been there all along.

As soon as he'd got his feet comfortably under the GBH table, we went off on tour. A two month tour of the States. Even by our standards, it was our most chaotic to date. In no small part, that was because we took Pedro and Boring John with us, the Morecambe and Wise of punk rock.

Both of them had roadied for Motörhead, and each of them swore blind that they'd done the sound. I think the truth - at best - is that neither of them did anything more than walk past a monitor desk once. If they were sober they could pick one out of a police line-up, and that was about it. Neither of them was Big Mick, but on this GBH tour, one of them was supposed to be doing the sound, the other was looking after backline. What they did in reality was up for debate. They definitely got drunk. They absolutely bickered like an old married couple. And above all, they fought. They fought over who was going to drive the van, over who had first dibs on the Jack Daniels, over this that and the other. If Pedro said it was Tuesday, John would tell him to fuck off, it was the weekend.

They were very entertaining.

One day we did a matinee show. Pedro wanted to do the sound, and John wouldn't let him, so the two of them had been arguing all day. Pedro's argument was simple.

You never did sound for Motörhead.
I fucking did.
Didn't.
Did.
Didn't.

They kept it up for hours. Eventually, Pedro pushes his way to the desk and goes *I'm doing sound!* And John snaps. He finishes his bottle of beer, looks at it, looks round the venue, looks at the bottle again, and then cracks it over Pedro's head. Pedro's wiry, frizzy, curly hair gives him some protection, but he still feels it, so he turns round and lamps John good and proper. And away they go, swinging punches and screaming at each other till we dive in and pull them apart.

They were like that all the time. Off their heads, and out of control. How the fuck we're still here I don't know, because John was like that whether he was in the venue or driving the van. As far as he was concerned, any drinking at the wheel was balanced out by a selection of powders, which meant he was straight, and fit to drive. Even for GBH, that was going it some. Jimmy did his best to minimise the madness, but seeing as he wanted to play as well, he was never really going to get anywhere. Truth is, anyone would have had their work cut out with us - especially on that tour - because the natural inclination of everyone involved was to do the exact opposite of whatever they thought someone wanted.

We did get through it, though. For the first month, we toured with Agnostic Front, who were great. They're New York punk rock pioneers, and they're good mates to this day, and we love them to death. Back then, they had a precocious Italian-American drummer called Joe, whose path we'd cross again later, they had a pit-bull called Tarbaby, who'd sort out anyone who tried to fuck with them, and they had a little trailer-caravan they pulled along behind their truck, because Agnostic Front didn't do hotels. They went camping. So we did too. We'd do a gig, head out into the wilderness, find a place to park up, build a fire, and sit round drinking. If we had a day off, we'd stay out there, and sit round drinking, have a game of football, play some baseball, drink some more.

Our last gig with them was at Fenders Ballroom in Long Beach, California. We were doing two nights there, and the first of those was the last one on the tour with Agnostic Front. We'd had a great time with them, and we were really sorry to be saying goodbye, so at the end of the show we called them back on stage - and presented them with a baseball trophy engraved with the score *GBH 13 - 7 Agnostic Front* because on one of our wild camping trips we'd beaten them at their national sport, and we weren't ever about to let them forget it.

The next night, in the same venue, our adventure with the Cro-Mags starts. Our old mate Harley Flanagan was the bass player, and he'd got this band together. A revolutionary New York hardcore metal punk band. The guitarist was Doug from Kraut, John Joseph the singer was one of the Bad Brains crew, and Mackie was a top drummer who'd played with loads of bands, Bad Brains included.

Just like Agnostic Front, these guys didn't do hotels. That was where the similarities ended. The Cro-Mags were straight-edge, they were vegan, and they were Hare Krishnas. So they didn't stop at hotels because they'd stay over at Krishna temples instead. Trying to have fun with them was next to impossible, because they had this Hare Krishna kick going. They were sociable enough, but parties weren't their thing, so we spent a month on tour with them living in two parallel worlds. On stage, though, they were something else.

I can honestly say I'd never seen anything like it. They were incredibly intense. Agnostic Front had been great live, but these guys - maybe with the explosive combination of John Joseph and Harley together in the same band - took it to another level. I watched them do their set when they played with us at Perkins Palace, watched as John Joseph climbed to the top of the PA stack, and watched as he took a swallow dive off the top. I was convinced he was about to get killed - after all, even if he cleared the orchestra pit, he'd die when he crushed some poor sod in the crowd and hit the floor. But John Joseph knew better. He just put his arms out and over he went. He fell through the air, and the crowd caught him. I don't know how the fuck they did it, but they did.

So, another incredible month with them. And while they might have been straight-edge, we weren't. My inevitable tour drugs story? That happened on a Cro-Mags gig. We were in Morgantown, West Virginia, playing a venue called the Underground Railroad, and people kept giving me things.

First of all - for no particular reason - some kid gave me a tape of horror movie soundtracks. Then a lady called Marsha gave me some dope. A huge amount of dope. So, of course, I swallowed it. Soon I started feeling weird, then I started hallucinating. Everywhere I looked, this kid's head would appear. It'd be behind bushes, on top of trees, looking out of parked cars. Was he fucking with me? Then there were bats flying round my head, which I swear were actually there, though given that I was stoned out of my gourd and

140

hallucinating, that may not be the world's most reliable evidence. The only way I could think of damping this all down was to reach for the booze, so that's what I did.

We're doing a matinee show, and by the time we're due to start, I'm bolloxed. It feels like someone's turned the planet's gravity way up. I can barely lift my limbs. I just about crawl on stage thinking to myself that this has got to wear off soon. I'm just going to keep my head down, and get through the set, and then I'll go and lie down somewhere quiet and hide. We start the set, and I'm playing 'Feel alright', banging it out like a good 'un, and it's lasting forever.

Fuck me, when are they going to stop?

Finally I manage to raise my head up so I can look around. I'm the only one playing. Colin's at the mike, looking at me, Jock's staring at me and shaking his head, Kai's sitting at the kit with his drumsticks in his lap. They've stopped playing five or ten minutes ago. Everyone in the whole venue has been waiting for me to finish, and I've been playing along to the echo of my own bass on stage.

Oh dear.

Colin asks someone to get me a chair, and I play the rest of the gig sitting down. Next day was the first time in my life I missed breakfast. However rough I've been, however much I've pushed the boat out the night before, I've always made breakfast. This time I just couldn't face it. We were playing Philadelphia, and I couldn't stand up, never mind eat. It took me a week to crawl out of the hole that dope put me in, a week for it to wear off.

I didn't know it yet, but the next tour of the States would be more of the same.

good, bad, inexplicable

If there's one thing for sure, it's that life in GBH has never been dull. It might have been drunken and chaotic, but it's always been full-on. I think that's because we can't stand boredom, and we enjoy meeting people. As simple as that. Whether it's the bloke in the chip shop, or the owner of the greasy spoon we're eating in, or the people we end up chatting to when we're at the bar, we're up for having a natter and a bit of banter. We've made some great friends this way. We've met some arseholes, too. But whether they've been good, bad, or ugly, it's always beaten being bored.

Well, almost always.

Every now and then we find ourselves in situations we'd have done well to avoid. In the summer of '86, on a day off in Genoa during another tour of Europe, we got led astray by a Guinness sign. We'd wandered into town, and there it was, winking at us from above the pub doorway, luring us in. And we didn't need much luring at the best of times.

So we spent the whole day in there, drinking, and then it was time to pay the bill. That was when the penny dropped: none of us had cash. All of us - bar Pedro - were out of the door and doing a runner in double quick time, but being pissed and not knowing our way round the town, we ran round in a circle and ended up back at the pub just as Pedro was coming out at speed. When the penny had dropped for him, and he'd realised we'd left him in the lurch, he was out of there too. As we scarpered up the road I remember thinking it was a good job we weren't going to be coming back to Genoa any time soon.

Then Jimmy added a date to the end of the tour. In Genoa. And now we had a problem. The pub we'd been drinking in had been full of guys with very short hair and right-wing persuasions. It had been dodgy enough being around them just once. We'd been in the pub about five minutes when one of them heard me use the word *Nazi*. He was nose-to-nose immediately.

Hitler was a nazi. We are fascists!
Right...
We are not nazis!
It's OK, Col, they're not nazis! They're fascists! Everything's fine!

I mean, we'd have hated to get on the wrong side of them by calling them the wrong name.

We've had a fair few run-ins with folk of their political persuasion over the years. I used to take a cricket bat on tour with me. I called it Excalibur. In quiet moments I'd thwack Boring John across the kneecaps with it, just to keep him on his toes. One time we were playing a club in Toulouse, a nice club, and me and John went out to the van to get some more merch. There were some short-haired right-wing people outside who hadn't been allowed in the gig, and they saw the two of us and they circled round.

Oh fuck, here we go. I grabbed Excalibur, and John picked up whatever he could find. This wasn't looking good, but if we were going down, we were going down fighting. Then someone tapped me on the shoulder. I turned round, and half the punks from the gig were there.

You fight. We fight with you.

With the odds evened up, our right-wing friends decided a ruck wasn't such a good idea, and they got in their cars and fucked off sharpish. But that was Toulouse. When we came back to Genoa for the gig, the short-hairs were waiting for us. Six of us, about thirty of them. It was one of those scrotum-shrinking moments.

They weren't happy with us. Not only had we run out of their pub without paying for anything, which was bad enough on its own, but while we'd been in there we'd assured them we weren't going to be playing in Genoa. And here we are. That means we lied to them, and their manly right-wing pride is hurt by the thought they were taken for mugs. To be fair, that's exactly what they are. But this probably isn't the moment to tell them that. Instead, we decide to wheel out our old friend the noble art of diplomacy, and hope that it can save our skins. And it does, kind of. We can be very diplomatic.

But at the end of the gig, when Jimmy comes out of the venue with our money in his briefcase, they try and mug him as he gets in the van. There's a tug of war, with us holding onto Jimmy's top half as the van starts moving away, and them hanging onto his legs, trying to pull him out of the van. Then, just before Jimmy gets ripped clean in two, they let go, and we drive off. Admittedly, Jimmy's dodgy shoulder - which would pop out if he threw a punch, say, or if he got pulled in two different directions by GBH and a bunch of fascists - has got dislocated, but then that's the mark of a good manager, to lay your body on the line for the cash. And Jimmy, for all his faults, could be a stand-up guy.

One time he came up trumps was when we played this freaky pub-club in North Carolina. It had the best jukebox in the world, crammed with punk rock classics, it had a lovely crowd, and we were having a wonderful night. But - and this remains one of life's little mysteries - the place was run by rednecks. What were they doing running a punk gig? I've no idea.

We were supposed to be getting the door money, and Jimmy was on the door collecting it all. Then the chief redneck told Jimmy there'd been a change of plan. *You collect the money, we'll be taking it.* Jimmy thought fast, and had a quiet word with Ken, the tour manager for the other band on the bill. While we were on stage and the rednecks were all outside comparing pick-ups, Jimmy grabbed the cash, slipped away, clambered into the boot of Ken's car, and made his escape.

The rednecks weren't best pleased. We came off stage and they were waiting in the dressing-room. Where was Jimmy? We told them we had no idea, Jimmy had ripped us off as well. *Man, he always fucking does this!* We called him everything under the sun, they got marginally less moody, and finally we were allowed to go back to the hotel without any important bits missing. Half an hour later we looked out of the window and there were more rednecks, all with guns and pick-ups, bad attitudes and worse haircuts, wanting to check our rooms to make sure Jimmy hadn't been waiting for us in the hotel and they hadn't been taken for fools. *Check our rooms! The little fucker's gone!*

So they did.

Luckily, Jimmy wasn't there. In the end, they left, saying they'd be back in the morning and would take us out for breakfast - which was nice of them considering they were out of pocket - and that's exactly what they did. They turned up in the morning, took us out for breakfast, and made us sign this statement they'd written, promising - before God, naturally - we didn't know Jimmy's whereabouts or what had happened to the money. So good as gold, we ate, we signed, and we went on our way. And good as gold, we got to DC and there was Jimmy, with the cash.

It didn't always work out that smoothly, though. On the first or second tour of the States Jimmy did with us, we played some venue which was a ropey old strip joint somewhere in New Jersey. I can't even remember its name, and to be honest, I don't want to. At the end of the night, Jimmy goes to the manager's office to get paid. The manager locks the door behind him. There's a Doberman at each end of his desk. He sits down, pulls a revolver out of the desk drawer, looks Jimmy in the eye and says *I ain't paying ya*.

He was right. He wasn't paying us. Put in an impossible situation, Jimmy said OK, gathered us together and got us in the van. But he wasn't fazed. As far as he was concerned, sometimes everything went smoothly and you got your money, sometimes you hid in a car boot, and sometimes you got threatened with dogs and a gun. You took the scary moments, you chalked them up to experience, you remembered who the bad guys were, and you moved on. And when you moved on, you found the good guys who made up for everything else.

The first album we did with Kai as drummer was *No Need To Panic*, which was recorded at The Old Smithy in Kempsey, a lovely little village in Worcestershire on the A38. There was a house up the road for us to stay in, there was a shop where we could buy our fags, and there was a pub. When we weren't in the studio, laying down tracks and giving engineers nervous breakdowns - we broke the first one, and he ended up discovering Jesus - it'll come as no surprise that we spent the odd hour down the pub, supping a medicinal Guinness or two, along with some medicinal tequila and the odd medicinal pharmaceutical.

There was an old guy called George Pimlott who used to sit in the bar, nursing a pint. Everyone took him for granted or took the piss, but - being GBH - we went in, bought him a few drinks, and got chatting. Next thing we know, he's pulling his trousers down. *See that?!* - he's pointing to his arse - *That's a bullet hole! See that?!* - pointing to his leg - *That's a bullet hole!*

It turned out George had been in the Paras in World War II, and had been part of the operation to take the bridges at Arnhem, by flying troops in by glider. His glider crashed, George kicked the door open, and he ran for cover with bullets and machine-gun fire ripping the earth up around him. One of the bullets hit him in the arse, and threw him into some bushes. George's war was over, and once his wounds had healed, he was taken to a POW compound near Bergen-Belsen concentration camp, where he spent the rest of the war.

Everyone took the piss out of us for talking to George, but he was a great bloke, full of stories. The next day, he's there in the pub with a little bag. He pulls out the bullet they took out of his arse, he gives me his cap badge, and he gives Jock his uniform insignia. Things that were really precious to him, which he'd hung on to for years, and now he was handing them over to a bunch of drug-addled punk rockers, because we'd bothered to sit down and talk to him. That said a lot.

From then on, whenever we went to The Old Smithy, we'd make sure we spent time with George. Sometimes we'd just have a drink, sometimes we brought him a bottle of whisky. He had to have one of his legs amputated, and he ended up in a home, but that didn't slow him down at all. One day we arrived in Kempsey to see him cycling along. With one leg. When he wanted to stop, he just rode into a wall. Very carefully. He rode along parallel to it, going slower and slower, and when the bike stopped moving, he leant against the wall, got off the bike, and hopped away.

Unsurprisingly, the staff who ran the home put an end to these escapes - they couldn't have some drunk old bloke with one leg cycling up the A38 and going under a truck - so then we'd go and visit him in the home, smuggle him in a bottle of whisky, and spend some time with him. We even named one of the albums we recorded in The Smithy in his honour, *A Fridge Too Far.* You can hear George singing on one of the tracks.

The album title, by the way, came up when we were playing an outdoor festival in Avignon in France, and these French punk girls gave us some windowpanes of acid. We took them, and in a moment of madness and inspiration, this play on the film *A Bridge Too Far* – which was about the assault on Arnhem – came up. Brilliant. Then we had to play the gig, tripping our tits off. Jock was away with the fairies, Colin was doing his thing at the front of the stage, and I put my bass down and went to lamp some guy at the side of the stage who was making faces at me. But he turned out to be a bunch of cables in the back of the PA, so I stumbled back to my bass, and carried on playing, laughing away to myself, and listening to Kai chuntering away behind me on the drums. He hadn't wanted any acid, but Jimmy had slipped a windowpane into his beer, and he'd come up strong. All I could hear all through the gig was Kai going *You focking bastards! Focking acid! You bastards!*

We were tripping, and the gig was an absolute shambles. But then, the whole crowd were tripping, so I don't think anyone cared.

So that's the good and the bad. The inexplicable? It's this. In January 1989, a plane trying to make an emergency landing at East Midlands Airport crashed just before the runway. 47 people died, and just about everyone else was seriously injured. One of them was a lad from Northern Ireland called Steven McCoy, who was a champion boxer, and a fan of GBH. Now he was in hospital in a coma. His family asked us to come over and speak to him, to say something, to offer some words of encouragement. So we did. We went over to Nottingham Royal Infirmary, and his family were there, and we said a few words to Steve, and held his hand, and his family went *Come on, Steve! The boys are here. They've come to say hi. Give them the thumbs up!*

And the thumb on the hand we weren't holding moved. It twitched. It kind of came up. Steve came round eventually, after two months in a coma. He's in a wheelchair, but he's alive.

What did we do?

We went down the pub with his family and got pissed. We couldn't explain what had just happened. And getting pissed was the thing we always knew to do best.

broken

September '87, and another tour of the States. Another big old, self-drive tour for a couple of months with new tour buddies, The Accused. Splattercore. The same routine as ever: jump in the van, pick up the hire gear, and toddle off into the distance. Except that this tour would be a little different.

In Winnipeg, we were on stage, and some muppet decided he'd take potshots at us with a BB gun. I'm playing along, and I can feel these *pings* as things keep hitting me. At this point, we've no idea what's happening - it was only when we got off stage we learned what had been going on. Suddenly Colin's head goes back like he's been shot. We come off stage and we're all covered in welts and bruises where the pellets have hit us, and Colin's got a lump right next to his eye, just on the brow.

A good while later on that tour, we were in New Orleans, and by now the lump on Colin's eye is huge. Naturally, we've got no medical insurance, so we have to go along to the poor hospital to get him treated. It turns out the pellet is still in Col's face. He was a fraction away from losing his eye, just because of some idiot with a gun. A lesser man might have been knocked about by that, but not our Col. We were in New Orleans, and it was my birthday, and we went out drinking.

Pretty soon I was off my tits on a cocktail of tequila, opiates, and marching powder. And somehow all the French I'd learned or half-learned at school came flooding back. I was chatting to two French guys, in French, and understanding every word. I have no idea how it happened. Or what we said, come to that. I was pissed, after all.

The opiates weren't something that I'd planned.

About halfway through the tour we'd played the lovely Santa Monica Civic, and we'd hung out with the Dickies and we'd done a great show. The gig finishes, and there's twenty minutes till the Mucky Duck shuts, so I'm racing over there so I can get a couple of pints in. One minute I'm doing the Chelmsley Wood sprint, the next I'm flying through the air like Superman. *What the fuck??!!*

There's a shin-high chain-link face around the edge of the car park, and I haven't seen it in the darkness. I just have time to put my arms out in front of me, then I hit the ground and there's two loud snaps which I feel as much as hear.

I get to my feet, stagger to the pub with my arms held up in front of me, and order a Guinness. John has to hold it to my mouth so I can drink, because I can't even hold the glass, never mind pick it up. As soon as I've finished he tells me we really should go to hospital. And that's when it hits me - if John's being responsible then things really aren't too clever. This is bad.

We make our way to Cedars Sinai. By now I'm in agony. They take some X-rays and tell me that I've cracked my left arm straight down the elbow, but that the right one's fine, which is weird, because the right one hurts every bit as much. But doctors know their stuff, I guess. They put a guard round my left arm and send me on my way.

Next morning I wake up in the hotel room and I can barely move. We're driving to Phoenix, Arizona, and as soon as we get there I go straight to a doctor, because my arms are killing me. He takes a look. The bad news is I've cracked both my elbows. The worse news is they can't be put in plaster. The vaguely good news is he can give me something for the pain. So he gives me a prescription for something called Tylox, and warns me it's very addictive.

Letting me loose on that was asking for trouble. But it did the trick. I necked two or three to get rid of the pain, and ten minutes later I was away with the fairies, which was great. There was talk of me flying home to recuperate, but I was having none of that. Broken arms or not, I was staying out on tour. OK, I couldn't play bass, but we could work something out. I spent the afternoon giving Alex - The Accused's bass player - a crash course in GBH songs. That night he filled in for me, and did a great job too.

Everything was going to be all right. Thank fuck for that.

Alex, mate, if there's ever anything I can do for you, just let me know, OK?

By the end of the day I was back at the hotel, I'd drunk a bottle of vodka, I'd had a couple more Tylox and a prescription from our South American doctor, and I was well away. Business as usual. Next day, I got Pedro to put the bass on me, just to see if I could play it. And I could. I could just bend my fingers enough that I could play, although the pain was horrendous, and the bass had to be lowered on to me and lifted off after, a bit like Henry VIII getting lowered onto his horse when he was wearing his armour. Give me a week or two to heal, and maybe I'd be fine. For now, only drink and drugs were keeping the pain at bay.

The following day, Alex calls in his favour. Tommy, the Accused's guitarist, has hepatitis, so he's going home. Alex is going to play guitar, and they need a bassist.

He wasn't even kidding. And I owed him.

So for the rest of the tour I played two sets a night with two broken arms.

I was dropping these painkillers left, right, and centre, drinking a bottle of vodka a day, and taking prescriptions from Dr José on top of that. So I was well and truly loaded. And then we bumped into GWAR, and everyone dropped acid. Everyone apart from me.

By now, I knew I couldn't take any more. I was running at my limits. I was in constant pain, I was so full of drugs I rattled, and I couldn't get food or a pint or a fag to my mouth because I couldn't bend my arms. At every gig I had a nurse to help me because I couldn't even feed myself. I say they were nurses, but whether they had nursing qualifications or not wasn't the point. What really mattered was that they looked good in a tight white uniform, and were prepared to be motherly, and spoon-feed me one minute, then chop me out a line and throw a couple of Tylox down my neck the next.

And after all that, I went out on stage every night.

And played bass in a punk band with my friends.

fitting in

GBH itself is a family unit, a circle. While this means we look out for each other and are a tight bunch of friends, a lot of people who hang around with us for a while but aren't part of the unit, they end up in a mental institution, or discover Jesus, or they simply disappear and are never heard of again.

Sometimes that's just down to our natural high spirits. One time we had a guy come in to the studio to record some saxophone on 'Needle In A Haystack'. He'd played with loads and loads of bands, and came highly recommended. We took him straight down the pub and filled him full of tequila, Guinness, and whatever else we had going. He did his sax track, alright, but then he walked out of the studio and just dropped out of sight and off the planet.

Sometimes it's less benign. Someone doesn't click with us, and we just want him gone. For example, there was this driver on a tour of North America. We'd be driving along and he'd say *Wow! Look at the size of that building! Awesome!* Our bullshit detectors would kick in. He lives in New York and he still finds big buildings *awesome??* Hmmmm. Worse than that, he had no idea about van etiquette. That's very important when you're in the same van with the same people, hour after hour, day after day. You need to have a few simple rules so you're not at each others' throats. One of ours was that we took it in turn to play tapes. If you didn't like what was on, well, it'd be your choice soon enough, just wait. This guy fast-forwarded tapes he didn't like, or he'd turn on the radio and surf from one channel to the next so you only got snippets of songs. It may sound petty, but this meant he had to go. When you're on tour, with all the pressures and the stresses and the exhaustion and the lack of privacy, the van is possibly the nearest thing you've got to home. And it's *your* home, and the driver - important though he is - is just a guest. This one was shown the door.

The fat driver who spent his time picking his nose was never going to last long, either. First day on tour we were driving along, and he pulled out a pearl of a bogey and ate it. Then he did it again. And again. He did it all day, day after day. It was incredible - where did all this snot come from? - and it was repugnant, and he was impervious to our suggestions he should stop. So he had to go. By about four days into the tour we're writing messages on pieces of paper, and putting them behind the sun visor in the van so they drop in his lap when he pulls it down.

I am so fat I'm a prisoner of my own body and I pray for death.

Cheery stuff like that. He went. I think the snot had become a comfort food for him by the end.

So yes, we can be bastards. But when someone fits in and becomes our friend, they become part of our family, too. From the moment he'd arrived, Kai had been such a perfect addition to GBH that it was hard to imagine how we'd ever got by without him. He was a good lad, he was popular with the ladies, he liked his drink. If there was an opportunity for misbehaviour, Kai would be grabbing it with the rest of us. And whatever happened, he took it on the chin.

When we'd spiked his beer with acid in Avignon, he'd dealt with it. *Focking acid! Focking bastards!* while he carried on hitting the drums. When we left him on his own in the house one night while we went down the pub, and then came back in through the window pretending to be burglars, and found him hiding behind the door getting ready to brain whoever he could with a table lamp, and fell around laughing and took the piss out of him *Fock! I knew it was you! Fock bollocks!* he dealt with it. And when England lost to Germany - again - in the European Championships, and I told him I didn't want to talk to him for a couple of weeks, he understood. He'd been around us enough to know how much football meant to us, and how much losing to Germany hurt, so he went out to a rock club in Brum for the night, then had to leave when they found out where he came from. *Focking English! Fock you! Bollocks!*

So when we finished recording *From Here To Reality* and he told us that he wanted to leave the band, that he wanted to move back to Germany and settle down with Steffi his girlfriend, that he'd do one last tour of the States with us and he was gone, it was a sad moment. He'd been through so much with us, he'd dealt with our piss-taking for so long, and he'd been such an integral part of the band. He'd been a proper GBHer.

Having a fight with him on his final tour would very nearly kill me.

The tour was massive. A self-drive, of course, but sixty-one dates through more than two months of 1990. On this one, our tour buddies were Aversion, from Orange County. Their rhythm section, Joe and Eddie Tatar, were brothers. Eddie played bass, Joe the drums, and they'd been playing together since they were kids in their dad's cabaret band, with their sisters doing backing vocals. So they were tight. Really tight. Over the years there's been a few bass players who've really influenced me - Jim Lea from Slade, Rainy from Discharge, Tufty who used to be in Toxic Reasons - all of them made a real impression on me. And Eddie was another. His bass playing was incredible. He was part of a rhythm section with his brother who he'd been playing alongside since they were knee-high, so they just knew exactly what to do and what the other would be up to without having to think about it, and it was a joy to watch. Eddie was a star.

He was a star, but his roadie saved my life.

There'd been the usual tour excess of alcohol and powders, but perhaps we were starting to get a bit frayed round the edges, a little more ready to snap. Or maybe that was just me. Kai and me had already had a bit of a tiff, a vodka-fuelled row over nothing, and then we played the Masquerade in Atlanta. My memory is that the owner had just re-decorated the place. I know he was really proud of it, and wanted to show it off. We walked into the dressing-room and there was this huge, brand-new mirror on the wall. He smiled.

Whatever you do, guys, don't break my mirror!
We nodded.
No problem. Wouldn't dream of it.

As soon as he shut the door we got stuck into the booze. It was all good fun. We did the gig, it was great. We drank some more. It was even better. And then - being my usual fucked up self - I got pissed off with something and wouldn't let it go. Next thing you know, me and Kai are having a fight in the dressing-room. I pick up a chair and throw it at him. It misses. And goes straight through the fucking mirror.

I take one look at the chair sticking out of what's left of the owner's pride and joy, and decide it's time to make a quick exit and leave everyone else to deal with the fallout. I head off to a bar with Eddie and Rob - Aversion's roadie - and we find a table and drink tequila and lime juice, and then more tequila and more lime juice. And some more. And finally, the world goes black.

I wake up on the floor. It's daylight. I'm in a van. There's a towel thrown over me. I have no idea how I got here. I look out of the back window, there are palm trees. I look under the towel, I'm naked. Not a stitch on me.

What the fuck?! Where am I?? What's going on???

I don't even know what day it is, my heart's racing fit to bust, and I can feel panic starting to rise. Then I see familiar faces. *Ah-ha!* I'm in Aversion's van. Now we're getting somewhere. I'm amongst friends. I want to ask what the fuck I'm doing in the back of their van with no clothes on, but my tongue is glued to the roof of my mouth and my head's glued to the floor of the van, and speaking is beyond me. Rob looks at me, all stern, and shakes his head. *Brother...* he says, *brother...*

After I'd blacked out, he and Eddie had carried me to their van so I could sleep there. Yes, I was blind drunk, but at least I'd be out of harm's way, somewhere neither Kai nor the venue owner could find me. The two of them left me in their van and went on their way. And then - for some reason he couldn't explain - Rob decided, half an hour or so later, to come and check on me. He found me blue in the face, gagging on my own vomit. So he sat me up, punched me in the back to clear my lungs, and watched as I covered myself head to toe in sick.

Rob did the decent thing. He looked after me, cleaned me up, made sure I wasn't going to be sick again, took my clothes off because they were absolutely minging, and threw a towel over me. He did far more than that, too. He saved my life. If brother Rob hadn't come back to the van, I'd have died, pure and simple, so it's him I've got to thank for being here. In all the years of drinking and getting bolloxed this was the only time I came so close to dying, which is a surprise in itself really,

158

because I sailed close to the wind a good few times. Later, in the dark years, I'd think of actually ending things - but we'll come to that. This was the only time I nearly did it just by being stupid.

So that's how I came into Florida. Stark naked and lucky to be alive. Next day I saw Kai again, and - just like when I'd fought with Wilf all those years before - we made up immediately. Kai thought the whole thing was hilarious.

The focking chair sticking out of the mirror! Ha! Ha! Fock! You should have seen the guy's focking face!

Er... right. Can we just forget about that, please?

Fock you, mirror man! Here, have a beer! That focking chair, Ross! Ha!

Thanks, Kai. Say... has anyone got any clothes?

hand of god

We came back from the Aversion tour, all more or less in one piece, and Kai said his goodbyes and headed for Germany to be with Steffi. It was hugely sad to see him go, because we'd been through so much together. We'd taken the piss out of him ruthlessly, and he'd taken it right back. The perfect GBHer. And now he was gone.

We needed a new drummer.

We got in Joe from Agnostic Front. He was more than happy to be leaving Howard Beach, because there was a lot of gang-related trouble going on, and his friends were all winding up dead. I think that's the quickest and best way to explain what was going on. The final straw was when his mate Mike rang him from a call box somewhere in Howard Beach. Joe was talking to him on the phone when he heard the gunshot. He jumped in his car, drove round to where he knew Mike had been, and found him dead in a pool of blood, with the back of his head blown off. As far as Joe was concerned, our offer of a fresh start couldn't have been better timed. He came over to England right away.

We might have done him a favour by getting him away from Howard Beach, but we weren't able to offer much more. After years of endlessly gigging and continually rehearsing and putting out one album after another, GBH was suddenly having a quiet patch. I couldn't put my finger on exactly why, but we weren't going in the studio, we weren't making records, we weren't going over to the States to tour.

None of this was anything to do with Joe. He was a great bloke, and having him join the band really put the cat amongst the pigeons. Me and Jock and Colin had been together for forever and a day, and we knew each others' boundaries, and we knew how to give each other space. Joe was a one-man whirlwind, and he ruffled our feathers and shook things up, which was no bad thing, but we didn't know how to handle it. We'd never had to deal with anyone like him before - an Italian New Yorker who was one-hundred-miles-an-hour from the moment he got up in the morning till the moment he went to bed. We all stood back and waited for someone to deal with it, to take the lead, to show us what to do. Maybe for the first time in our lives we got an idea of what it was like for *other* people dealing with *us*. It was an eye-opener, that's for sure.

Joe was a force of nature, and he was a fucking caveman on the drums. He changed our sound a lot, because he used a double-kick, and he played at speed. Did it all gel, musically? I'm not sure. There's a live CD from a tour of Japan in '91-92, and some of the songs are so fast they're unrecognisable. How I ever played them, I don't know, because I was doing the same bass lines as ever. A song like 'See You Bleed', which has a tasty bass line to it, with Joe on drums I was playing that a hundred times faster than before. On the one hand, I was marvelling that I could. On the other hand, maybe musically it didn't show us at our best.

But like I say, none of our problems were really to do with Joe. He'd watched his friends get murdered, and he had a lot of anger to get out, but he was incredibly generous, and there were times when he did more than anyone to keep GBH alive and kicking. A few short years ago we'd been courted by MTV. Now it felt like we were on the ropes.

A lot of things contributed to that. As a band, we'd run ourselves into the floor. On top of that, the scene was changing, and while we were trying to navigate our way through it, hang on in there while we caught our breath and worked out what the fuck to do next, we'd no energy or enthusiasm left to drive things forward. We moved rehearsal studios. We moved again. We wrote a few songs, but the idea of recording an album made our blood run cold. We gigged a bit, in the UK and Europe mostly, but we were more fragile and less coherent than ever.

Even at this low point, though, we still managed to have some GBH adventures.

Argentina was certainly one.

This Anglo-Argentinian guy, José Luis, asked us over to Buenos Aires to play a couple of gigs. We'd never been before, and we're always up for going somewhere new, so we said yes, hopped on a plane, and twelve hours later there we were, in Argentina. José met us at the airport, showed us the van that would take us into town, then mentioned that he was on his motorbike - and he had a spare helmet with him, if anyone wanted a lift. I leapt at the chance. The opportunity to be on a bike after so long cooped up in a plane wasn't something I was going to miss out on.

So we're heading along the road into Buenos Aires from the airport, and I'm soaking up all the sights and smells, revelling in the newness of the place and the exhilaration of being on a bike, when José slows down, pulls over onto the hard shoulder, and stops. Just off the side of the road is the biggest billboard I've ever seen. It's absolutely massive, and written across it are just four words: *Las Malvinas son Argentinas*.

The Falklands belong to Argentina. You see, the Falklands war might have been ten years earlier, and Argentina might have lost, but no-one in the country believed that had changed a thing. As far as they were concerned, the islands were theirs. We were the first UK punk band to play in Argentina since the conflict had ended, so in every interview we did there were a few quick questions about our music, and then they'd get down to the important stuff, the nitty-gritty. What did we think about Las Malvinas?

What could we say?

Sorry.
Nothing to do with us.
You can have the fucking things!
Have your penguins back. Really.

After all, we were guests in their country. We didn't want to make enemies of all forty million of them. And as hosts, once the Falklands question had been settled, they couldn't have been nicer. For example, José knew we liked football, so he arranged for us to go and watch Estudiantes v Boca Juniors. The game was being played at Independiente's ground, which was surrounded by shacks and derelict houses where people had set up kitchens and stalls selling hot food - sheep burgers, dog burgers, or whatever - to the fans. As a Blues fan I felt right at home. Then we bumped into some of the hard-core Argentinian hooligans on their way to the game, and José decided it would be a great idea to tell them we were English.

Oh fuck. Here we go. The Falklands. We're going to get battered.

One thing saved us: the Hand of God.

When Maradona scored with his hand in the World Cup quarter-finals of 1986, and helped Argentina beat England, he'd given the hooligans bragging rights, and they knew it. There was no need for a punch-up, they just chanted Maradona's name and mimed knocking a ball into a net with their hand.

163

Hey, Inglès! Maradona! Maradona!!

It wasn't the only time his name came up. We were staying in a grand old hotel in the centre of Buenos Aires, and one morning we get woken up by the sound of trumpets. It's six o'clock in the morning. Which is way too near the middle of the night. We've been busy getting radged on good old Argentinian hospitality which only ran out of steam a few hours earlier, the room is full of people I don't know in various states of undress and disrepair, the windows are open, the curtains are billowing in, and outside there's some idiots playing trumpets. And they're not even playing anything tuneful, either.

I stagger to the window, step out on to the balcony, and look around. The street is rammed with men on horseback. Argentina's cavalry is milling about in the main drag outside, and there's thousands of them, all playing their trumpets and getting ready for the big May parade. It's a right racket.

Harry our roadie joins me on the balcony. *Oi!* he shouts. *Keep the fucking noise down!*

The cavalrymen look up. They're puzzled. Why are two half-naked men shouting at them? Then the penny drops and they twig where we're from. The trumpeting stops.

Hey, Inglès! Maradona!
Fuck off!!
Maradona! MARADONA!!

We must be the only punk band in history to have the entire Argentinian cavalry wave the Hand of God at them.

I think the whole country cared about that more than they cared about the war, in honesty.

slipping away

Argentina was a rare high point, truth be told. Yes, the whole Hand Of God thing was a laugh, but in the real world we were struggling to get by. All was not well on planet GBH. We thought we'd worked out the reason for the problem, so we did something about it.

We came back from Buenos Aires and sacked our manager.

I think it had started to dawn on us that Jimmy wasn't on the level. It seemed that he was always doing really well, and we were always skint. And then Colin managed to get his hands on a statement for the band's credit card, which Jimmy looked after, and there was personal shopping and booze on it, receipts from Threshers and Asda which had nothing to do with the band. And suddenly the penny dropped. Along with the pfennig, and the cent, and every other coin you can think of.

Naively, I'd always believed that the five of us - the band, and Jimmy - had been sharing everything on a five-way split, because we were mates. In my world, in the punk way of doing things, that's how it would work. Now I learned it wasn't so. The more we delved, the more we found out. None of it was good.

We cancelled the credit card. Jimmy rang up wanting to know what was going on. We told him it was over, he was sacked. I think he was a little bit shocked. I know he asked Colin to keep the credit card going for another couple of weeks because he needed it. Hang on - how do *you* need our credit card? Fuck off.

Learning how Jimmy had creamed us, and done it for

years, took the wind right out of our sails. Not that there'd been much left. We'd been telling ourselves we were all in it together, all mates, and now we knew the truth. And the truth was that we'd been idiots. We'd been so busy drinking and partying and enjoying the ride - while we let someone else look after the cash - that we hadn't seen what was really going on. We'd lost our way, we'd got no money, and that two-day special for MTV was so long ago it might have happened to a different band. I'd wake up every morning and wonder how I'd ever trust anyone again. What would we do? Who'd look after us? Who'd rip us off next?

What was the fucking point?

It was a proper kick in the nuts. As if that wasn't enough, the stresses and strains of life in a band that spent so much time on the road were starting to take their toll. Some of the gigs we did were OK, others were less so. We were exhausted, we were short of money, we were out of ideas. And on top of that - on a personal level - my relationship with Karen had gone west, and I was hiding, more than ever, in drink and drugs.

By the time we went to Germany, we were running on way beyond empty. The gigs weren't great - the bands were, but the crowds were poor - the atmosphere had changed, Joe was badgering us about money which none of us had, and Colin wasn't talking to anyone.

I think the final nail in the coffin for him was when we got to one venue, looked at the flyer, and couldn't find our name. Had they cancelled the gig and not told us? And then we saw this band *Gee Bee Aje* in the listings. *Gee Bee Aje*. You're fucking kidding. What halfwit's done this? Colin was having a rough time anyway, but to turn up somewhere and discover that after all these years of touring and slogging our guts out they couldn't even spell our three-letter name right, as far as he was concerned, that was it.

We got to Freiburg, our second home, full of old friends, and I managed to have a chat with him in the toilets. As you do. I asked him what was wrong and he said he just wasn't enjoying it, he wanted to go home. In all the time we'd been on the road together, I'd never heard him so low. None of us were having a great time, but the show had to go on, you know? *Come on, Col! We're on tour! You can't just leave!* We had two more gigs to do, then there were a few days off, so all he had to do was hang on in there for a couple of days and everything'd be fine, that was how I saw it. I hadn't given many pep-talks in my time, but I gave it my best shot. It would be OK, I knew it. Col would stay.

Next morning, my phone rings. It's Joe. *I've gotta talk to ya! Colin's gone!* There's a note on the table in their room saying *Sorry.* There's a big pile of money next to it. But there's no Colin. He's disappeared and left us to it.

It turned out he'd got someone to buy him a plane ticket back to Brum, and done one. For now though, our bigger problem was what we'd do about the gigs. The promoter already wanted to cancel the shows, now we had no lead singer he was keener than ever. But we needed the money. Which meant we needed to play.

There was only one solution. We went on stage that night, told the crowd what had happened and why Colin wasn't there, and gave them the option to leave. For those that stayed, we played. And I did vocals. That is, I *vocalised.* You couldn't call it singing. It was a unique style all of its own, born of desperation and not much more. At the end of the show some guy came up and said it was the worst GBH gig he'd ever seen. He said I sounded like Lemmy - which can't be all bad, right? I tried to explain the circumstances to him, that our lead singer had gone AWOL, that we didn't want to let people down, but he wasn't having it. Before I knew it, I had him up against the wall. We were doing our best, we were trying to do right by people, and he still wanted more. It was too much. Way, way, way too much.

We did two gigs like that, and then we flew home. Harry had a girlfriend who worked for Lufthansa and sorted us out some cheap flights, else we'd have ended up walking, and we landed in Brum and there was Colin at the airport. He was full of apologies for leaving, and he looked a lot happier – or at least less unhappy – which was the main thing. We just gave him a big hug and his share of the little bit of cash we'd made, and went to the pub.

Much as we tried to pretend everything was OK, that this was just the latest in a series of mishaps we'd shrugged off and that life in GBH was back to business as usual, the truth was we weren't in a good place at all. We were hanging on by our fingertips, living from hand to mouth by the skin of our teeth. And all Joe's generosity couldn't change that. He might moan at us about money sometimes, and drive us crazy with it, but other times he'd see we had no cash, and he'd go back over to New York, do whatever it was he did there, and send money over so we could eat. He moved heaven and earth to try and patch things back together, bless him, but it was beyond even him. Things were as difficult as they'd ever been.

Looking back, I'm surprised we got through it, that it wasn't the end of GBH, because it easily could have been. It happens all the time. A band burns itself out after a few wild years on the road, or they fall out, or they can't handle being skint anymore, and suddenly it's all over. Done. Finished. That could have been our story too.

That it wasn't is down to Joe as much as anyone. We weren't getting on. Me, Jock, and Colin weren't talking to him. We couldn't talk to him. It was impossible to talk to him.

We were still reeling from the shock of learning we'd been ripped off, and we couldn't deal with Joe wanting money we hadn't got, or wanting us to do gigs we had no stomach for, or wanting us to go in a studio when all we wanted to do was hide. A lot of guys would have said *Fuck you* and walked away. Instead, Joe got our mate - Stevie Young from the Starfighters - in as a mediator. He got us all in our old rehearsal space at Concert Lighting, and he made us talk. I remember thinking Stevie should keep his fucking nose out, that this was a band matter the four of us should be sorting out on our own, but I was wrong. Joe did the right thing, he got us talking and that helped clear things up. By the end of that meeting, three things were clear.

We were in a hole.
We were still a band.
We needed to put an album out.

So we put our differences aside for a bit, and went to Rhythm Studios in Bidford, just outside Stratford-on-Avon. Out in the country, near a pig farm. I remember walking up the path to the studio one day, and there was the biggest rogue porker you've ever seen. It was a pig about the size of a Vauxhall Corsa, and it had escaped. Everyone from the village was trying to get it back to its hangar - it wouldn't have fitted in a pen - and they were herding it with dustbin lids, and the occasional tractor. If they'd had a tank, they'd have used a tank. It would have evened things up a little.

When the Bidford pigs weren't on the loose, we got on with making an album. *Church Of The Truly Warped* might not be one of our best, but at least we'd got ourselves moving again. Walking, if not up and running. On the back of that, and to help ourselves get further over the episode with Jimmy, we decided we'd get out of the country, and go tour the States.

We wanted some good news, something to enjoy, something to look forward to. And GBH did nothing better, and was never happier, than when we were out on the road. So we contacted Andy Somers from The Agency group, who'd stuck by us over the years, and asked him to fix up a tour. He did.

We should have been careful what we wished for.

The tour was a disaster.

civil war

It all started well enough. We flew to the States and were picked up by a tour bus. This time we'd be touring in a bit of comfort, travelling through the night from gig to gig, living in a little home from home, with bunks to fall into whenever we wanted. We climbed on board and Colin opened a can of beer. This was our new start. We were celebrating the departure of Jimmy, the end of self-drive, and the resurgence of GBH. America here we come! This was going to be great!

But the truth was that we hadn't toured America for three years, and a lot of people thought we'd split up, or died, or they'd forgotten who we ever were. Or some kid - who'd be sitting in a nice Lincoln Continental, like as not - would take one look at the tour bus and give me grief because he reckoned I must be living in a mansion, when the reality was that I was one step away from being homeless and my life was anything but good.

There were still some good times. Living on a bus meant we had somewhere we could invite people back to for a beer before the show, or a party after. The back lounge became the party lounge, the bus nightclub. We christened it *Latrine's*, and that was where the fun happened. I remember dancing to Stereo MCs in there one night with Beaker, our t-shirt guy. Both of us off our head on ecstasy. I'm down to my underpants, having the time of my life, and suddenly - and to this day I have no idea where they came from - the lounge is full of half-naked girls with their tits out, and life gets even better. I make eye contact with Beaker, we give each other the big thumbs-up, we pump up the volume. *Wa-hey!!!*

For the most part, though, the tour was hard work. Hard, hard work. Numbers were shit. Some of the gigs were OK - the west coast was even respectable - but overall it was a grind. The novelty of being on a tour bus wore off, the poor turnout at shows meant we were barely breaking even, and living cheek by jowl with Joe was anything but easy. Me, Jock and Colin knew each other inside out and had lived in vans since forever. Trapped in a small space, Joe was like a caged animal. I'm not slagging him off, because I loved Joe, but he didn't know how to relax. Being on a bus with him on a tour where everything was running smoothly might have been manage-able, but this tour wasn't running smoothly.

Inviting people back on the bus wasn't always a good move, either. One night Colin had to spark a guy out when he got rowdy. His mates called the police and we had to do a runner, make it out of state before we ended up under arrest. On top of that, Joe wanted more money and the money wasn't there - we were living on $20 a day and even that looked like it was pushing things - and that wound him up even more. Everyone was tense. Every day the friction grew.

Then there was talk of the bus disappearing because we couldn't pay for it. The driver took me on one side and warned me *It's nothing personal. You're a great bunch of guys, but if there ain't enough money to pay for the bus, I'm outta here, and what-ever's on the bus comes with me. Personal stuff or not. You understand?* He was giving me a chance to make sure I kept my stuff with me, and from then on I did. It never actually got to the point where the bus left, but it was close.

So it was all a little bit fraught.

By the time we made it to the last gig of the tour, in Baltimore, we'd all had enough. We just wanted it to be over, so we could go back home and re-group, because we were exhausted. We were beaten and battered, and we couldn't understand what had changed, why venues weren't packed like they used to be, and why we were out of favour. We'd arrived in the States convinced we were taking the first steps to a GBH resurgence. Now it wasn't turning up on demand, and that was hard to take.

We still had time for a typical GBH gesture, though. We arrived at the venue and there was a homeless guy hanging around. We ended up chatting with him, then we invited him onto the bus for a beer. We gave him some smokes, and a few dollars to get some food, and he went on his way. A few hours later there was a knock on the bus door – he'd spent the money on a hooker and was going to get laid. Was there any chance we could spare a bit more cash so he could buy a condom? You had to admire his optimism. It was one of the few bright moments in a dark, dark day.

I never saw the fight coming.

I don't know what the audience thought, watching a band implode on stage. But watching it happen when you're part of that band is incredibly painful, and raw, and impossible to believe, all at the same time.

What kicked it off? Loads of things. Frustration. Disappointment. Exhaustion. A sense of betrayal. Take your pick. The trigger on the night was that Jock thought Joe was taking too long between songs, leaving a big gap between one and the next. Jock wanted things moved along, and Joe wasn't having it. He's from Howard Beach, and he's lived his life not being pushed around, so he tells Jock *Fuck you!* and wipes himself down slowly with a towel, flexing his muscles, making a big show out of not being intimidated, nodding at Jock all the while.

Next thing I know, Jock just picks up his guitar amp and hurls it at Joe.

Did I just see that?!

Then Colin wraps his mike stand round Joe's head, and Harry jumps in too. He said, afterwards, that he was trying to break things up, but from where I was it looked like he was throwing punches with the best of them.

I couldn't believe what I was seeing. I took a step away. Then another. And another. I ended up at the bar, still with my bass and my wireless pack. Back on the stage it was a brawl. Jock, Colin, Joe, and Harry were taking lumps out of each other, the drum-kit was flying everywhere, it was complete chaos. What the fuck was going on?

The guy behind the bar leant over to me.
Say, nice stage show!
I shook my head.
Mate, this is for real.

Security broke it up, in the end. But the gig was over. Joe stormed off somewhere, and the rest of us clambered back on the bus to lick our wounds and have a beer. One thing was certain - we couldn't let Joe back on the bus, not the way things were. Luckily, three girls we knew had come down from Pittsburgh to see the show, so we asked them if they'd drop Joe off in New York on their way home, gave them some money for the gas, and hoped that was that. Maybe a couple of days away from each other would help everything settle down and let us work out what to do next.

It wasn't much of a plan, but it was all we had. Unfortunately, it didn't work. Twenty minutes later the girls climb back onto the bus and throw our money back at us, saying they aren't taking Joe anywhere – he's grabbed their keys, got behind the wheel of their car, and almost crashed it. He's raging, and they're scared. One of them's telling us this and Joe storms in and slaps her round the face. And everyone jumps him.

I just want it all to go away.

So I walk away, into the back lounge, shut the door on them all, take a nice cold bottle of Jaegermeister out of the fridge, and start glugging. And I keep on glugging till it's gone.

It all calmed down eventually, more or less. But not till after the homeless guy had turned up again. He wanted to know if he could help. We'd been good to him, now it was his chance to repay our kindness.

This Joe guy – you want me to kill him?
No, mate.
You sure?
Yeah.
'Cause I'll do it, if you need it.
Appreciate it mate, but it's not like that.
Really?
Really.

We drove on from Baltimore with Joe on the bus, crying his eyes out, telling us stuff from when he was a kid, about life in Howard Beach, about watching his mates killed by gangs. You had to feel for him, poor bastard. We took him back to Howard Beach, sat with him, said our goodbyes, and left. We didn't talk about the fight, or what had just happened.

What was there to say? Joe's life was a mess.

And mine was no better.

nose dive

The truth was, I'd never been much good with people. Right back from when I was a kid, I found talking to people impossible. I was way too shy to even make eye contact, never mind say anything. If I had to talk to girls, I'd make silly noises - like nervous tics - or do anything which meant I didn't actually have to talk to them, or have a conversation with them. Because it terrified me. I even went through a period of wanting to be called Dave instead of Ross, because - in my mind - Ross was a bit of a loser. So I think it's fair to say that right from the start my self-esteem wasn't that high.

Then, like a lot of teenage boys, I found my refuge in music. I rigged up a speaker to an amp in my bedroom, and spent all day every day in my bedroom, miming along to Slade, Alex Harvey, or Thin Lizzy. One day I'd be the drummer, the next the guitarist. Sometimes I'd even pretend I played bass. I'd dream of being a cool rock star, because cool rock stars seemed to have none of the problems I had. They had their pick of girls, they were confident, everybody loved them.

But however much I loved music, and found an escape in it, I was still painfully shy. When I first started learning guitar, my friend Roy introduced me to the Alex Harvey Band. I spent days learning the chords to one of their songs, and then I invited him round. *Come on! Listen to this! It sounds great!* But the afternoon he came round to hear me play along to my Alex Harvey record, the idea that someone would actually witness me playing guitar was so utterly scary that I had to shut the door and make him stand outside the bedroom so he couldn't see me. He could listen, but he couldn't watch me play. No way.

That was with a good mate I'd known for years, so you can imagine how much more difficult I found it when there was a whole crowd at a gig. I'm constantly amazed that I walked on stage with GBH that first time back in The Crown, because when Jock and Col and Wilf offered me the gig, it was touch-and-go whether I'd play, or just have to do a runner and apologise to them afterwards. I was on the verge of legging it right up to the moment we walked on stage. If there's one thing that kept me going through the dark days I was about to hit, it was knowing that – in The Crown that evening and at every gig since – I'd somehow found the resolve not to run away when someone had offered me a pop at my dreams.

Without GBH, I don't think I'd be here, tell you the truth. I think I just wouldn't have made it, mentally. And if you think that means I'm saying this band has saved my life, you'd be right. But it wasn't easy, and it was a long hard road.

Every time we had a gig coming, I'd wake up in the middle of the night in a cold sweat and a blind panic. On the one hand – and this kept me going – I was in a band with my mates. On the other hand – because of how I am, and how hard I find it to relate to people – the whole thing was immensely traumatic. Every single time.

So why put myself in that situation? Why spend so much of my time hiding away, then get up on stage and play a gig? I don't know. It's a question I can't answer, but I know I'm glad I did. It's one of the paradoxes of my life that I made myself have to deal with people when dealing with people was the most terrifying thing I could do. But that involved bolstering my confidence with alcohol, in industrial quantities. It meant I was busy drinking and taking drugs so I could take myself to a place where I could talk to others because I was too battered to be able to worry about it.

I did it for years.

It had done nothing for my relationship with Karen. The whole time we'd been together I'd been off on tour, or away recording, or back in Brum but hanging out and partying with my mates. Doing all of that meant I was never there, and that meant Karen was getting messed about. Yes, she'd had whatever money I'd had, but a lot of the time I hadn't any money. We came back off tours with loads of great experiences, but no cash. And my experiences didn't pay her bills. Acid trips where I met god didn't put food on my daughter's plate.

A couple of years before the Baltimore bust-up with Joe, our relationship had ended. I'd come back home and all my stuff – not that there was much – was packed. From there on, there was just me and the band. So when GBH flew back to England without Joe, without any money, and with no idea what we were going to do next, I felt as though the one solid thing in my life, the one thing that had always been there, was at risk of coming to an end. Without GBH, what was I? Who was I?

Any band would have been shell-shocked in our position. And we were. It was a difficult time for us all. For me personally – I can't speak for the others – it felt like the world was ending. I just wasn't ready. I'd spent the past nine or ten years hiding from the things that terrified me. I'd hidden in plain view, with my mates, in front of audiences all over the world, while we'd ridden the wave, played our music and had a name and made some money – for other people if not ourselves. Now it looked like that success was gone. We'd found out our manager had ripped us off and sacked him, we'd watched success slip through our fingers, and we'd come to blows in the most public way possible. The future wasn't looking good.

Patching up the band might just be possible. At a stretch, I could imagine that.

I wasn't sure it was going to be for me.

dark days

One of the hardest things about the US tour which finished with the Baltimore brawl - given that watching the band fall apart was out there in a league of its own - was having people assume that the fact we were on a tour bus meant we'd sold out, that we had more money than sense, that we all lived in punk palaces the size of Texas. They knew *nothing* about our lives and there they were, pointing the finger. It did my head in.

The bunk on that tour bus was the nearest thing I'd had to a home since I'd left Karen's. Since then, I'd been couch-surfing, kipping at mates' houses, or hanging out at the studio. I wasn't actually sleeping on the street, but I wasn't far off, and I think I half-expected it was only a matter of time. At some point I was bound to run out of sofas or mates, wasn't I?

It was Harry who got me out of the shit. Big time. First of all, he said I could come and stay at his. Suddenly I had a roof over my head - and the same roof every night - which meant I felt a little bit less transient. Before we went to the States on that fateful tour, Joe was living there too, so at that point Harry had kind of opened a drop-in centre for itinerant musicians with fucked-up personal lives, bless him. And then when we came back off the tour, Harry turned round and gave me the keys to his place. *Here you go, Ross.* He was heading back to the States to get married to a girl he'd met there, and he didn't need the flat any more, so now the flat was mine.

I was sketchy as you like, but at least I had a place to live - until the council realised that Harry wasn't there, and wanted the keys back. But that would be weeks away, and when you're

179

living minute-to-minute that's so far off in the future you don't have to think about it. So I didn't. I just hid in the flat with my new acquisition, Titan. He was a pit-bull - I'd got him when his original owners had a kid and decided it wasn't safe to keep him - and a bit of a handful. One morning I wake up and Titan's sitting on my chest, staring at me, trying to be top dog. *Hmmm. This isn't good.* He's trying to intimidate me, so I know I've got to intimidate him back, which means there's only one thing to do.

I sneak my arm from under the bedclothes and punch him full in the face as hard as I can. *Have that!* Titan falls off the bed, gets to his feet, shakes his head and wags his tail, and decides he knows his place. From that moment on he was as good as gold. If only my other problems had been as easy to resolve.

Those weeks in Harry's flat bought me some breathing space. It didn't sort my head out at all, but by the time the council kicked me out I'd found somewhere else to go. A mate had introduced me to an eccentric Indian guy who had a few properties to rent, and he agreed to rent one of them to me. So in January '94 I moved into this four-bedroom house on the other side of Brum.

That might sound great. It wasn't. The house was big, and cold, and empty. And I mean empty. It was freezing cold, all bare floorboards everywhere, and all I had was a sofa bed with a thin foam mattress which me and Titan slept on downstairs near the kitchen in the hope being close to the cooker might help us feel warm. It felt like I was living in a fridge in some apocalyptic wasteland - even the chip shop was a twenty minute walk. I'd given up on hiding in plain view. By now I was just hiding. From everyone. The band wasn't doing a massive amount - everyone was just licking their wounds after the US disaster - and that meant I had nothing to do except sit around in this big empty house and get lost in my own head. And that's exactly what I did.

All my life there'd been this nagging thought at the back of my mind that there was something wrong with me. Now it took centre stage. After all, I had all the proof I wanted, didn't I? My relationship was over, I didn't know how to deal with people, I was skint, the band was on its way to being history, I was living on my own with a dog I had to punch in the head to keep in line, and I didn't have a clue how to do anything about it all, because I didn't believe I deserved anything more.

Put like that, it sounds innocuous. Takes just a couple of lines to explain, so it can't be that serious. But when those thoughts are banging around in your head every minute of every day, from the moment you wake up till you finally fall asleep, so that you've heard them so often you're convinced they must be true, and when you're freezing your nuts off on your own in a house that's little more than an uncared-for squat... then, it's a different story. A very different story. For the ten months I lived in that house I stayed up all night every night, drinking, tearing myself to shreds, beating myself up about what a fuck-up I was. And because there was no-one there to put the case for the defence, I was able to sit and wallow in my misery to my heart's content.

Things didn't really get much better when I moved. The council put me in a two-bedroom flat in Highgate, which was heaven in comparison with where I'd been. There were carpets, there was heating, there was an Indian takeaway next door and a chip shop down the road. It was walking distance to our rehearsal space in Rea Street, and just a couple of minutes from any number of pubs. The Lamp Tavern, Town Crier, Queen's Head, and more. I knew them all. But - however welcome it was - the change of place didn't change what was going on in my head. I'd stand on the balcony of my fifth-floor flat in the middle of the night and think about jumping, because then my worthless, miserable life would be over. Especially if I did it head first.

For two years I barely picked up my bass. The band still practised, but even though I lived closest of all of us to our rehearsal rooms, I hardly ever turned up. I might drop by and have a drink, but that was as far as it went. Even at the best of times, music can actually put me on edge, or rouse me to anger, and these weren't - by any means - the best of times. Once, I'd been able to find the courage to stand up and play in front of huge crowds. Now, even the thought of walking down the road and rehearsing was too much to deal with. So I'd hide in my flat with Titan, and get drunk.

And then, in the middle of the night, I'd walk out on to the balcony and wonder whether the best thing to do was jump.

mexico

Outside in the real world, away from my slow self-destruction, life was going on. GBH even did a few gigs in the UK. We did them with Joe, which might come as a surprise, but there was none of the tension which had marred the tour of the States. Baltimore was history now, and Joe was still a mate, and there was no animosity. Maybe that was because we knew these were his last gigs with us, so we could relax. And so could he. It definitely made things a whole lot easier, but we were short of gigs - which meant we were short of cash, and that would always be a problem - so there was still a sense of relief when Joe left and went back to the US. It meant we needed another drummer - we seemed to be working our way through drummers at a rate of knots - but fortunately we had someone in mind.

Scott had been hanging around with us for a few years already. He'd begun by watching us practise, and then he'd started filling in on drums if we were rehearsing and Joe was in New York, and then he'd ended up playing drums in Bomb Disneyland when he wasn't hanging out with us. He used a double-kick, like Joe did, but his style was very different, and he was the obvious candidate to take over now Joe had gone.

We asked him. He said *Yes*. And now we had a drummer from our own backyard rather than one across the Atlantic. Which had to be good. We promised him that any cash we made would be divided equally between us now we had no manager, but warned him that there might not be much cash. Or even many gigs. One thing was for certain though, it would be fun. Sometimes. Then for his first gig, we took him to Halifax. He enjoyed it.

His second gig was a riot in Mexico City.

I'm not high enough up the food chain to know how we got the gig. When all's said and done I'm just the bass player. I keep my passport and my toothbrush and my bass guitar to hand, and wait for someone to tell me what to do.

We've a gig in Mexico, Ross.
OK.

It doesn't ever need to be more complicated than that. Anyway, we fly in to Mexico City and the promoters meet us and look after us and drive us to the venue. We're headlining an outdoor gig at some basketball court, with a list of local bands as long as your arm on the bill before us, and a couple of thousand Mexican punk-rock kids ready for the show. It's absolutely heaving, and all the local bands and their mates want to hang out with GBH and have a chat and a few beers, which is fair enough. So while Col and Jock and Scott head off into town to do some shopping, I stay in the venue and get battered with the locals. All in the name of Anglo-Mexican relations, naturally.

By the time we go on stage the place is going mental. It's a cracking gig. And then, about three or four songs into our set, there's a bit of a commotion. Outside the venue there's another couple of thousand kids who haven't got tickets but who want to see the show, and they force the gates. This tidal wave of people pours into the venue, and the crowd just swells and swells and swells till every square inch of space is full. Pretty soon there's only one place left for them to go.

The stage.

It fills up. In the blink of an eye there's two or three hundred people on stage with us, and they're after anything that's not nailed down. I turn round, and there's people trying to dismantle my amps behind me. Someone else is trying to steal the strap off my bass while I'm still playing it, half-a-dozen kids are taking the laces out of my boots, and an army of them are dismantling the drum-kit. All of them are smiling, and none of it's malicious, but half the kids in Mexico City are grabbing whatever they can get their hands on so they can have it as a souvenir, like a plague of little Mexican locusts.

Obviously, the gig is over. But what's going on in the venue is only half the story. Outside, there's a full-blown riot. Cars have been overturned and set on fire, the police have turned up in force and are firing tear gas like there's no tomorrow, and there's helicopters overhead. We assess the situation and conclude it's definitely gone a little bit tits up. Any moment now they'll be sending in the tanks. It's time to go.

We got out of there with the clothes on our backs and not much more. I managed to hang onto my guitar - just - but we lost tuners, cymbals, leads, all the small stuff. And Colin's passport went missing, which meant we'd be hanging around in Mexico City till he got a new one sorted out. It was quite a day.

When the rest of the band went out that evening, I stayed in my room and watched TV. I was trashed from drinking with the locals in the afternoon, and I really couldn't handle any more excitement or any more people. I'd found the news channel and was watching the report on this punk rock riot *Ha! Ha! That's me, that is!* and then I fell off the bed.

Funny, I thought. *I'm not that pissed.*

It's an earthquake. A big, big earthquake. Everything in the hotel room is shaking, the coat hangers are rattling around in the wardrobe and falling on the floor, and I'm wondering whether I should be hiding in the bath or staying where I am or running for the stairs. What the fuck do you do when the earth quakes? I must have missed that lesson at school. Then my phone rings. Maybe it's someone offering advice. I pick it up. It's Harry. *Wa-hey, Ross! Earthquake!!* Thanks. I knew.

So, a weekend in Mexico and we'd played a gig which turned into a riot and now there'd been an earthquake. It could only happen to GBH. And Mexico wasn't done with us yet. We spent three days there while Colin got his passport replaced, and when we finally got to the airport to fly back to the States so we could catch a flight home, there was Linda Carter, the actress who'd played *Wonderwoman*. The woman who launched the libidos of a million teenage boys.

Harry's pissed. He sees Linda and starts doing the *Wonderwoman* moves. To be honest I'd forgotten she ever did moves, but I remember the costume, and the breasts, and I'm fairly certain Harry hasn't got the figure. Still, he's giving it his best shot, and when we get on the plane and she turns left to first class while we turn right for our seats in cattle class, Harry turns left too. He follows her up the aisle giving it the moves and shouting *Yoo-hoo! Wonderwoman! Over he-re!* A stewardess grabs him and escorts him back to his seat, but as soon as she turns away, he's off again, heading for first class. *Yoo-hoo!*

Fair play to Linda, she didn't bat an eyelid.

Life in GBH. You really couldn't make it up.

work

For most of the mid-90s, if you ignored riots and earth-quakes, GBH were pretty quiet. We didn't make any albums, we didn't go to the US. We just did low-level tours of England, with the odd foray into Europe to spice things up. This meant I had very little to distract me from my main activity, which was sitting in my flat in Highgate and driving myself insane.

They were dark times. Partly, that was because there was no money coming in from GBH. Mainly, though, it was because I was just rotting away in the flat. I'd always got past my fear of talking to people by getting pissed and talking complete bollocks, but now I had a lot of days where just the thought of going down the pub was too much to handle. I felt raw and exposed and uncomfortable around other people. I wanted to hide. On those days, everything I did was organised round avoiding human contact.

Something as simple as nipping down the corner shop became a logistical and emotional nightmare. Before I could leave the flat, I had to walk out onto the balcony, and look up and down the street. If I could see just two or three people, well, that was a crowd. And that meant I was going nowhere, not until they'd gone. Once the coast was clear, I'd run down-stairs - I couldn't use the lift because the thought of meeting someone and having to share a confined space with them gave me the cold sweats - and leg it to the corner shop. And if there was a queue in the shop I'd have to walk round the block and wait till it was empty before I could go in and buy my bottle of vodka. Then I'd leg it back home again, get pissed, and spend the rest of the day beating myself up and thinking about jumping off the balcony.

Mentally and physically it was unbearable.

This was as low as I'd ever been. When you can't even make it to the corner shop without it scaring the shit out of you, things clearly aren't good. I can't even tell you how I turned it round, same as I can't really tell you how I found the balls to walk on stage in The Crown that first night all those years before, but thankfully I did. Somehow I found it in myself to make it down the pub once in a while. That might not sound like much, but for me it was a huge step forward. I'd have three or four pints, level myself out, and manage to spend some time in the outside world. I was talking to people again – or rather I was listening to mates because I'd nothing much to say – and I wasn't running screaming through the door. I'd spend a few hours there, do a passable imitation of being human, and then I'd go home and polish off a bottle of vodka on my own. This was progress. I was still bumping along the bottom, and there were days where the header off the balcony still seemed the way to go, but now there was a glimmer of hope. Maybe there was light at the end of this tunnel.

One thing really helped. Mates kept trying to get me on the crew.

Every major city has a crew. If there's a venue in your city with a capacity of a couple of thousand or more, the sort of venue where bands turn up in tour buses, and bring PA and lights with them in a truck, then your city has a crew. Because somebody has to unload the truck. The band don't do it. Their engineers don't do it. They need a bunch of locals who aren't afraid of hard work and unsociable hours, who they can rely upon not to mess things up too much or too often, and those people are the crew. A small production tour with one truck might need eight local crew. On an arena show with five or six trucks it can be forty, maybe more. They turn up first thing in the morning to put the show together, and they're back at the end of the night to throw it all - ever so carefully of course - back in the truck.

Shows don't happen without them.

The Birmingham crew, Stagecraft, was known to everyone in it as the rockstars' graveyard. When I turned up for the first time, I looked round and realised it was full of people like me. People who were in bands but who had no money and nothing to do. People who needed work till the next tour or the next album, or even their next band. For all these people, crewing was the ideal way to get by. You could fit it in round other commitments. You could go away on tour for a few weeks and pick it up when you got back. You could have a good laugh and put money in your pocket at the same time.

Given how terrifying I find it being around people - and especially how difficult I was finding it at the time - turning up to work on the crew that first time was incredibly difficult. I walked into the venue at the NEC - the same NEC I'd helped my dad build when I was a nipper - knowing that I had to spend the next five hours of my life with the twenty or thirty people in front of me, and all I wanted to do was turn around and run away and hide. But I didn't.

I knew I had to stay, for my own physical and mental well-being. If I walked away from this, then I'd end up back at the flat and it would be only a matter of time before I jumped off the balcony. Deep down, I knew I didn't want that. So I swallowed my fear and I stayed. It wasn't ever for the money, it was simply so that I'd survive.

I was spending most of my time off my face, and that didn't really change just because I'd joined the crew. I'd spend the night down the pub, fall out of it at five or six in the morning, realise I had to be at work in a couple of hours, get straight on the bus, and turn up at the venue bolloxed. I remember one morning where I stumbled in with Punky, a mate on the crew, and our boss took one look at us and told us both to go somewhere quiet and have a lie-down. He'd seen us in some proper states, so we must have been bad. We staggered off to the hampers where the venue kept their drapes, crawled in, and crashed out for a few hours while our mates covered for us. That's what I loved about crewing - it was good work, with good people, who'd watch your back, cut you some slack, and take the piss out of you. And after all those years in GBH, that was a world I understood.

Now I could see why Joe had been crewing when he was over in Birmingham. Yes, it brought in some money, but it was also about having a laugh with mates, and about burning off some of the energy you could otherwise turn on yourself. And for anyone who's in a band, it does you no harm at all to get stuck into unloading trucks once in a while and learn how much work goes into making your gig happen. You see the touring crews who come round and appreciate the graft the locals put in, and then you see the touring crews who come round and treat them like shit, who think they're somehow better than the local crew just because they're on a tour bus. I hate that. And I'll tell them, too.

If there's one thing I've learnt, it's that sometimes the tiny decisions you make, the ones where you shrug your shoulders and think *Well, why not?* that are the ones that really matter, the ones that move things on. For me, taking up crewing turned out to be another one of those moments - like giving up the milk round, or going on stage at The Crown - which changed my direction. To say it marked a turning point might be putting it too strongly, there wasn't light at the end of the tunnel - not yet - but at least I was beginning to pull myself out of the dark place I'd slipped into. The balcony stopped looking like a possible solution.

Maybe there would be a future after all.

crew

Seeing as I've been singing the praises of crew, and how important they are to a band, I guess it's time for an honourable mention for the guys who've worked for GBH over the years. Some of them have cropped up already. Most of them are mates from Birmingham who've spent at least a couple of years coming out on the road with us to live the dream, get pissed, have a few adventures, and crawl out of the wreckage more or less alive.

First up was the legend that was Boring John, nicknamed Whizzpig – which gives you some idea of where his interests lay. He was an old mate who'd been a roadie for Motörhead, and who'd worked for Sham 69, and he was a sound man, of sorts. We had one gig in Germany where half the PA stack caught fire and he didn't even notice. There was another in America where he decided to take a broomstick and push all the sliders on the sound desk right up to full. Loud was good, so louder was better, and now he could get on with the important business of finishing his bottle of Jack Daniels without having to worry about the sound. The fact people were leaving the gig with their ears bleeding, telling him this was fucking disgraceful, only made him happy. So far as John was concerned, if they were in pain, that was an achievement.

In 1984, John was joined by our mate Pedro, who'd turned up at Colin's house one day and whose main claim to fame was that he'd worked in Spain as monitor man for the Pope. According to Pedro – and you can take this with as many grains of salt as you like – he'd been responsible for setting up the PA for John Paul II when he'd been doing a series of open-air masses in Spain. They'd become good friends, him and John Paul, even though the Pope had to give him a ticking off when he found Pedro in his dressing room about to use his mobile phone - *Hi mom, it's me! Can't talk long, the Pope's not got much credit.* And it was when he was working in Spain for the Pope that Pedro had picked up this Spanish name - his real name was John - and always kept it.

We didn't believe a word of it. But we loved the idea of Pedro making sure the Pope could be heard by the faithful thousands, of John Paul II doing the soundcheck with his foot up on the monitors *Give it a bit more bottom end, Pedro!* and even though Pedro was as mad as a fish and had more tall tales than you could shake a stick at, or maybe because of it, we took him with us.

He sacked himself. Regularly. We'd do something that upset him, and he'd walk away, but then seeing as he managed to upset us quite a lot too, we were pretty much quits. And after he'd taken a bit of time off and put his toys back in the pram, he'd come bouncing back and join us again, and tell us about life on tour with the Pope.

So when we played Pontiac in 1987 on our tour with The Accused, and realised the Pope was in town too, doing another of his open-air masses - presumably with someone else filling in for Pedro on monitors - we nipped over there, bought a poster of John Paul II from one of the thousands of stalls selling mementoes of the day, and signed it. Then we wandered back to our ever-so-slightly smaller venue, where we'd sell less merchandise in a lifetime than the Pope flogged in five minutes, and found Pedro.

Just met your mate round the corner, Pedro.
Who?
The Pope.
No! Really?!!

Yep. He says 'Hi'.
Bostin'!
And he sent you this.

And we give Pedro the poster of the Pope, which we've signed *Pedro! Lots of love, JP!*

Pedro is made up.

Thanks a lot, bag! Told you I knew him!

I'm stopped dead in my tracks. Is Pedro having me on? Or does he really think he knows the Pope? I still don't know. I'm not sure I ever will. I'm not sure I want to.

Next up was Harry. He was a spiky-haired young punk, one of the Pigeon Park crowd, who'd started hanging round watching us when we rehearsed at Concert Lighting. When the place got burgled and our guitars got robbed we'd pointed the finger - briefly - at him, and then had to grovel and apologise when it turned out we were wrong. *It wasn't me who said you'd nicked the guitars, it was... Jock. No! Not Jock. Someone else. I don't know who. But we know they're sorry.* That was the beginning of a beautiful friendship. Harry came with us to Argentina, and he'd been with us on the disastrous tour that ended up in the Baltimore brawl. He also came with us when we went to Israel in 1993.

We're playing two gigs in Tel Aviv, and we've barely got off the plane and collected our luggage when these two dodgy-looking guys are asking us if we want to buy any hash. Given that we're still in the airport building and haven't even got to Customs, we're hardly going to say yes. This stinks of a set-up. So we tell them to fuck off.

They usher us all to one side, where the policemen are waiting. We're all taken into a little windowless room, and told to strip. So we do. We know this is all about humiliation, about making us stand there with our tackle out, about them making sure we know they're top dog and we're playing by their rules.

They haven't counted on Harry. Nothing - and I mean nothing - is going to intimidate him. He's a well-endowed young man, and he knows it, so he starts waving his cock at them, pulling the foreskin back and forth, laughing at them. *You ain't got one of those, 'ave ya?*

It's not what the police expected. Harry's taking them on, and suddenly they're not getting a kick out of making five foreign punks get their kit off. We're all sniggering and their authority, that petty abuse of power they prop themselves up with, is ebbing away. This is going to be more trouble than it's worth. They mutter at us to put our clothes back on, and let us go. Nice one, Harry.

We picked up Geoff not long after the tour of the US where we'd rubbed shoulders with the Pope. He'd been roadie for The Accused - that's Geoff, not John Paul II - so we'd spent a couple of months on the road with him and got on really well, and then he came and joined us on a tour of Europe and Japan. It was attritional. For Geoff, at least.

In Amsterdam he parked our van too close to the tram lines. As he opened the door and got out, a tram was passing. The tram hit the door, the door hit Geoff, and Geoff went flying through the air and landed on his head. We knew nothing about this - although we had vaguely wondered why it was taking him so long to park the van - till Geoff came back from hospital with his head so thickly wrapped in bandages it looked like he was wearing a turban. He spent the next two weeks not being entirely sure who he was, or where he was, or what he was doing. Which meant he fitted in perfectly.

He'd just about recovered when we played in Prague. For

those of you who don't know, Prague is the capital of the Czech Republic, a landlocked country in central Europe with a very high percentage of beautiful women, and I don't know if it was because he thought he was on a promise, but Geoff had taken his bandages off, and he was down at the front of the stage while we did our thing. Then some punk in the front row reaches out and rips out one of Geoff's dreadlocks. I remember watching it happen. I can see the lad holding this lock in his hand, showing his mates, and I can see a big empty circle on Geoff's head, oozing blood. Geoff is too stunned to move, or do anything about it, so at the end of the gig, we go out into the venue and find the kid who's done it. We drag him back to the dressing room, lock the doors, and tell Geoff to go to town.

The kid was like a cornered rat, looking for a way out and finding none. Like we cared. He deserved everything that was coming. Geoff stood there, holding this big long lock in his hand, still in shock, and shook his head. *No*, he said, like the decent, peace-loving guy he was, *I don't want to do this*. And he told us to let him go.

The kid was lucky. If Tomo had been on that tour, he'd have knocked seven shades out of him.

Tomo was a mate of Scott's who used to come down Concert Lighting and watch us play, back in the days when Metallica were practising in the next room. He was another Birmingham punk, and we got on, and we took him away on tour with us, all over Europe. Most of the time he was either missing with the ladies, or sparking people out. If there was the tiniest hint of any trouble, Tomo would be in there, like a rat up a drainpipe. And you could guarantee that when it kicked off, he'd be in the thick of it.

We lost him in Italy.

We were in Florence, and it was a day off, a long day's travel to the next gig. So before we left, we sent Tomo off to the shops across the road from the hotel to buy fags and booze for the journey. Off he goes on his skateboard. An hour goes by. Then another hour. *How long does it take to buy some packs of fags?* We need to leave, but we can't go without him, so we start searching the area. We walk up and down the streets all round the hotel, and we check in the alleyways, looking for a gobby little punk on a skateboard. Or the remains of a gobby little punk on skateboard. We find nothing. We even phone the police. No joy.

We end up staying that night at the hotel. Next morning Jimmy – he was still with us at this point – goes down to the police station to make an official report of a missing person. He's describing Tomo, mentions the skateboard, and the cop's eyes light up in recognition. At the back of the station they've a crèche for lost kids. Sitting in it, amongst the teddy bears, hugging his skateboard like it's the only friend he's got in the world, is Tomo.

He went out to the shops and couldn't find his way back. And he couldn't remember the name of the hotel either. Eventually, after wandering round Florence for the day, he'd gone to the cops, and they'd put him in the crèche. Which was our fault, obviously. The fact we'd been looking in bins for him counted for nothing. When we turned up there, *he* went mad at *us* for leaving him stuck in a crèche for twenty-four hours. And he'd smoked our fags.

But Tomo was eminently forgivable. And a lot of fun. If you wanted to get hammered on tequila, Tomo would be ready to do it with you. If there was a fight, he'd watch your back. If there wasn't a fight, he'd start one.

And then there was the goldfish.

We were at some Dutch kid's house, E-ing our tits off. Tomo wasn't even our roadie anymore, but he'd got well into his dance scene and he'd blagged a lift to Amsterdam with us to spend the weekend raving it up while we played a couple of gigs. Anyway, we're in this house and one of the kid's goldfish goes missing. Or that's what he reckons, though I can't see how on earth this would happen. I might be off my head, but I know fish don't just disappear. Then I look at Tomo, who's sat next to me. He looks me right in the eye, completely deadpan, and opens his mouth. There's a goldfish flopping around on it.

Did I just see that??!!

I look again, but Tomo's mouth is firmly closed. I'm not sure whether he swallowed the fish or put it back in the tank. I don't think Tomo's too sure either. He did like his pills.

We had to drop him off in Kent on the way home, though. He'd insisted on playing rave music the whole way back. None of us were into it at all - even when I was off my nuts on E it did nothing for me, in fact I'd got myself thrown out of one rave for badgering people about their shit taste in music - but if we didn't like it, Tomo didn't care, and when Colin said something about him giving it a rest, Tomo bust his nose open. So we pulled over, dumped him in a car park, and told him to get back to Brum on his own.

Next afternoon there was a knock on the door of my flat. It was Tomo, come to say sorry. He wasn't playing rave music, which was a relief.

Come on in, mate. Have a cup of tea.

After all, he was a proper GBHer. All the guys who worked for us were.

197

enzo

We were kicking around in Brum, not doing very much of anything, when out of nowhere we got a phone call. It was from a guy called Enzo, telling us he wanted us to come and tour Italy. He'd got contacts and he'd got clout, and he reckoned he could put together a tour of venues all round the country. They'd be big venues, too. Up to 2500 capacity. Were we interested?

We were. We piled in the van, took Tomo as our roadie, and headed over to Milan. Maybe, at last, our luck was changing. Maybe the good times were back. We drove across Europe, got to the hotel where we're meeting Enzo, checked in, and then joined him in the pizza parlour downstairs to have something to eat and unwind after the journey. We're being fed and watered and we're about to start a tour, so we're all in good spirits. When the bill comes Enzo tells the waiter he's left his money upstairs and it'll just be easiest to charge it to his room, and there's a bit of an argument over it, but I reckon that's just because the waiter's not happy about not getting a tip. I mean, these things happen. Storm in an Italian teacup, nothing more.

Enzo goes back to his room to sort out a few last-minute details for the tour, and we adjourn to the bar to have a few beers with some guys from one of the other bands. A little while later myself and this guy Marco decide we should invite Enzo to come and join us all for a drink - after all, we're going to be working with him for the next couple of weeks, so we might as well be sociable. We go up to his room. He's on the phone to someone, speaking Italian, and he's clearly pretty pissed off. Marco translates. He tells me Enzo's talking to the venue we're playing next day, and he's upset because the venue haven't printed enough tickets for the gig, which means loads of people who want tickets won't be able to get them, which means they're going to be upset, which means Enzo's not happy. Well, I think, that sounds all right. Looks like he's got his eye on the ball. The tour's going to be a good one!

The next day we get up and Enzo's done a runner.

Some of his luggage is still in his room, but he's nowhere to be seen, which means that any minute now the hotel will throw us out on our ear. We go through his stuff in case there's a wad of money we can appease them with, but all we find is a journal. Marco starts reading it. We're still searching the room for money when he puts his head in his hands and moans. *Cazze! Fuck! Cazze!*

Our Italian isn't brilliant, but we guess this isn't good.

It turned out Enzo was in love with a prostitute who had a smack habit. She spent her time taking the piss out of Enzo because he fucked up everything he turned his hand to - whereas her life was one screaming success after another, obviously. *So,* Enzo writes, *I shall prove myself. I shall get GBH over to Italy and have a successful tour with them and prove to her I am not a failure.*

So he'd brought us over to do a tour so he could win the love of a junkie prostitute. That was a new one, even for us. All I could think - once I'd got past wanting to kill him - was this was typical GBH. How many other bands could end up in the situations we did? Who else would travel halfway across Europe to play packed out venues and find the whole thing was nothing more than the desperate imaginings of some crazy Italian flake?

We went to the first gig anyway, more in hope than expectation. It was a tiny film noir cinema which could hold about 300 people. Not quite the 2500 capacity venue we'd been promised, but I don't think any of us were too surprised by that. We'd dealt with worse, and we could deal with this. We are GBH. The show must go on!

We started getting our gear out of the van and taking it into the cinema. And then the cinema owners told us - via Marco - that there was no gig. Yes, it had been booked in, but Enzo had cancelled it. There were no lights brought in, there was no PA, there'd been no publicity. Nobody knew about this gig except us.

Now we were really in the shit. We'd been ready for small gigs, but we'd never considered the possibility there were no gigs at all. This was a disaster. No gigs equalled no money. No money equalled no getting home.

Marco saved us. He stepped in and took us back to Turin and let us stay in his dad's apartment. That, and that alone, was good. Then, in the space of one day, he arranged a gig in a squat in Turin and got enough people to turn up for us to scrape together the money to get home. Which was way beyond the call of duty. Things got a little bit hairy when the people from the squat across the road came over to argue the toss about the fact we were playing in a communist squat and not playing there instead, and the whole gig nearly turned into one big brawl, but in the end everything got sorted out, nobody died, and we were able to put just enough petrol in the van to get us back to Brum - as long as we took it steady, and coasted when we went down hills.

By the time we got to Birmingham, the van was running on fumes. OK, so the tour had never happened, but thanks to Marco - who we owed big time - at least we'd made it home.

We brushed ourselves off, found enough money down the back of the sofa to buy a bag of chips and some scratchings, and went down the studio to rehearse. Music was all we had to take our mind off the fact we'd been screwed over yet again. Yes, we'd met some great people who'd helped us out of the mire, and we were grateful for that, but we were skint. Absolutely rock-bottom skint. Which meant Frank Lea caught us at a bad time.

Frank - whose brother Jimmy had been in Slade, and been one of my heroes - wanted to talk with us because he'd just bought Clay Records. He offered us a deal. If we sold him the rights to all our Clay recordings, he'd give us £10,000. We hadn't got a penny. So we didn't even think about it. We just looked at each other and thought of money when we had none, and we said *Yes. Just show us where to sign.*

From that moment on, we got no royalties from any sales of any of the songs we'd done on Clay. That wasn't a good deal. Not that it was Frank's fault - he made us an offer and we said yes and that was all there was to it. But he'd caught us at a bad time, and I still feel aggrieved that we sold so much of our work for so little, all because we'd just struggled back from Italy from a tour dreamt up by some sad knacker in love with a heroin-addicted prostitute who wanted nothing to do with him anyway.

And I'll bet that never happened to The Clash.

punk junkies

In 1996, we went back in the studio. And came up with *Punk Junkies,* which was a brilliant album. The best we'd done in years. Maybe ever.

I don't know where it came from or how it happened, but everyone was on top form. Why? I haven't the foggiest. Was it because we'd had some time off? Because we'd been through a dark time and come out the other side? Did the change in personnel help? Or had we just become better musicians and honed our craft over the years? Maybe all of these things and none. Perhaps we just hit that first chord at the moment all our stars lined up, and some butterfly farted in Sumatra - that makes as much sense to me as anything - and from then on it was destined to be great.

Jock's guitar work was immense. Whatever it was he did on *Punk Junkies*, he'd never done it before and I'm not sure he's done it since. Scott, on his first venture into recording with us, proved he could cut the mustard - and proved Joe's barbs about his drumming wrong - by turning in a great performance. Col's vocals were spot on, and the bass playing wasn't bad either.

For me, it's my favourite album. Musically strong, and fun to make. It even had a throwaway track called 'Enzo Is A Cunt'. The title pretty much says everything you need to know. It's blunt and to the point, and it allowed us to get the Italian fiasco off our chest, and turn another one of our misadventures into something loud and brash and vicious. To this day we've no idea where he is, whether he's haplessly chasing after his smackhead love, dreaming up new schemes to win her over, or being hounded for money for pizzas he never paid for. Who knows? Who cares?

What we did know was that - somehow - we'd stumbled on the makings of a really good album. So it was a massive disappointment when it failed the cassette test. See, whenever we recorded an album we played it on a car tape deck to see how it sounded. Did it work? Or didn't it? *Punk Junkies* failed, and it failed when we played it at home as well. That was a major setback, because we were all too aware that we couldn't afford to go back in to the studio and record it all again, and we couldn't work out what was wrong, why these songs didn't sound amazing on tape, when they'd sounded so fantastic in the studio.

Luckily for us, Paul the engineer - who was a great bloke, and one of the few we never broke - sorted it out. When we trooped in to the studio the morning after the cassette test fail, he had a plan.

Right. I've got this little box of tricks here. We're going to plug it into the desk... like this... and that comes out of the other end... like that... and this goes back into the master... like so... and Bob's yer uncle.

He played the first song, and within twenty seconds - whatever it was he'd done - the sound just pinned us back against the wall and we screamed *YES! That's it! Don't touch anything else!!*

And that was how we got the perfect sound on *Punk Junkies*. I've no idea what Paul was using. It looked like a little microwave oven. Maybe it *was* a little microwave oven. I don't care. It did the business, this magical mystery box. Even Paul was blown away.

For those of you who care, I think the magic number was 12. Whatever that means.

Now we had an album which sounded like GBH should sound. We loved it. And it seemed that everyone else loved it too. I've read some comments about it being *vastly over-produced*, as if we spent weeks sitting in booths laying down tracks, or stayed up scratching our heads till the small hours of the morning, worrying ourselves stupid about every tiny detail, and I just laugh and think *You're kidding.* Do you know how long it took to produce that album? About as long as it takes to play.

We were in the studios ten days, as always, with two more days to mix it. Down at Rhythm studios in Bidford, where the pigs are the size of houses. And most of that twelve days was spent down the pub, or chasing pigs round a farmyard. Or being chased round a farmyard by pigs. Me and Scott had laid down drums and bass in the first two days, so after that we only went to the studio to get drunk and have a fuck about while we watched Col and Jock do their thing. *Punk Junkies* was made the GBH way, with a minimum amount of fuss and a maximum amount of cheap vodka. And it's fucking great.

It got us a lot of critical acclaim. Certainly more than we'd had in a while. It wasn't enough to get us back to the States, but it did bring in a lot of gigs in Europe. The fact we were now on a German record label - We Bite, from just outside Stuttgart - didn't do any harm either. They even put up the money for a video for one of the tracks, 'Crying On The Hard Shoulder', so we knew things were going fairly well.

The song was written about Boring John. He'd been with us in the van, and he was having one of his miserable fits - John would have these from time to time and there was precious little you could do about it - and he wanted the van to stop, and stop right now, so he could get out. So we pulled over to the side of the road, John got out, bawling his eyes out, and told us to leave him. So we went *All right* and fucked off.

We didn't go far. We just circled round and came back and picked him up. Pulled him back in the van and told him he shouldn't be daft enough to think we'd really leave him crying on the hard shoulder, he was our mate.

So Colin had written a song about it, and now the record label wanted us to shoot a video. We went to a nightclub in Wandsworth in the middle of the day, and met the producer. He had this plan for the video. It would have naked women chained to the wall, being whipped.

Er… what's that got to do with the song?
Nothing.
Right…
But it'll look great!
No, mate. I don't think so.

In the end he hired in some dancing punk girls, who kept their clothes on. I don't think he was too happy about that. I'm guessing, because I was pissed the whole time, but it's a fact that not much of the footage got used. But in conjunction with the shots of us miming in Piccadilly, and in a subway, we got a half-decent video out of it.

On the back of *Punk Junkies* we were getting gigs, and we'd done a video. It looked like things were picking up. We were still pissed, and we were still skint, and we could never undo the mistakes we'd made, but – on the basis that what doesn't kill you makes you stronger, if nothing else – life was getting a little bit easier. The band was still tight, we'd made a great album, and I still hadn't jumped off my balcony. Everything was all OK.

the wernt

Punk Junkies was a real shot in the arm. After so long of feeling so miserable, being involved with a GBH album that gave me a complete buzz, well, it was just what the doctor ordered. Suddenly it felt as if the world was opening up a little, as if there were new possibilities. As if things could be fun again.

Me and Jock had earned ourselves a bit of a reputation over the years for being musical slags, for jumping in and playing with mates in other bands if we were asked and the fancy took us. It was always just a bit of fun, a chance to do all the things we did with GBH, but with some different people and some different tunes.

We'd done a few demos and a couple of gigs with Fun Scandals from Walsall - one night we did a cover of 'CID' by UK Subs and Charlie came on stage and sang it with us, which we hadn't expected. Jock was nearly crying with happiness, and even I thought it was a bit special. It's one thing having Charlie as a mate, it's something else to do a Subs song with him belting it out next to you.

We played with a band called Free To Conform as well, and when our mate 'punk-as-fuck' Stu got himself in with Sensa Yuma, who were from Stafford, we joined in with that too, went in the studio with them, and released their back catalogue as an album.

So, like I say, word had got round that Jock and me were always up for banging out some tunes and supping the occasional beer. Not long after we'd recorded *Punk Junkies*, GBH did a gig at the Q Club in Brum with our old mates English Dogs, and when Pinch - their drummer - mentioned they had some old songs they'd never recorded and weren't going to use, and Jock mumbled that we had some riffs we'd never found a home for, a plan was hatched.

Pinch said he'd send us a tape of the songs so we could have a listen and see what we thought. I didn't hold my breath. People were always saying they'd do this that or the other once they'd got a few drinks inside them, and then they sobered up and did nothing at all, but Pinch was as good as his word. The tape came through the post, and it sounded like something that could be worth messing around with, so we went down to Peterborough to practise with them, check out their chip shops, and see what happened.

It worked, right from the off. We gave the band a name – The Wernt – we brought their songs together with our riffs, and it all just fell into place. This was way more than any of us had expected, but we still didn't think anything would come of it – other than it being a bit of fun, hanging out with some mates – and then our mate Tommy Proctor put up some money so we could go and record an album, and suddenly our possibilities opened up some more.

The studio we recorded the album in was on a farm in the flatlands somewhere outside Peterborough, slap bang in the middle of nowhere, with no chip shop within a hundred miles. That isn't our natural environment. It shouldn't be anyone's natural environment. We had to fly in emergency supplies, Red Cross parcels of chips from elsewhere, so we didn't starve.

Pinch was on drums – he'd laid the drum tracks down before we got there, which made things a little tricky – Wakey, who turned out to be a mental genius front man, was on vocals, Jock played guitar, and I was on bass. We had a £500 budget, we spent £400 of that on beer, we came out with an album called *Wrecking Temples*, and we had great fun making it. As you do when you spend £400 on beer.

To our surprise, we got loads of gigs on the back of it. They went well, and we even got ourselves a bit of a reputation. The Wernt was never going to be a second GBH, but it was a laugh and a good time, and I had room in my life for both. We borrowed a mate's VW campervan to travel round in. It was old, and eccentric. But then so were we. We took it out on the road for our gigs round the Midlands, went down to London in it, played with the Dwarves a few times, and then we headed up north to do a stint of gigs there.

We're hauling our way up the M6 and the VW isn't liking it at all. At Carlisle, a wisp of smoke started coming out the exhaust. Thirty miles later, the smoke was billowing out in clouds. We ignored it, and hoped it would go away. That didn't work. We got as far as a place called Annan, and the van went belly up, and we had to pull over.

It was a beautiful part of the world, but we didn't want to be stuck there. We had gigs in Glasgow, Edinburgh and Newcastle left to do, but it was pretty clear we wouldn't be getting to them in the van. It was going nowhere any time soon, not without a tow truck. I got out, stretched, and looked across the fields. In the distance I could see what looked like a farmhouse. Beyond that, there was a tiny village. I had an idea.

I stomped across the fields to the village, found a pub, and got the beers in. I necked a pint, ordered another, asked the barman for a phone directory, and phoned a car rental place which was - amazingly - just round the corner, and could do us a van. An hour later we've all had a pint and grabbed a bite to eat. We've been to the rental place, hired the van, thrown our gear in it, and dropped in on a garage to ask them to collect our mate's VW from the hard shoulder of the M6.

Will they tow it away and sort it out? Yes.
And we're on our way.

I was really chuffed that I'd sorted everything out. Just a couple of years earlier I'd been living as a recluse, terrified of leaving my flat in case I bumped into someone. Now, I was booking hire vans and dealing with garages, resolving problems instead of telling myself I was good for nothing and living my life to prove it. I'd even rung my mate Tony Quinn to get him to come up and collect the VW while we did our gigs. I couldn't have dreamed of doing a fraction of that before. Doing it felt really, really good.

We did the gigs, actually made some money on them, and made our way back to Brum. Where we discovered that our mate's VW was gone forever. The garage had dumped it in a supermarket car park with a note in the window apologising for leaving it there and promising it would be collected. But Tony had never quite got round to getting out of Brum to go and pick it up like he'd said he would, and the van got vandalised and then it got confiscated, and our mate had lost his pride and joy. If I ever win the lottery and have the cash, I owe a good mate a camper van. Mind you, it's been a few years and I've never had the money yet, so I don't think he's holding his breath....

Apart from losing the van, the gigs had all gone really well, and been a lot of fun. In pretty quick time we made the decision to go back to Peterborough, back to the studios in the middle of nowhere, and record a 7-track single. Unlike the tracks on *Wrecking Temples,* these were new tracks we'd written from scratch, not the rescued fragments of tunes from other bands. In some ways, this made The Wernt seem like a real band, in their own right. And that had repercussions.

We'd never considered - me and Jock - that Colin might get a bit upset about how well things were going with The Wernt. Given that GBH were still fairly quiet, and that the two of us were putting so much effort into this new project,

I suppose it shouldn't have been a surprise. We didn't see it coming, though. But when Colin and his missus called us over to their house for a meeting, we felt like we'd been summoned, like two naughty schoolboys going to see the headmaster. And we knew exactly what it was going to be about.

Thing was, we'd been mates for so long there was no drama. Colin put his point of view, and we put ours. There were no arguments, there was no falling out, no-one threw anything at anyone or broke anything. We just chatted. Me and Jock re-assured Colin that what we were doing with The Wernt wasn't ever intended to be a threat to GBH. We pointed out that we weren't doing much and this was just a bit of fun, a bit of money in our pockets, that was all. This was no different from what we'd done with the other bands, before. GBH came first.

One of the strengths of GBH - and one of the things that's kept us together through the hard times and the lows over the years - is that we can sit down and talk things over, come back to them if we need to, and know that we're still mates. Once we'd had that chat with Colin, everything was fine. The Wernt carried on being something Jock and me dropped into for six years, on and off, right up until Pinch joined The Damned, got married, and moved to America. That kind of drew a line under it. But they were six years of fun, that little side project. And we will do it again, one day, with a new drummer. The world needs us.

detroit rumble

By the end of the '90s, things were looking up. As a band, our lowest point - and there'd been a few to choose from - had probably been the Baltimore brawl. For me personally, it had been the years just after. But *Punk Junkies* had put us back on the map, signing to We Bite had given us a profile in Europe, and I'd just about hung on in there long enough to find some kind of light at the end of the tunnel.

Now, we were starting to enjoy something that looked a little bit like a renaissance. In 1999, we did a pretty big tour of Eastern Europe - all through the old DDR, Poland, and the Czech republic - organised by this guy Olaf from Chemnitz, which had been called Karl-Marx Stadt when the communists were in charge. Everything was changing. Towns had different names, borders had gone, there were no East German police guarding the socialist showpiece, no little wooden Trabants, and money was pouring in. Eastern Europe was in transition. A massive transition.

It was one of those rare tours that ran like a dream. We were on a bus, so we had a taste of the luxury of the US in '93, our tour buddies were two great bands - Lousy and Bambix - the gigs went well, we had a good laugh, and we even made a few quid. We came home feeling pleased with ourselves, and then Andy Somers from The Agency fixed us up a tour, a truly massive tour, of the US.

This would be the first time we'd been back since the disastrous tour with Joe. Our last memories of the States hadn't been good ones, but Andy seemed confident we had nothing to be nervous about, so we picked up our passports and our toothbrushes again, and off we went.

The displaced Anglos of Billy Club were going to be support. Karl from the Exploited - who's an even bigger rocknroll slag than Jock and me - was on guitar, Tezz from Discharge was on bass, Matt played drums. They were all English, but living in the States. Apart from Johnny Zito, their tour manager, only the singer Dave and Danimal their roadie were American, and they were from Texas, which is a law unto itself.

So we flew over, climbed in a van, and tootled off to the first gig. I think it was in upstate New York. That first night, and the few that followed, made one thing very clear: this was going to be noticeably better than our last tour of the States. Numbers were up, the atmosphere at the gigs was better, people loved seeing us play. It was a huge relief.

Why was it so different? I've no idea. You can analyse what lies behind that kind of thing till you're blue in the face, and still get nowhere. Had we changed? Had the US scene been going through a slump last time we'd been over? Had *Punk Junkies* woken people up to the fact we still existed? Someone else can argue the toss about it. All I wanted to do was have some great gigs, and get pissed. And touring with Billy Club - who were a bunch of old mates anyway - gave me every chance to do both of those things. I spent a lot of the time travelling in their van, just for the *craic*.

Tezz is one of the most lovable men you'll ever meet, and a devil with the ladies - I think he met wife number five on this tour - but if you get on the wrong side of him, he'll spark you out. Billy Club had done a few gigs before our tour started, playing their way across to New York, and Tezz had clearly used the opportunity to get some practice in. If people took the piss, he punched their lights out. It was par for the course, this simple but effective way of sorting out problems, and it meant that while you didn't want to cross him, he was a great man to have on your side. If you needed it.

Pedro and the Fujimotos

Harry and me

leather, studs, and bristles

happy drummers: Joe and Kai

photo: Tim Bramlette

work...

... and play.
Beaker, after a night in Latrine's

doing what we do best....

...straight as a die

me, Pedro, Nikki. Niagara's, NYC

wedding day, Ka'ena Point, Hawaii

Somewhere in this A-Z is Highgate...

Charlotte

Samantha

Mostly, we didn't need it. The tour was going well, it was a vodka frenzy like they always are, and Pedro's expertise in restoring broken dressing-room furniture with judicious use of gaffa tape to get me out of the shit - a valuable skill in any roadie worth his salt - reached new heights. Billy Club were old mates with a great set, and the other band touring with us - a ska-punk outfit with a brass section called Against All Authority - were a good bunch of lads too. The tour was one big happy party.

And then we rolled into Detroit.

Our merch seller, Jimmy, had a video camera with him and was documenting the tour from his point of view, and seeing as we were playing the infamous Harpo's - this disco venue with a flashing dancefloor - he was filming the place while he was setting up his stall. Suddenly, this huge guy is standing in front of him. He's an absolute shithouse, with mutton-chop sideburns, and he's wearing a big red t-shirt with a swastika in a white circle.

He's a nazi. And he's not happy that Jimmy's got a camera.

You filming?
Yeah...
I want a copy.
Er... why?
You make me look bad and I'll fuckin' kill you.

And he writes his address down for Jimmy. *666 White Avenue.* We didn't know about any of this till after the gig, but when we found out we couldn't help but wonder... was that a real address? Was the nazi just fucking with Jimmy's head? Or did he actually live there? Because he was the kind of person who'd hunt down that address and make life hell for whoever lived there until they handed it over to him instead. Even if he was the only white guy in a black neighbourhood.

The first we knew about all this was when we were watching Against All Authority open the show. From where I'm standing at the side of the stage I can't see what's going on in the audience, but Colin's nearer the front, and I can see him shaking his head. He calls me over. *Come and look at this!*

Mutton-chops and twenty or thirty of his mates are standing right in front of Against All Authority's brass section. They've singled out the Puerto Rican horn player, and they're giving him the *Sieg Heil*. Endlessly. The atmosphere is ugly and intimidating. There's maybe five or six hundred people in the audience, and these thirty nazis are ruling the roost. If anyone gets too close, mutton-chops or one of his mates are kicking lumps out of them. Even the people who normally mosh in the pit are keeping well clear, which means that - apart from the nazi cluster - there's this big semi-circle of clear space in front of the stage. I've never seen anything like it.

It's no better by the time we go on stage.

We're two songs in, and this big kid with long hair dances a bit too close to the nazis and they start whaling in on him. We stop playing. We put down our instruments, Colin jumps into the pit and starts swinging at nazis, and Jock follows him. Then Scott jumps in. Some kids in the audience are yelling *Fuck the nazis, keep playing!* but that ain't going to happen. This is a proper old ruck, and it's just carnage. I'm wading through it, pulling one nazi off Scott, seeing him get hit over the head by a bottle, dodging fists as best I can. Boots and blows are flying everywhere, Colin tries to harpoon one of the nazis with a mike stand and misses, I'm holding on to another of them so he's out of the fight, and we're hoping that someone's going to step in and help us, because we're outnumbered.

214

We might have done the right thing by jumping in, but now we're getting pummelled by nazis.

No-one in the audience is getting involved.

And the bouncers aren't getting involved, which is a bit of a surprise, and isn't helping us any.

We're going to get battered.

And then Billy Club step in. Good old Billy Club save our bacon. Tezz wades in to the fight, marches up to mutton-chops, who's clearly the nazi big cheese, and kicks him in the balls. The guy just wavers a bit. Tezz looks over at me, shrugs as if to say, *OK, he asked for it*, draws back his fist, and hits mutton-chops as hard as I've seen him hit anyone. The guy's knocked clean off his feet and goes flying down the stairs. And when he goes down, the fight goes out of the nazis, and everything stops. They re-group, retreat, and leave.

We're still in one piece. Thanks to Tezz, we've nothing worse than cuts and bruises. The fight's over, everything's calmed down, and no-one's getting killed. And now the bouncers - who are all big black guys it would have been useful to have on our side five minutes earlier - are wandering round carrying shotguns. I couldn't believe it. I went up to one of them.

Come on, you saw that shit, why didn't you do anything?

He looked me in the eye, and told me it was against club policy. And maybe it was. I remember the club owner was furious with us, wanted to know what the fuck we thought we'd been doing. And lots of the people who'd stood by and watched and done nothing were telling us
You shouldn't be fighting!
We're all white together!

That kind of bollocks.

The kid who'd been getting beat up when we'd leapt in? He was made up that we'd put our instruments down to save his skin. So in my book that counts for more.

There's a coda to this story. A few years later, we play Detroit again. A place called St Andrew's Hall, run by really good people. We pull up in the van and there's two cars opposite. It's the nazis, scouting us out. Two of them get out of one car, go in the club, come back out, nod at us knowingly, and they drive off. It's territorial pissing, we know it. They're letting us know that they know we're there and they can come in if they want to. They didn't, mind. But they were letting us know that they chose not to, that they weren't running scared.

I don't know why people want anything to do with that hateful shit.
Life's too short.

And we've got Tezz on our side.

death

It was March 2001, and I was sitting in the Moseley Arms
– the pub round the corner from my flat – getting completely
plastered, as usual. At two or three in the morning, my mobile
phone rang. It was my daughter, Charlotte, telling me my
mom had been rushed to hospital.

For years, my mom had worked at the hospital as a nursing
auxiliary. That evening, she'd finished her shift at six, taken
the bus home, and gone upstairs to change. Then she called
down to my dad to say something had happened, she couldn't
feel her left side. She'd had a stroke. My dad rang *999*. An
ambulance turned up to take my mom away, and while they
were driving her to hospital she had another stroke, and lost
consciousness. By the time I got to the hospital, half-drunk in
the small hours of the morning, my mom was in a coma.

I'd never been able to talk to my parents. I'd always visited
them, and my mom was good as gold, but I'd always kept them
at a distance. From as long ago as I can remember, the thought
of being touched, or mollycoddled, had been enough to give
me the screaming ab-dabs. That's me. It's just how I am. And
now I sat in front of her while she lay in a hospital bed, and
didn't know what to do with myself. So I went outside to have
a cigarette, and while I was out there, smoking, she died. She
was sixty-five years old.

I felt nothing.

It's how I've always been. Whenever anyone I know has
died, that's what I've felt. Nothing. I know I *should* feel
something, but the truth is that I don't. I can't. I watched

217

Charlotte being upset her nan had died. I watched the people who'd been working with my mom the day before turn up to start their shift in the morning and learn that she was cold and dead and in the morgue, and saw how hard they found it. I watched my dad being a proper trooper, but knew he was gutted. Me? I was nonplussed. My mom was gone and I didn't feel anything at all.

I tried to make myself cry, a couple of days later. I tried because I thought that was what I should do, because everyone round me was doing it. But I couldn't. I haven't, ever. There's something inside me that means I just cut off. I don't feel. When we scattered my mom's ashes, I was there, I watched it happen, but I felt nothing. We were just scattering ashes. It might as well have been sand. The person's gone. All this means nothing.

Everyone had been at the funeral. It was up at Yardley Crematorium, and my mom's family were there, and my dad's family, and the all neighbours from Sheldon, and the people she'd worked with at the hospital, and people I didn't even know. All my friends were there too, because - from when I'd been a kid right up to the day she died - my mom had always been good to them. I'd always been able to bring anybody back to the house, and my mom would make them welcome, cook them pancakes or make them a meal. When Tony Quinn was on the run from the police, my mom let him stay at ours. The coppers came round at four in the morning, and found Tony trying to hide under the bed, so her career in harbouring fugitives never came to much, but Tony never forgot my mom for helping him out. Helping out was what she did.

So there were hundreds of people there, all come along to the service to show their respects. The crem was packed. People were standing outside. The same happened when my Auntie Pauline - my mom's sister - died last year. It must be a family trait to be loved by so many.

Me? I felt awkward for feeling nothing. I wanted the fuss to be over. I was uncomfortable. My mom's service finished and I looked at the people turning up for the next one - it's a crem, you know what it's like, they do one service after another with barely a pause - and they had ten or fifteen mourners where we had this crowd, and that felt wrong. I can't explain it, but I had this bizarre desire to go up to them and offer them a few of our lot so they could swell their numbers. But I didn't. I knew it wasn't appropriate. They wouldn't have taken it well.

My mom's death was just one among many.

Titan, my pit-bull terrier, had been with me since I'd been sleeping in the empty house in Hockley, losing the plot. He was from a long line of recognised fighters. He'd been tattooed, he'd been castrated, and he'd been insured for pretty much everything bar radioactive poisoning if he took it upon himself to attack a nuclear power station. Other than that, he was covered. He died at Xmas, the year before my mom.

I know it'll seem weird - wrong - to mention the death of my dog in the same breath as the death of my mother. But, to me, the way I react is one and the same. I feel the same *nothing*. I'm not one of those people who doesn't give a toss about humans but goes to pieces when a pet dies. I'm equally insensitive to both. I always have been.

When I was a kid and our pet parrot, Juanita, went feet up on the floor of her cage, I didn't feel anything. Even though she used to sit on my shoulder, or come to my rescue if anyone had a go at me, I didn't fall apart, didn't blub in the way kids do. I just grabbed the shovel and buried her in the pet cemetery in my parent's back garden.

Dead was dead. Life goes on.

At least it does if you're lucky. Sometimes the good ones go young, and the ones you wish would die keep going forever.

I was sitting in my flat one night and I got a text from Jock.

Brother John has left us.

Our legendary friend, roadie, and svengali-figure, Boring John, had hanged himself.

He'd been suffering with depression for quite a while. Although he wasn't working for us anymore, we'd still hang out, if John would let us. Sometimes he'd come down the pub, but sometimes he just didn't want to see us, to see anyone or talk to anyone, because he was too low, too miserable, and he'd just lock himself away and hide.

One day, he took things that one step further.

It's hard not to wonder if we should have done more. John had been unemployed, short of money, drinking a lot. I knew what all that was like. I'd been there. He'd been stealing half-bottles of vodka from supermarkets and making no attempt to hide what he was doing. He knew he'd get caught. Was it a cry for help? Did he want someone to save him from himself?

I've no idea.

From my own experience, I know that sometimes - however miserable and lonely you are - the last thing you want is to have people come round and jolly you along, tell you to snap out of it. Being told you should pull yourself together doesn't help. If anything, it makes you feel worse and more lonely than ever. You want people to tell you that they care, but when they do, you don't believe it.

John was loved by hundreds of people, but it didn't make any difference to him. In the end, I walked away from my balcony. He couldn't. The world would have been better if he had. I wish he hadn't taken his own life, but if I think of him I prefer to remember the good times we had together, out on the road.

I remember us rescuing John from the owner of the B&B in Osnabrück who'd set his dog on him for something John had never done. Laughing with John when he got arrested in Stuttgart because Colin had reversed the van through the plate-glass windows of a shop when he was pissed and the copper thought John looked guilty. Watching John and Pedro, our comedy double act, bicker and fight like a couple of kids, and John smash a bottle over Pedro's head. Sitting in a van, with John behind the wheel telling us that he'd cancelled out the booze he'd drunk with some big fat lines of speed, so he was absolutely good to drive.

Everything will be fine, boys. Just watch.

He was Whizzpig. A proper GBHer. Sorely missed.

grab it

The downside of life in GBH in 2001, was that too many people we knew were dying.

On the plus side - such as it was - we made another album.

We recorded it at UB40's Abattoir studio in Digbeth, now demolished. *Ha Ha* was OK, as an album, but it lacked that special something which had made *Punk Junkies* feel so good. Maybe there weren't enough great tracks, and too many fillers. Maybe it just needed the magic microwave box. Our old mate Tezz was hanging out with us a lot in Brum at the time, carrying on in his own inimitable fashion, and we asked him to come to the studio and put a guitar track down on 'Punk Rock Ambulance'. He did. It sounded great. But when he'd gone, and we tried to mix it into the song, we realised it didn't quite work. Whatever we did, we couldn't get it to fit, so we got Jock to do it again. Tezz isn't a man to cross, so we made sure he never knew.

And as long as he doesn't read this book, he never will.

Another of the songs on *Ha Ha* is about a friend of ours from our days in The Crown who'd been murdered. It might seem a little morbid to be writing songs to murdered friends, but that wasn't going to stop us. The old saw about the only guarantees in life being taxes and death isn't far wrong, and over the years we've lost a lot of friends one way or another. Trixie - who'd nursed me in Richmond when I'd been touring with broken arms - got strangled by her boyfriend in an argument over drugs. John was dead. Lumberjack had died. Joe's heart gave out. Given all it had been through I suppose it wasn't such a surprise, but it was a sad loss. There were more.

When you're living fairly attritional lives, some people would say you cut the odds on dying young. But we've been on the road a long time, and we've seen that death isn't picky about who it takes.

In 2009, we were doing the VANS Warped tour, and we were on the way to San Francisco. We stopped at a rest place to have a piss and stretch our legs, as you do. There were some people in a car doing the same. I remember there was a bloke driving, a woman in the passenger seat, and another couple of guys sitting in the back. When we set off again we followed them out onto the highway. They picked up speed, got to about 70mph, and then their car started rocking. First it rocked a bit, then it rocked a bit more, and when the driver completely lost control, it smashed into the big grass median, took off, flipped over, and cartwheeled end over end down the carriageway. By the time it came to a halt, the two guys had been thrown out of the car, and the woman in the passenger seat, who must have had her seatbelt on, was hanging out of the window. The whole of her face had been ripped off. Gone. Her breasts were ripped off. Gone. She was dead. Gone. The guy at the wheel was still there, bolt upright and in shock, and the two guys in the road were alive, but mangled, but she was just ruined flesh. There was a little bit of hair on what was left of her head.

You always imagine you're going to be a hero in a situation like that, but all I could think was *I'm not going anywhere near this*. John the tour manager got out and did what he could to help, and someone threw a coat over the woman out of respect, so she had some kind of privacy in such a public death. And I couldn't help wondering what it must be like for the guy who was driving - five minutes before he'd been on a day out with his wife and some mates, and now her face was left on the tarmac. What on earth was he feeling now?

Events like that make you aware of your own mortality and no mistake. And of how blind luck and chance can tip the balance, make the difference between a near miss you survive, and a body bag you're zipped up in.

Later on that tour, we were almost statistics ourselves.

I was driving the van. We were on our way from Arizona to New Mexico, and I was overtaking an 18-wheeler. Sometimes, as you're overtaking them, there's a vacuum effect that sucks your vehicle in, and – sure enough – as I was passing the truck, the wheel was just snatched out of my hand and the van started swaying and rocking. Then the side of the van just banged into the trailer of the truck.

All I could think about was that car crash we'd seen earlier. Everyone in the van was yelling and screaming, and I'm pretty sure we were all thinking this was it, we were about to go under the truck. We'd seen other people die. Now it was our turn to have strangers scrape us off the road. Then, suddenly – and I can't explain this – I knew with absolute certainty that we were going to be OK. Sure enough, the van straightened up, the wheel came back into my hands, and we passed the truck. I looked round. Everyone was grey with fear. *Wow*, I said. *What the fuck was all that about?*

I think the truck driver thought we were going under the truck as well, because when we finally passed him and it was clear this was a near miss and nothing more, he wound down his window and gave a blast on the horn and was leaning out whooping and hollering and every bit as glad we were alive as we were. I didn't stop, I just carried on. We had another 300 miles to drive till we got to the gig, so we just kept on going.

You see, you never know when your number's up. We've done a lot of miles, and we've seen bodies being hauled out of cars, we've seen vehicles on fire, we've lost friends. There's no rhyme or reason to it, either. Just blind luck. If there's one thing I've learned from that - and it's not something that comes naturally to me - it's that perhaps you really ought to seize the day.

It might not be a good idea to put stuff off till tomorrow.

love

In 2003, GBH went back to the States again, and did a huge tour with our old friends the Circle Jerks, and another band called The Bronx, who had one of the best front men I've ever seen. He was like a punky Norman Wisdom. The tour was great. It was fun, it was successful, it was largely sold out. We played in pubs, in clubs, and in theatres. We went back to places like the Electric Banana in Pittsburgh, which is always a joy to play because it's run by an Italian couple who feed visiting musicians some of the best Italian home cooking you're ever going to have.

When you consider how hard life is for small venues, and how difficult it is for them to keep going, it's wonderful to find that places like the Electric Banana - clubs that we've been playing since we first toured the States in '83 - are still on the circuit. You pull up outside, and you know you're going to be seeing familiar faces, touching base with people you've known for years, and that - whatever else is happening on the tour - this will be a good day.

There were a lot of good days anyway. We were enjoying ourselves, doing what we do best, which is being on stage. This tour couldn't have been more different from the nightmare of '93, and when it finished we hung out in Manhattan with good friends there - Italian-Americans who feed us well and like the odd beer - and partied. We'd come through the dark times at last, and that was worth celebrating. Now it was time to kick back at the end of a long tour, unwind after a lot of miles on the road, and take it easy.

That meant we spent a lot of time in bars.

One night we drinking on the Lower East Side, and ended up in a bar called Niagara's. I nipped downstairs to the toilet, came back up, looked across the bar – and saw this vision of beauty. Right there and then, I fell in love.

I'd been in a few relationships since the break-up with Karen. Some had been brief, a couple of on-off ones had trundled on for years, one had even given me a daughter. But none of them had made me feel anything like this. I floated across the bar towards this girl, muscled my way in past Pedro – who was standing next to her – so I could cut him out of the loop and introduce myself, and promptly spilt everyone's drinks. As first impressions go, I guess that gave a pretty good picture of what life with me could be like. For some inexplicable reason, it didn't seem to deter her.

We chatted. We swapped addresses. I told her I was from Birmingham. She told me she was from Hawaii. I was on my way back to the UK, and she was on a stopover for a few hours before she flew back to the middle of the Pacific. We spent twenty minutes chatting in Niagara's, then we went on to another bar called Manitoba's, and then she left for the airport. I knew I'd fallen for her big time. Was she equally smitten? I didn't know. I knew she was called Nikki and she knew I was called Ross, she'd gone to another bar with me, and she hadn't run away screaming or reached for a gun or called the police, which I was fairly sure were good signs. Or at least not bad ones. But whether she thought I was the best thing since sliced bread, or had lobbed the piece of paper with my address on straight in the bin the first chance she had, that was a mystery.

If I was honest, my money was on the bin.

After a few more days partying in New York, GBH flew home. I got back to Brum, walked in to the flat in Highgate, turned on my phone, and there was a message from Nikki.

Now *that* was a surprise.

From there, things snowballed. While I was at home, we spoke to each other on the phone every day. When GBH went off on one of Olaf's tours to Germany, I phoned her every evening from whatever town we were in, told her how my day had been, and listened about hers. And once the tour was over, Nikki flew over to Brum and stayed with me for three weeks. Then she flew home for two, then she came back for another three. By Xmas that year, her mom was flying over with her to come and check me out. In a few short months, my life had been shaken up and changed in a way I'd never dared to imagine was possible, and I was loving it.

Things were going well with the band, too. In January '04, GBH went back to Japan. This time we didn't lose Jock, we didn't meet up with Wilko Johnson, and we didn't fill the bath with crabs. It was still a great tour, mind. We played all over the country, the gigs were big and the crowds were bigger, there were six or seven bands on the bill each night, and it was a huge amount of fun. Then this promoter turned up. He wanted us to stay on in Japan once the tour was over, and play a couple of festivals in Osaka and Tokyo. They were big festivals, and the fact he wanted to add us to the bill just underlined how successful our tour had been – which confirmed to us that we were back on our feet as a band – but the truth was we weren't that keen on doing them. We'd been out on the road a lot, and Colin was adamant that once the tour was over we were going home.

So we told him thanks, but no thanks. Two days later he's back with an improved offer, and this time we all looked at each other and thought *We can't turn that down. We're stupid, but we're not that stupid.*

We stayed on in Japan, played the festivals, and made ourselves some cash. Then everyone else flew home.

And I flew to Hawaii.

aloha

I'd been wanting to see Nikki again, and those two unexpected festivals in Japan had made all the difference. Suddenly I had the cash. So while the rest of the band flew back to Blighty, I booked myself a flight to Hawaii, and headed off there for six weeks instead.

Writing it like that makes it sound easy. The reality was this was the first time that I'd gone off and done something on my own since I'd caught the train to Harrogate so I could join the army, back when I was still in school. Since then, I'd been a lot of places, but I'd travelled to all of them with the band. It had made me an expert at navigating my way around, but it had also been done with familiar faces, a little protective pod of people I knew. This was going to be different.

I wasn't scared. Yes, heading to Hawaii on my own was a big deal, but I reckoned I could handle it. I said goodbye to Colin, Jock, and Scott at the airport, found the gate for my flight, realised I had twelve hours to wait till it left, sat myself down, and went into a trance.

If there's one thing being in a band is good for, it's teaching you how to wait. In between the adrenalin rush of the gigs, there's a lot of dead hours spent hanging around in venues, hotels, and vans. You learn to be patient. You get used to being bored. Twelve hours in an airport was nothing I wasn't used to, and it did give me time to think. About lots of things. About my life. About the band. About how important it can be to hang on in there when you hit the low points and think of jumping off your balcony. Because you never know what's coming next, whatever you might tell yourself, and sometimes what comes along is so good it blows your little socks off.

I was nervous, but I knew this would be fine. Even being the only white, English-speaking male on the plane from Japan to Hawaii didn't faze me. And it would be great to say this confidence carried me right through, that I landed in Hawaii and met up with Nikki and everything was smooth and easy as could be, and it was all happy-ever-after, because Hawaii was the most incredible place I'd ever visited, like nowhere I'd ever been, and Nikki was beautiful, and there was rolling surf and sunshine, but the truth is I got there and thought

I'm from Birmingham. What the fuck am I doing here?

and everything went a bit pear-shaped. My confidence evaporated and I plunged headlong into panic and self-doubt. It simply couldn't be possible that someone as beautiful as Nikki could want to have anything to do with me. It simply couldn't be possible that someone like me - with all my problems - deserved to enjoy life in a place like Hawaii. What had I been thinking? I was an idiot to believe we had a future. I was an idiot, full stop. There was absolutely no way it was possible for this hare-brained scheme to work.

For two whole weeks I beat myself up with a vengeance. That meant I clammed up and didn't talk to anyone, including Nikki. And it could have ended there and then, I guess, but somehow - just like I did when I found the balls to join GBH, or do all the other things I've done - I soldiered on. I realised that my panic was brought on - in part at least - by being on my own away from the rest of the band for the first time in years. I got over my post-tour exhaustion, came through the other side, and began to relax. It didn't come naturally, but I gave it a go.

As soon as I did, I saw that Hawaii was stunning. OK, there are parts of the island which aren't picture postcard pretty - there's industrial estates and military bases, and so on - but set against that there's a lot of surf and a lot of beaches, and I was hanging out by the rolling surf of the North Shore. Trust me, there's worse places to be.

Nikki rented a house there with two other people, up on the side of a mountain, and she had her own little business, growing flowers on a farm up on the mountain, then selling them in pubs and clubs at night, and getting home at four in the morning. She'd get in, grab a few hours kip, and then she'd get up, and go surfing, because Nikki lived to be out in the surf. Every moment possible, she was out there. I knew nothing about surfing - there wasn't a lot of call for it in Chelmsley Wood - but she looked like she knew what she was doing.

So she surfed, and sold flowers, and I hung around doing nothing in particular, and tried not to give myself too hard a time. Which got easier, the longer I was there. All too soon, though, the six weeks were up, and I was flying back to the UK to pick up my bass and go back on the road.

I can't begin to remember where we played. All I can tell you is that GBH did some gigs, but if you want to know whether they were good or we sucked, whether they were rammed to the gills or we played to one punk and his dog, whether they were in Wales or West Africa, well, you'll need to ask somebody else. I haven't a clue. My head was full of Hawaii. The instant the gigs were over, I grabbed my passport, stuck my toothbrush in my pocket, and flew back to see Nikki.

A few weeks after that, and despite the best efforts of my *I-don't-deserve-this* negativity, we got married. We drove out to the west side of the island, to Yokahama Bay, and carried on all the way to the end of the road, out to a place called Ka'ena Point. If you're going to marry a girl who's mad about surf, you might as well do it in the open-air, somewhere you can look out to sea and watch humpback whales leaping out of

231

the water, next to an albatross reserve, with the sky full of giant birds and the sound of the waves crashing on the shore. I recommend it.

Thing was, I hadn't really thought about what getting married would mean. I'd no idea it would turn my whole world upside-down. As far as I could see, we'd got married. That was good. Now I'd go back to Brum, and Nikki would come over and live with me there. That was my plan in its entirety. Me being me, living from day to day like I do, planning even this far ahead was a minor miracle, and I was really proud of myself. What I really hadn't grasped was that while this was as far as the plan went in *my* head, Nikki's plans went a good deal further.

My first inkling this wasn't going to be easy came when Nikki flew over to live in Brum. Overnight, she went from living on a mountain in Hawaii, in a paradise where she could go surfing every day and the sun shone pretty much all the time, to sharing a fifth-floor council flat in Highgate, in Birmingham. It didn't matter how hard you looked, there were no mountains, this wasn't paradise, and there was definitely no surf.

The penny dropped.

This was a big change, a monumental change, for her. And it wasn't going to be anything like easy. As soon as I realised how difficult it was going to be for Nikki, life became hugely difficult for me, too. How on earth was I going to make this work? How - realistically - could I expect anyone to trade Hawaii for Birmingham and not feel, well, at least a little disappointed?

If I'd been in Nikki's shoes, and I'd been hauled from Hawaii to live in a big industrial city with poor weather, then - even if it had great chip shops - I'm not sure what I'd have done. I imagine I'd have been just a tiny bit depressed, or I'd have been furious with the world. Either way, I'd probably have ended up down the pub. Nikki was made of sterner stuff. She took one look at Birmingham, rolled up her sleeves, and took it on.

All my life, I'd walked everywhere. Occasionally, if I was feeling particularly flush, I'd go wild and splash out on the bus. Nikki was American. She needed a car like she needed air to breathe. So we spent two days looking for a car. In the end we took the bus to Coventry and bought a second-hand Rover. Now, Nikki's never driven in the UK before, and I've only ever been in cars as a passenger - which generally means I've been pissed - and I've only the vaguest understanding of the Highway Code, so it's a recipe for disaster. But we jump in the car and Nikki drives away. She's doing OK, and then we come to a roundabout.

They don't have roundabouts in Hawaii. They don't have them in the States in general, come to think of it, so this is the first one she's ever seen. And the roundabouts on the Birmingham ring road are monsters. They're roundabouts on steroids, with an attitude problem, roundabouts that can make grown men cry. And this was when I first recognised how determined Nikki can be when she puts her mind to something, because she took a deep breath, and handled that roundabout like she'd been doing it all her days.

Now we had a car, she had an escape route. Next weekend we went down to Cornwall for the surf. We were camping, and it was typical Cornish weather - so Nikki sat in the car while I put the tent up in the rain. Then we went to South Wales, past Swansea, down to The Mumbles. It was freezing cold again. But nothing stopped her. I remember watching her running down the beach in the thickest wetsuit possible - with neoprene booties, a neoprene hat, and neoprene mittens to match - just so she could go and surf in sub-zero temperatures. The wind was blowing a hoolie and it was so cold even the fish had overcoats on.

You're stark staring mad, girl.

But she's a sea girl. She's grown up with it, she's lived on it and in it, and she simply had to get her fix. Me? I learned all the surf spots within a day's drive of Brum, I got adept at putting up cheap tents in extreme weather, and I learned all the surf terminology. Just as you have a back-seat driver in a car, I'm a brilliant back-seat surfer. I've never done it but I know everything there is to know about *how* to do it. Nikki can look at a picture of water and tell you which way it breaks, where the rip is, and what the fish there had for breakfast.

I can tell you it's a picture of water.

She was a one-woman dynamo. She got herself a job in a flower shop, and she signed herself up for a course in a college in Brum. If I was working - crewing for Stagecraft, or away gigging with GBH - and I wasn't around when she had free time, she'd go off and do stuff on her own. I'd get a phone call from London because she'd caught the coach down so she could see Buckingham Palace, or she'd ring me from Stratford.

Ross, have you heard of Shakespeare?

We were both giving it a go, but it wasn't always easy, and it wasn't perfect. There was a certain amount of bullshit to get past, and there was a fair amount of attrition, of knocking the corners off each other. That kind of thing. But I thought we were doing OK. And then one day she sat me down, looked me in the eye, and asked me

Where do you want to be in five years, Ross? Where do you see yourself going?

234

plans

Where did I want to be in five years?

Christ, I didn't know what I'd be doing next week. And that was an improvement from the days when I didn't know if I'd make it from one moment to the next. I didn't have a fucking clue what I'd want in five years, and just being asked to think about it terrified me. Add to the mix the fact that this was the first time I'd tried living with someone - properly - since Karen, and I think you can see it was a lot for someone like me to take on.

Nikki had been in my life for no time at all and already she was sitting me down like a naughty schoolkid and asking me what my plans were, what my goals were for the future. I heard her say something about a five-year plan, and I looked in her eyes and I could see she wasn't joking.

Uh-oh. This is serious.

I hadn't bargained for any of this. I'd married Nikki because I loved her, and that was all the thought I'd put into it. It didn't need anything more, did it? The day she flew over to live with me, I tidied up the flat, made a bit of space in the wardrobe for her, and threw some rose petals on the bed. Then I stood back and admired my handiwork. Pretty fucking good. What more could a girl want? This was going to be marvellous. Then Nikki arrived, took one look at it, and went mad. Everything needed changing. T-shirts I'd had for a thousand years were thrown out. Stuff was moved. Things were cleaned. I think I went into shock.

And now? Now she wanted plans.

I'd never had a five-minute plan, never mind a five-year one. Being asked to draw one up took me well out of any kind of comfort zone. And Nikki was between me and the door, so legging it down the pub was out of the question. I had nowhere to run, and that really set the alarm bells ringing. I got scared. I started to sweat. My stomach shrank. My testicles shrivelled up. This really wasn't good. I'd got married because I wanted someone to go to the pub with, or sit and watch telly with, and I'd ended up with a fucking alien who wanted plans and spreadsheets and a course of action. Sweet jesus.

Could I punch her in the face and snap her out of it?

Or would she just hit me across the back of the head with her surfboard?

I think Nikki sensed my unease. And my panic. And my fear. But she was relentless, and she was determined to make me do something I'd never done. Which meant there was no escape. In the end we whittled the five-year plan down to a two-year plan, but the whole experience was so traumatic that I instantly erased that two-year plan from my memory. The moment the discussion was over, I had no idea what we'd agreed to, or what I'd said. Although I'm guessing it must have been something semi-coherent, because Nikki did let me out of the room alive.

I guess it says something for both of us, how it worked out. She came in all-American, needing plans and goals and targets, and came slap bang up against my inability to plan at breakfast what I'll be doing come tea time. And yet, the two of us found a compromise. I managed to agree to a two-year plan, even if I didn't know what it was, and Nikki settled for less than the exhaustively detailed five-year plan she wanted, and recognised how difficult I found the whole thing.

See, Nikki will have a sheet of paper with a list of things to do each day. And as she does them she'll tick them off the list. I can't even find a piece of paper. There's the difference. Everything she wants to do, she ends up doing, and in a way it's good to be around someone like that, because you realise you don't have to keep on living the same way you've always done. You can make plans. You can set yourself goals. You can do things differently. I get the concept, even if I haven't got round to putting it into practice.

It's possible that writing this book is proof I'm starting to get my head round it, but it's still scary stuff. What if I write something down, and can't put a tick next to it? That's terrifying. Maybe it's better not to make a list so you can't fail. That's the way of thinking I was in for years. It still makes sense a lot of the time, if I'm honest. And even though that was how I was, and even though it must have driven Nikki up the wall, I never found *assassinate good-for-nothing husband* on one of her lists, which was - frankly - a relief.

So, Nikki hadn't killed me, and we had a two-year plan. Whatever it was. Agreeing to it made her happy, and allowed me to pretend nothing had changed. Even though Nikki reminded me - regularly - that the most important part of the two-year plan was to move to Hawaii, I wasn't worried. Two years off was so far in the future that it was too far to think about. It was so far in the future that it might as well be never. I had plenty of time to mould her by then so she'd have learned to love Highgate, chip shops, bad weather, and roundabouts. Everything would carry on just like it was now. No problem.

I should have known I was kidding myself. You don't mould people like Nikki.

237

For now, though, we carried on as if everything was fine. If GBH were gigging, Nikki came along. If that wasn't possible, she did her own thing. When we went to Brazil, she went to Vegas. When we did a gig in Leeds and then flew to Madrid for another, she went surfing in The Mumbles. She wasn't the kind of girl to sit at home and do nothing.

The Leeds gig had been a corker, and the next day we drove to Liverpool so we could fly to Madrid. I've got on the plane, found my seat, and I'm texting Nikki to tell her I love her, when this rottweiler of a stewardess appears and snaps *Don't send that text!* I look round. The plane doors are still open, there's still people getting on. What's the fucking problem? She insists I mustn't send it. I tell her that I will. We exchange words. That escalates to a row. In the end I thrust the phone at her, tell her to take it.

And go fuck yourself while you're at it.

Next thing I know there's two security guards by my seat. The stewardess has told the captain I'm a security threat to her and the rest of the passengers, and now the band are flying to Madrid without me. The guards escort me off the plane, with the stewardess following behind, smirking. She's really pleased with herself. The world's a safer place now. Let people text their partners when a plane's still on the ground and who knows where the madness will end. Stuff her. I get to the top of the steps, and decide I might as well have the satisfaction. I turn round and tell her exactly what I think of her.

I think even the guards were shocked.

I wave to everyone as I cross the tarmac, I collect my luggage, and I make my way back home. I know Nikki's going to be pissed off at me for getting thrown off the plane and missing a gig, and I think about not telling her, but I'm a crap liar and I always get found out, so I decide I'll let her know. Honesty is the best policy, I tell myself.

And in this case, it is. It turned out the Madrid gig was in a sex club, with live sex acts, and GBH was the entertainment in between the sex. Which was a new one, even for us. Explaining that gig to Nikki would have been tricky at best, so the rottweiler stewardess did me a good turn in the end. And with GBH being GBH, I still got paid, even though I never made it off the runway.

If only things always worked out that well.

As the deadline for the end of the two-year plan got nearer, and the move to Hawaii loomed larger, tempers got a little frayed. In 2005, we were back in the States on tour, we were in the Henry Fonda Theater, and Nikki and I were having a row, an argument over something and nothing.

I'm already over it - my knees had been hurting and a mate who was rocknroll doctor for the day had slipped me a pill, a painkiller which relaxes you, numbs the pain, and chills you out - but Nikki isn't. She's keeping the argument going. So to bring it to an end I decided to punch the door.

This wasn't such a good idea. The door's a steel door, and it's a lot harder than me, and the instant I hit it I know things aren't good. I feel an electric shock all the way up my arm, I look at my hand, and I see that all my knuckles have disappeared. Now they're living in the middle of my palm. In my slightly woozy, not-quite-with-it state, knowing my knuckles don't really belong where they are, I decide the best course of action is to push them all back to their original position. There's lots of cracking and crunching, and my hand feels like a bag of spanners, but I get them back to more or less where I think they need to be.

And then I pass out.

I wake up in a dressing-room full of firemen, ambulance men, and policemen. There may even have been a coastguard or two, I'm not sure. Do I want to go to hospital? I don't know. Hospitals are for serious stuff, like when you break your arms rushing for a pint of Guinness, and even then they don't really seem to help. This is just a flesh wound. And it's on my picking hand, which still - somehow - has two working fingers, which means I can play bass.

So, no. I won't go to hospital.

I'll play punk rock instead.

upheaval

The start of 2006 brought a lot of changes. In fact, that doesn't do it justice. The start of 2006 pretty much conspired to turn my whole life upside-down. First up, on January 12th, Nikki flew back to Hawaii. This suddenly made the two-year plan real, because I'd kind of hoped that - if I didn't think about it - then it would all just go away and everything would carry on as it was, with the two of us living in the Highgate flat, and me going off on tour with GBH from time to time.

Now it was clear that wasn't going to happen. Instead I'd be leaving Birmingham, which meant leaving my comfort zone. That took the shine off things for starters, but on top of that my dad - who'd lived in Brum all his life - wasn't well at all. He'd been living on his own since my mom died, and he'd been less and less himself. He'd crashed his car, he'd had a couple of strokes, and he'd spent a lot of time in hospital. Even when he was home, he wasn't right. I'd been round there and found him lying on the settee, doing a fine impression of a dying man, talking to my mom, talking to other people I didn't know - none of whom were there - with the house wrecked around him because every time he got up he fell over because the strokes meant he couldn't walk properly.

You didn't have to be a doctor to work out that he couldn't look after himself any more. And I could barely look after myself, so even if I hadn't been leaving Brum I wouldn't have been much use. In the end, my dad went to live in a care home down in Plymouth where he could be nearer to my sister. It might have been the best option, but it was still upsetting and depressing, because he was a proper Brummie, and he'd spent his whole life in the city, and now he was being taken away from everything, everyone, and every single place he knew.

He was being uprooted. And so was I. The difference was that I was in control of my move. It was my choice. At least in theory.

In reality, it didn't feel that way. Every night I'd wake up in the middle of the night, and lie in my bed and stare at the ceiling, knowing that in a few weeks I'd be leaving England, and it put me in a complete panic. I didn't want things to change. Not this fast, anyway. I had just a few more gigs in England with GBH, and then we'd be going to the States with Goldblade to tour there, and when that finished, I'd be moving to Hawaii.

All I wanted to do was run. And I couldn't. This was all part of the two-year plan, and I'd agreed to it, and - just like when I joined GBH and knew I had to walk out onto the stage in The Crown or walk away forever - there really wasn't any choice. But knowing that I had to do it, that this move to Hawaii was inevitable, just took the gloss off the tour for me. It went well enough - it was a good tour by all accounts - but I don't remember much about it. In my mind, the whole tour was just one long, slow countdown.

The only thing that does stand out is the riot.

We were playing a festival in San Bernadino. It was called 'British Invasion', most of the bands were from the UK with a few US punk bands to make up the numbers, there were 3-4000 people there, and I was dog-tired. So as soon as we got there I went to sleep in the van. An hour later I woke up because the van was rocking. *What the fuck??!!*

I look out of the window and there's a full-blown riot. Apparently the local nazis have put in an appearance, it's all kicked off, and now the police have waded in too. There's a helicopter overhead, there's clouds of tear gas, and everywhere I look there's a fight. I clamber out of the van and some guy

242

goes to punch me and misses. I walk into the gig, and notice the Jack In A Box across the road is being looted and there's lines of punks passing out burgers. It's hungry business fighting cops and getting tear gassed, I guess.

I find everyone else. Then we go and find Jock's daughter Bridget who's doing merch. She's a proper trooper – even though there's tear gas swirling round the stadium she hasn't left her post. Just in case someone takes a break from rioting to see if we've a t-shirt in their size. We get her out, we get the t-shirts out, we get everyone in the van and we trundle away from San Bernadino, past Jack In A Box, watching punks handing out burgers.

It's the only gig on the tour I remember, and we never even played.

I've seen pictures from that tour, and I look tense and preoccupied. Partly that was because my dad had been shipped off to Plymouth, and partly it was because I was off to Hawaii, but it was also because I knew that when we finished the tour at the end of March I'd be loosening my ties with the band, for a while at least.

I'd told Colin and Jock and Scott about this, but I think they felt that – me being me – I couldn't and wouldn't go through with it. I knew I was. I didn't have a clue what would happen when I got to Hawaii, but I wanted to be sure I didn't let the guys down by leaving them without a bass player while I was there, so I'd already spoken to my mate Micky and asked him to fill in for me while I was gone. Whoever took over from me for the gigs I couldn't do needed to be someone who I knew and trusted, and who the band knew and trusted, and Micky was that man. He'd been part of the GBH family for years – and that's not just lip-service – and he was more than happy to step into my shoes.

So Micky was sorted out as stand-in bass player. Then, when the tour was over and we were hanging out in LA, Jock announced that he wanted some time off too. I was off to Hawaii, and Jock wasn't getting on the plane back to Brum either, instead he was going to hang out in LA for a while and see what happened. Colin wasn't happy about that at all.

From his point of view it seemed like the band was falling apart. After all the hard times GBH had been through, what with the fight in Baltimore, and Jimmy ripping us off, and the dark times we'd had over the years - some of which we'd survived by the skin of our teeth - suddenly it looked to him as though our adventure, our life together as mates who'd stuck by each other through thick and thin, was coming to an end.

I didn't think I was leaving the band. Jock didn't think he was. We just saw it as a little bit of time out after twenty-six years of gigging. For us, this was just a chance to do something different. But Colin took a bit of convincing. GBH had gigs lined up in the UK, and now he'd have to do them with a new bassist and a new guitarist. And he had no-one to play guitar. Not yet. It's no wonder he was worried.

They were a tumultuous few days. But we ended them as we'd started them. As friends. And when they were over, Jock slipped away into the LA jungle, Colin and Scott flew back to the UK, and I made my way to John Wayne airport, Santa Ana.

I was flying with Aloha airlines, and as I stood outside the airport, I went through my pockets to make sure I didn't have anything on me I shouldn't. I pulled out my pouch of tobacco, looked at it, and threw it away. I'd thought about stopping before, but thinking was always as far as it went. I'd been smoking since I was nine years old, but right then and there, outside Santa Ana airport, I stopped.

I didn't need cigarettes any more. I was off to my new life.

I was catching a flight to Honolulu.

hawaii

I didn't really have any plans beyond arriving in Hawaii. I knew - vaguely - that I'd probably have to think about getting some kind of occasional work somewhere down the line, but that was too far off to worry about. My plan when I'd got married had been simple - *I love Nikki, we'll get married, life will be wonderful* - and I'd given pretty much the same amount of thought to things now. If I had any kind of plan, it could have been written down on the back of one of the fag packets I no longer needed.

I'm here, there you go.

After all, what more could a woman possibly want?

I should have known Nikki would expect more than that. She already had her flower business back up and running, and she had another two-year plan - worked out in meticulous detail - for how it was going to grow. On top of that, she'd sorted out somewhere for us to live while I was on tour, and on top of that she'd made another plan for what she'd do if I didn't turn up, because she wasn't entirely convinced I'd keep my side of the bargain and join her in Hawaii.

It seemed I'd surprised everyone by doing that.

So while I was really pleased with myself for doing what I'd said I would, and even more pleased with myself for giving up smoking - which was a big deal after thirty-five years - and knew this was me wiping the slate clean and starting again, Nikki saw the same old Ross, who'd dragged his heels about getting there and who didn't have the tiniest idea what he'd do now he'd arrived. She wasn't impressed. Five minutes after

I'd landed, before I'd even had a chance to re-acquaint myself with the beauty of Hawaii, I was promising I'd knuckle down, get a job, and earn some money.

I hadn't a clue how I'd begin to go about it.

Fortunately for me, Nikki's mom was around. Without her, I'd have been sunk. She's every bit as good as Nikki at getting things organised, but with less of the drill sergeant about her. First thing she did was take me to a solicitor to see about getting my green card. Yep, he said, that would be easy. It just cost $4000.

I hadn't got $4000 in the world. So a green card was out of the question. To me, this sounded like a disaster. No green card meant no work, didn't it? Not according to Nikki's mom. *This is Hawaii, Ross. Everyone's running away from something. Everyone's working under the table. It'll be fine.* This was my first real encounter with the Hawaii way of doing things, the *Why worry, what's the rush?* mentality. There's always a way of getting things done. I might not be able to get a green card, but I had got a one-year work permit from the tour with GBH. The work permit meant I could get a social security number, and as soon as I had a social security number I had a foot in the door, because that meant I could get a line of credit, and that would make anything possible.

First, though, I had to get a job. This would appease Nikki and show I was taking my responsibilities seriously. As seriously as someone like me can take these things, anyway. Left to my own devices, I'd probably have spent all my time hanging round where we lived in Pearl Harbour, because I loved it there. We lived in an apartment above a Filipino lady called Mercy, who was our landlady, and was certified schizophrenic. When she was taking her medication she was fine. I'd sit downstairs with her and have a cup of tea and talk to her about the Queen as though we were best friends, and she'd lap it up, but when she stopped taking her meds - which was a lot of the time - she could be quite scary, screaming and shouting and accusing Nikki and me of being squatters, not paying the rent, and having guests she didn't approve of. Once or twice a week we'd have the police knock on our door.

Hi. Mr Lomas?
Yeah.
Officer Kapono here again.
Hi, how you doing?
Fine, Mr Lomas. I've a few questions...
Fire away.
You've paid your landlady the rent?
Yeah.
There's no problem with that?
No.
And there's no-one here who shouldn't be?
No.
So you don't have the devil living up there with you?
No officer, we don't.
I thought not. Goodbye, Mr Lomas. Have a nice day.

With Mercy downstairs, and the old couple next door who were in their nineties and who loved each other to bits even though she knew that when he invited me round he'd want to talk about the war and tell me how his only visit to Birmingham had been to fly a bomber there from East Anglia so he could pick up a consignment of ice-cream and fly it back to base - which made a change from people wanting to tell me an Ozzy Osbourne story - I'd have been happy not leaving the neighbourhood at all. But I had to get a job.

I saw one advertised online. A job at a furniture store on the outskirts of Waikiki. Nikki dropped me off there on her way to work so I could go in for an interview, but as soon as she'd gone the old fight-or-flight panic kicked in. Why put myself through this? I could just turn round, go home, spend the day listening to war stories and telling Mercy about the Queen, and when Nikki came home from work I'd tell her I didn't get the job. That would work. In fact, it sounded like a great idea.

But I didn't run. I went in.

This little 4'6" Italian-American guy looked me up and down and said *You start tomorrow morning.* So next day Nikki dropped me off again and I started work in the back of the shop, putting furniture together. I worked there, on and off, for the next eighteen months. I got sacked once, and I resigned twice, but the boss always took me back, partly because I loved hard work, partly because he couldn't understand a word I said, and partly because he had a soft spot for international oddballs, being one himself. His unfeasibly large-breasted wife was from Puerto Rico, he was part Italian, and I worked with a Hungarian called Tomasz who used to be a professional footballer, two guys from the States - Todd and Cullen, who became really good mates - and two Brazilian cagefighters who couldn't speak English. This was Hawaii, after all.

Working there got me out from under Nikki's feet six days a week, but I couldn't rely on her to keep dropping me off every day. By now, though, the line of credit was kicking in. I had a job and a social security number, and that meant companies were falling over themselves to offer me credit cards. I started collecting the pretty ones, the ones with pictures of eagles, or flags, or turtles, and before I knew where I was, I had more credit cards than you could shake a stick at. Suddenly I could get anything I wanted. I could pay the solicitor to get my green card application done, more importantly I could fly back to the UK when GBH had tours, and – above all – I could buy myself a vehicle of my own.

There was just one problem. I couldn't drive. Which meant I couldn't have a car. So instead I spent $1200 on a piece of shit Chinese scooter, and tootled back home on it with Nikki following in the car trying not to laugh as I weaved down the road. To make the whole experience more interesting, Hawaii's full of little old Korean ladies who drive cars and have less road sense than I do, and they're a menace. I got home safely, but I'm not sure how.

Next day the handlebars came off in my hands as I was heading down the highway on my way to work. The guy who'd sold me the scooter hadn't fitted them properly, so I took it back. He shrugged. It's Hawaii, these things happen. No big deal.

I wasn't so sure the scooter had a future.

One day I rode past a driving centre. On impulse I popped in to find out about getting a probationary licence. Twenty minutes later I'd got it, and went home happy as larry, like a dog with a bone. It was a good job too, because a few days later the scooter went belly up, just broke down and wouldn't start however much I swore at it. Seeing as I was near Nikki's workplace, I pushed it there so I could dump it with her and take the bus back home. She threw me the keys to her car.

Take that.

I shat myself. I'd never driven a car in my life, and Nikki's car was a big old Toyota station wagon, the *Starship Enterprise* with wheels. This could go horribly wrong. I took a deep breath, climbed in, plotted a course back home, and crossed my fingers. It worked. I got home. And I didn't kill any little old Korean ladies either. Which surprised me more than anyone.

This was just the latest in a series of big changes in my world. I'd moved to Hawaii. I'd given up smoking. I'd got a social security number, and taken up work. Now I'd learned to drive. All this in just a few short months. I felt like I was discovering a whole way of life. Learning that I could do things. Even when I took my driving test for the first time and failed, I wasn't fazed. I was amazed that I'd *failed*, because pretty much all you had to do was drive round the block and not crash the car, but hey it's Hawaii, these things happen. The second time I took the test, I passed.

I was surprising myself. Even though I was always telling myself I couldn't do this stuff, that I was bound to get it wrong, that I'd be better off not trying in the first place, I'd still go *No. I'll give it a chance.* Why do the same thing I'd always done? Why not try something different? What, after all, was the worst that could happen?

I was trying all this because of Nikki.

And for Nikki.

And in spite of Nikki.

I think she was proud of me. But I did have to be dragged along kicking and screaming for the first few months, because I found it incredibly hard to accept that I deserved to be somewhere so beautiful as Hawaii. I felt guilty about my dad sitting in Plymouth on his own, and I was missing playing with GBH, and I knew Micky was out with them instead. So it wasn't easy. For either of us. Nikki hated where we lived just as much as I loved it. She had plans for everything and I didn't. I was doing my best to change, but it wasn't fast enough for her. I'd always lived hand to mouth and she didn't want to.

We were in paradise, but life wasn't perfect.

And when, at the end of 2006, I told Nikki I was going back to tour round the UK and Europe with GBH while they supported Rancid for a few weeks, she wasn't happy. Not at all. This meant I would be away for Xmas, it meant I wasn't making an effort. Me going away with the band wasn't in her plan. So she stopped talking to me.

And I flew halfway round the world because - however lovely Hawaii was - I needed to pick up my bass guitar and play.

unravelling

Playing with GBH again was like slipping on a pair of old shoes. Almost. The one strange thing was that Jock wasn't there. When he'd decided to stay in LA, our old mate Karl Morris – who'd been guitarist in Billy Club – had stepped in, and by the time I came back for the Rancid tour he had his feet well and truly under the table. I didn't like this. We got to Italy and I got pissed and we had a bit of a bust-up. I knew I was way out of line, not just because Karl's a lovely guy and I had him pinned to the floor and was ready to punch his head in, but because – when we got back to the hotel – no-one else in the band would talk to me. And normally we forgave each other everything.

I apologised, as best I could, and Karl was cool as fuck about it, because he's a great bloke. Which just made me feel worse. I felt like life was spinning out of control. On the surface – on one level – things were looking good. I'd got married, I'd moved to Hawaii, and I was finding my feet there. Scratch a little deeper, and things weren't so rosy. Nikki wasn't talking to me, I felt guilty about my dad, and I missed my mates. Being somewhere new – however beautiful – was stressful, and I wasn't quite aware of it, but I was fighting off depression.

When I went back to Hawaii at the beginning of 2007, life went downhill very fast. Nikki wasn't happy at all. She told me she didn't see the point in us anymore. I thought

If you think I've been through all this for you to walk away and call a stop to it, if you think I'm going to just sling my hook, you can forget it.

But depression hit. A depression as bad as any I'd ever had. If I'd been in Highgate looking at the balcony, I'd have jumped. That's how bad it was.

Every day was horrible. Painful. I was in the most beautiful place in the world and it felt toxic, and foul, and empty. I was back working for Al the Italian in the furniture store, heading in there on my scooter when it worked because Nikki wouldn't lend me her car, and all I could think of was how to escape the pain. How to end it all. I'd never been big on plans, but now I was busy making one. I wanted a five-day plan which would get all of this over by the end of the week. I considered driving the scooter into the back of a bus, but that wouldn't be fair on the driver. I thought of heading out somewhere beautiful, like Ka'ena Point, slitting my wrists and bleeding out with the sound of the surf, but that wouldn't be fair on whoever found me. Everything had a hitch. Then I had a brainwave.

I could join Waikiki gun club, get my hands on a gun, and blow my head off.

This made sense. And knowing I had a way out from the depression gave me a kind of release. It sounds weird, but I was happy working out the details, planning how I'd join the gun club, learn to fire a gun, then turn it on myself. I know people say folk who kill themselves are cowards. I'm not so sure. I think it takes a lot of courage to reach the point where you say *I'm going to do this*, and then work it out and follow it through. Not actually doing it can be the cowardly thing, sometimes. That was the way my brain worked at the time, anyhow.

One day I was back in the apartment, and I picked up the phone book. Somehow I found the number for the Samaritans. In my mind, my choices were clear. It was the

Samaritans, or it was Waikiki gun club. One or the other. So I dialled the Samaritans, and got through to an answerphone. Typical. I left some kind of message - I don't even know what I said - hung up, and thought

Right, gun club it is then.

And then the phone rang, with some guy from the Samaritans - who actually sounded like he cared - ready to listen to whatever I needed to say.

By the end of the phone call I had an appointment to see some woman at one of the churches down in Honolulu. I went down there on the scooter after work, sat outside, and waited. I knew this was stupid. How could I talk to someone I didn't even know? Why would they ever want to listen? This was pointless, a complete waste of time.

Then this beautiful black woman came out and introduced herself, told me she was called CJ, asked if I'd like to talk to her. *Well, why not? I'll give it a shot.* I started talking and everything I'd ever done, everything that had ever bugged me or eaten me up just gushed out. I expected CJ to look like she didn't give a fuck, but she didn't. She stayed there, and she listened, and she looked like she certainly *did* give a fuck. I couldn't believe it. I'd told myself the Samaritans would just be bullshitters. Now it seemed they weren't. We talked for an hour, maybe longer. By the time I'd finished talking, the gun club wasn't really an option any more.

CJ suggested that, seeing as Nikki and I weren't talking, it might be good if we both came and talked to her. So a week later I was back at the same church, with Nikki, and she got a chance to talk about what was bugging her. Which was difficult to hear, to be honest, but now she felt better too. After a couple of these meetings I felt much better, Nikki and me were getting on better, I felt positive again, and when I walked out of CJ's office Hawaii was the beautiful open green place it had been when I first arrived.

There was just one snag. CJ wanted me to have a plan. I couldn't believe it. What was it with people and their plans? I hated plans. Getting me to make one was like pulling teeth.

What do you want, Ross?
Nothing.
You must want something.
Not really.
Well, what would make your life better?
I... no, it's stupid.
What is it?
I'd like... er... a green card.
OK. So if we make a list -
I've never made a list in my life.
If we make a list and put 'green card' on it...
Uh-huh.
... and you can tick it off when you get it, will that make you happy?
I guess.
Will it make you happy, Ross?
Yes. It'll make me happy.

So, courtesy of CJ's cajoling, I made my list. It had just one thing on it. *Get green card.* And a little while later, I did. Which meant I was able to put a tick by the only thing on the only list of the only plan I've ever made.

That counts as pretty good in anybody's book.

Suddenly, life was looking up. I had a green card, I'd passed my driving test. I was teaching the Brazilian cagefighters how to speak English, which meant they were saying things like

Everyone's a twat.

I was very proud of that. No-one in Hawaii could understand them. I was proud of that, too. At work, Al had thrown me the keys to the 10-ton truck full of furniture – *Here's the list. Go make the deliveries* – which meant I'd gone from building furniture in the back of the store to driving the truck round the island. Which is how I came to be up the side of a mountain, in the truck, with two Brazilian cage-fighters, looking out to sea. The Pacific Ocean is laid out in front of us, there isn't a cloud in the sky. We're sitting there in silence, enjoying the moment.

What do we think of that, guys?
Everyone's a twat, Ross.

Perfect.

It couldn't last, of course. On my birthday Al rang from the furniture store. The cagefighters had fucked up an order and he reckoned it was all my fault. So he hurled abuse down the phone at me and hung up. When I went into work next day he wouldn't apologise – typical short man, typical boss – and I ended up going for him. The cagefighters dragged me off him, and his wife with the unfeasibly large breasts came downstairs from the office and screamed at me to get out.

My pleasure!

So I left, and went looking for work. First I answered an ad for a stagehand to work with a magician. I got the job, then I learned what they wanted me to wear. They wanted me to stand on stage in a pair of black latex trousers, topless, with white cuffs round my wrists. I was a bit pasty, but they reckoned they could bronze me up. I knew what that meant – I'd look like a fucking Chippendale.

No thanks, guys. I'll give it a miss.

Over the next year or so I moved from job to job. First I worked at Cirque de Hawaii, operating motors for people coming out of roofs. Then I worked for an agency at Sears, refurbishing the store, getting high on cleaning fluid all day. After that I got myself a job doing removals for George the Hungarian, who had been a satanist trapeze artist but had now turned to god – really – and who had a fleet of wagons which just about rolled and were held together by duct tape and prayer. When I stopped working for George I started working with a bunch of Samoans, liquidating hotels. I loved it. I was living in Hawaii, working with the locals, picking up the local pidgin, having the time of my life.

But Nikki had a plan.

She wanted us to move to San Diego.

separation

To this day neither of us know why we thought it would be such a good idea.

We left Hawaii just as it seemed that everything was going well. Nikki had built up her flower business and got a good network of contacts, I had work, and we both had enough free time to have a decent social life. Occasionally I'd get up and play 'Blitzkrieg Bop' in a Ramones cover band in one of Hawaii's bars, and Nikki had taken up rollerderby. I didn't understand the sport myself, but seeing as it was girls in short skirts ripping chunks out of each other, there didn't seem to be much not to like.

We were finally getting into the Hawaiian way of life, and now she wanted us to leave these eight little islands out in the middle of the Pacific, and move to San Diego. It made no sense.

It didn't go well, either.

Before we left Hawaii, I used my new skills on the computer to book us a hotel in San Diego so we'd have somewhere to stay while we looked for an apartment. The one I picked looked OK - pretty enough, and not too expensive - but when we arrived it was pretty clear that the truth was it was the local knocking shop. Nikki wasn't happy about that. We moved to another hotel. Then we rented an apartment, with a pool. By now things had got a bit fraught.

Don't get me wrong, San Diego's lovely, but it was a poor second-best to Hawaii. We couldn't find jobs anywhere. Or at least I couldn't. Every day I'd sit down at the computer and look for work. In the six months I was there I applied for over one thousand jobs, and fired off more than one thousand emails. I got two replies. In six months I got myself one day's work doing removals. That was it. I couldn't survive on that, even if Nikki and I had been getting on. But we weren't. She thought I was doing fuck all, drifting back into my old ways, and I couldn't understand why she'd dragged us away from Hawaii. Each of us was pissed off with the other, and we were slowly but surely drifting apart.

After six months I took my only other option. My safety net was being able to earn money back in the UK, so I flew back to Birmingham, started working for Stagecraft again, and got back into gigging with GBH.

I was pretty much homeless. I'd sleep on the floor at Pedro's house, or I'd stay in a room in one of the pubs in Digbeth. Then I got a cheap room - the box room - in a house with some of the Stagecraft crew. All the time I was sending money back to Nikki, and resenting her for leaving Hawaii. And she resented me too. After a while she stopped answering the phone. Then she got a roommate. Then she didn't want me to send money over anymore. Then she moved somewhere new. The marriage was hanging on by the skin of its teeth. In my ideal world I'd have been in the band, and I'd have been in the States too, but 6500 miles is a big ask for a regular commute - for work or a marriage - so that wasn't happening.

I felt like a failure, and I was pissed off - obviously - but it wasn't the end of my world. When things had finished with Karen, and I'd been homeless and rootless and lost, I'd gone through a really dark spell. This time I wasn't. Even if things were falling apart between me and Nikki, I knew she'd done me a power of good. When I'd met her and fallen in love with her, I knew that if I was going to make any attempt to make things work between us, I was going to have to change. I had to grow up, if you like.

That meant Nikki dragged me screaming and kicking into the 21st century. I can honestly say, if I hadn't met her, I don't think I'd be here today. I'd probably have taken a header off the Highgate balcony years ago. She taught me there's more to life than ordering another double vodka at the bar. While I was with her, I got my first computer, I learned how to drive, and I moved halfway round the world to live somewhere new. My confidence built and built and built. So even though we were going our separate ways and I was having a rough time, I knew I could do anything. I could go online and book a ticket and be feral anywhere in the world I wanted. I wasn't trapped.

When I left Karen, I'd been lost. All I'd known to do was spend day after day getting pissed, and taking drugs. Nikki had forced me to rise to the challenges she'd set. She'd made me agree to a two-year plan I couldn't remember, and she'd kept on pushing, and that meant that now, instead of crumbling, I had the armoury to take care of things. I'd learned to take care of myself.

That was a very big deal.

There was another big deal in the offing, too.

For the two years I'd been in the States, I hadn't seen Jock at all.

While I'd been in Hawaii, Jock had been hanging out in LA with Bridget, his daughter from his marriage to Lia. The two of us had kept in occasional contact by text, but that was it, and although I flew back to play bass when GBH toured with Rancid, Karl was on guitar. Jock stayed in LA. Even when Bridget moved back to Texas to be with her mom, he stayed on, and turned into a street person. For quite a few months he hung out on Venice Beach with the homeless artistes, sleeping under the stars and adopting a monster dog called Roberta, who was the size of a horse. I think he loved every minute of it, because Jock's a proper bohemian given half the chance, so that crowd were right up his street.

In the end, though, he had enough of it, rang Lia, and asked if she could help him out. So she drove all the way from Texas to LA - which is a thirty-hour drive if you do it straight through, or three days if you take it easy - collected Jock and his monster dog, and drove them both back to Texas. For a while he lived with her and Bridget, and now he was coming back to Brum.

It was great to see him. It had been a couple of years since we'd all been together - Micky and Karl had been filling in - and you could tell Colin was happy to have Jock back. Now he had his team back together. Jock and I had gone off and had our adventures, while Colin had been busy keeping HMS GBH afloat on the high seas of punk rock, and now we were all back together again and it was as comfortable and familiar as ever. It was as if we'd never been apart. As if we'd just stepped back in the rehearsal studio after nipping out to the chippy. It felt good.

It felt very good.

It felt like time for an album.

perfume & piss

While I'd been in Hawaii Colin had sent me demo tapes of some new songs, with Micky on bass – which was a bit weird – and Karl on guitar. Listening to them was so traumatic I must have erased it from my memory, because I can't for the life of me remember what they were like. It's very strange to hear your band, playing without you. And the tapes had arrived at a point when I hadn't picked my bass up for months. I was just playing an acoustic and thinking about learning the ukulele. Every day I'd see school kids at bus stops, and just about all of them had schoolbooks and a ukulele under one arm, and a chicken under the other – don't ask me why – and I thought if they could play it then I could probably play it too. It would make a change from bass guitar.

So I started playing the ukulele. If I'd stayed in Hawaii long enough I might have adopted a chicken too.

Meanwhile, back in the UK, Tim and Lars from Rancid had got in contact with Colin to say they were thinking of signing us to their label, Hellcat. We'd always remained mates with Rancid – chiefly with Lars, because he'd ended up staying with us in Brum for a while when he'd been over with the UK Subs – ever since Lars and Tim had sneaked into our gig in San Francisco all those years before. Now they were successful, and were in a position to give us a helping hand, and they did. They always have. In 2001, when I was using some old plank of wood or other for a bass, Lars took me over to Rancid's rehearsal studio in Oakland, and Matt their bass player gave me one of his '75 Fenders. It was unbelievably generous, and I was deeply touched. Being me, I took the piss so I could hide my embarrassment, and complained

262

they hadn't given me a '71, but I know Rancid are proper punk rock family, who put their money where their mouth is. We owe them - hugely - and I know they've helped other bands out too. They're stand-up guys and I won't hear a word said against them.

So we signed to Hellcat, and then we got on with recording *Perfume and Piss*. This would be our first album since 2001, which is quite a long time when you think about it, but it was well worth waiting for.

I didn't enjoy recording it, though. We went into a studio in Birmingham, and there were songs we were recording which I was hearing for the first time. I'd no memory of the demo tapes, and so all the songs were alien to me. Normally, it's good to have got into a song before you record it, so you can play around with it, but this time I couldn't. On top of that, my fingers were hurting because I hadn't picked my bass up in so long, and all this added together to make me feel like I'd lost my mojo entirely. I can listen to old recordings, stuff I've done on other albums, and - even if it wasn't technically brilliant - there was a bit of imagination in there. But on *Perfume and Piss*, I just picked out the root notes.

I might have been stressed out, but Jock was on fire. He was coming out with all kinds of good shit, layering leads and harmonies, and as tight as he'd ever been. Two years in LA had done him no harm at all. The album is a top album, even though I struggled in the studio. I felt exposed, and I didn't like the way I sounded, which made me angry. So when I listen to the album, while I think the production's great, from my point of view - personally, and listening to my performance - it does very little for me.

All of which goes to show how your experience in the studio doesn't necessarily match the experience of the people who buy the music and take it home and listen to it. Because

Perfume and Piss was released on Hellcat, thanks to Lars and Tim, and from what I can see, everyone's got it. We got great feedback on it, but don't ask me how it sold. When it comes to stuff like that, no-one in GBH has a fucking clue. We're the same when it comes to merchandise. Everyone has GBH t-shirts, hardly any are ours. All I can really tell you about the success of *Perfume and Piss* is that it seemed a lot of people liked it, and it raised our profile, and we went off on tour on the back of it. GBH were hitting the road again.

Andy Somers at the Agency, who'd stuck with us since forever, bless him, organised a huge tour of the States, from one coast to the other, with a bunch of reactionary left-wing troubadours called Outernational. Musically, we were chalk and cheese. They're folky, with rock and reggae influences, they play harmoniums, and they're musically unique. But they're good musicians, and they're good lads, too. They had one song 'The Fighting Song', which Tom Morello of RATM - who was mates with them - had done vocals on, and when he heard they were going on tour with us, he warned them to be careful. I've no idea what he warned them to be careful of, but for some people we've got this reputation. Maybe they think we're drug-addled, thieving psychopaths. Who knows? Like most bands we've toured with, Outernational got on with us fine once they'd met us rather than worried about the myth, and we had some great adventures.

Every night I'd join them on stage and play ukulele on one song. During the tour there were a few crowds where they didn't go down too well, but they took it on the chin. Then we played Arizona.

Arizona had just passed this law where anyone who even *looked* hispanic could be stopped and searched. It's ironic when you consider that Arizona used to be part of Mexico, but there you go... So while Outernational were on, Miles the singer decided to make a little speech about what a bullshit law this was. And there were a good few Arizonans in the crowd who didn't like this. Down by the side of the stage where I was waiting with my ukulele, you could feel the atmosphere getting nasty.

Oh dear. Tools down, lads, it's another Detroit.

But instead of backing down, instead of thinking *Oh fuck what have I started?* Miles just looked out at the audience and said *Yeah, whatever. You just get your confederate bandanas out and go home and listen to Lynyrd Skynyrd.*

That just riled them up even more. I still hadn't done my ukulele spot, and I was looking at it thinking it wouldn't be anything like as much use as a bass when the fighting started, because I knew for a fact we were going to get batted off the stage. But we got away with it, somehow, by the skin of our teeth. Miles said his piece and we lived to tell the tale. They were a great band. So were Bronx, Krumb Bums, Whole Wheat Bread, and all the other bands we've played with. Fantastic people.

It was a great tour. We did some live TV as well, which is always good, and then we flew back to the UK for a few gigs there and in Europe before the next big chunk of gigs. We were off on our first ever tour of Australia and New Zealand, sandwiched in between two tours of Japan.

The whole trip was amazing. We knew Japan would be good, but Australia and New Zealand were too. Two new countries we'd never been to, and we went down well. The crowds were good for the most part, though I remember Perth being a bit quiet, and at Melbourne, the security were a bit heavy-handed. Midway through our set they grabbed this kid who was stage-diving. And instead of walking him out of the building, or throwing him out to the side of the crowd, they bundled him through this little door. I couldn't see what they were doing, but it didn't look like it was going to be good. So I jumped down and followed them. Sure enough, they were giving him a good pummelling. So I stepped in and took him back on the stage, where I knew he was safe. He was happy about that. He was from Colombia, and at the end of the night he came backstage, got everyone to be quiet, and made a big speech about how the people of Colombia thanked me for saving his life. I don't know about that, but the bouncers certainly wouldn't have done him any favours. I was talking to one of them outside later, and he told me they hadn't been best pleased with me stopping their recreational activities. When I dived in and stopped them it was touch and go whether I'd get my face pummelled too.

Nice guys.

That was just a blip, though. All in all, it was a complete buzz playing new places after so many years in GBH. In Perth, our mate Minnie the Minx - who has her own flying school - took me and Danny for a flight the morning after the gig. We got up at 6am, headed out into the bush, and Min took us up in the ricketiest old plane she could find. You felt every little pocket of air. If the wind blew, you felt the plane being taken with it. I loved it and I wondered what the fuck I was doing, all at the same time. It was another incredible GBH experience in a long list of incredible GBH experiences. From Perth we went back to Japan to finish the tour off. That turned out to be one of our best tours there ever, too.

That *Perfume and Piss* tour was the best way possible to get back into life in GBH. Jock and me had both had some time off and now we were back, we'd knocked out a brilliant album - even if I hadn't enjoyed making it - and we'd gone to the

States, to Japan, to New Zealand, and Australia. I couldn't believe how lucky we were. None of us could. It was a hell of a way to get back into things.

We'd been together thirty years, through thick and thin, and things just kept getting better.

gary critchley

GBH have never been known as a political band. Some bands wear their heart on their sleeve, and are always calling for the overthrow of this or the ending of that. We haven't. It doesn't mean we haven't got strong feelings or opinions, and people who know us well know what they are, but Colin's always had the freedom to write about whatever he likes, without having to worry about toeing the party line.

In 2010, though, we got well and truly involved in one campaign. It was the campaign to free Gary Critchley.

Gary was an old friend who'd been on the Birmingham punk scene back in the late '70s. He'd been at the first gig I ever did with GBH, that night I was scared shitless upstairs at The Crown. Just another face in the crowd. Someone who liked the same music as the rest of us, and didn't like the system.

In the summer of 1980, he went down to London to stay in a squat for a couple of weeks. One night, he was found crumpled up on the ground outside the squat, covered in blood, with a hammer wound to his head. He'd jumped out of a window fifty feet up and broken his back, his ankle, and a wrist. When the police checked the room he'd jumped from, they found the guy Gary had been sharing the room with was dead. He'd been beaten to death with a hammer. Gary got the blame.

I remember seeing him back in Brum before the trial. Gary was on bail and on crutches, and he said he'd never killed the guy, but his memory about what had actually happened wasn't too clear. He was sent to trial and found guilty of murder, with a recommendation he served 8-9 years. He was just seventeen years old.

Time went by. GBH were doing our thing, gigging and making records, and - like everyone else - I took it for granted that Gary had been released, that he was out there somewhere getting on with his life. So it came as a bit of a shock to find out that he was still inside. After all, it was thirty years since he'd first been convicted. A friend of ours, Carol, said he was in an open prison in Norwich and gave me the number, so I ended up chatting with him on the phone. I knew - vaguely - that there were miscarriages of justice, I'd never expected to find one happening to a mate.

Next thing you knew, people had got together and started a campaign to get him out. Let's be clear about one thing - getting that campaign off the ground was nothing to do with us. It was all down to Julie, Wendy, Tom, Sharon, and Carol, old Birmingham punks, who put in the hard yards, worked their arses off, and did everything they could to get Gary's story in the public domain. Because it was quite a story.

You see, Gary had been convicted of murder on the flimsiest of evidence. The hammer which had been used as the murder weapon didn't have a single one of his prints. Even though the poor bastard who'd been murdered had bled to death, and his blood was all over the room, not a drop of it was on Gary. Witnesses, who had seen other people entering the room, weren't called in court. No-one had seen Gary be violent, in any way, ever. And finally, Gary had always, relentlessly, maintained his innocence. Despite this, he'd been convicted of murder when he'd gone to trial, his appeal - a year after being sentenced - had been turned down, and the system had shipped him from one jail to another. For thirty years.

The campaign set out to raise public awareness, to make a song and dance about the fact Gary was still inside and should never have been there in the first place. They got MPs involved. They got letters of support from the Pope and from Downing Street and made sure they got that story in the papers. They refused to go away.

We just did what we do. We strapped our guitars on and we did some gigs to help raise money so the campaign could keep going, could post out letters and print flyers and contact lawyers to look at the case again. We wore the t-shirts, and we took Gary's story wherever we had a gig. That was the only part we played. Carol and Sharon and Wendy and Julie and Tom did the work. And they succeeded, too.

It really gets me when people say if you don't vote you can't complain, you've got no voice and you're sitting back and doing nothing. Rubbish. I was born into a political and social system which I don't agree with, but I have to exist within it and get by as best I can. You get screwed over whoever you vote for, so why should I vote for who's going to do it? Voting is one day every five years. It's what you do with the rest of your time that matters. Being involved with the Gary Critchley campaign and trying to right an obvious wrong did more good - just with that - than putting a mark on a piece of paper ever will.

In March 2012, Gary was finally released from prison after being in jail for over thirty years for something he'd never done. His imprisonment was a miscarriage of justice as blatant as they come. Now that's been set right.

But it's not over. The next step is to get him pardoned.

reflection

When GBH finished touring Australia and New Zealand, I went back to the States. Nikki still wasn't talking to me, and it was pretty clear my life was my own again, so I decided I'd go and visit a lady friend in mid-Texas, and spend Xmas with her.

I'd planned to fly to Dallas, get a hire car, and drive to her house. But my plans went tits up early on. First the plane out of Birmingham was delayed by ice. That meant I missed my connection at Schiphol in Amsterdam, had to stay in a hotel overnight, and take another flight to Dallas in the morning. When I got to Dallas, my luggage had gone missing. So much for a relaxing trip abroad. By the time I'd driven to her house in the hire car, I was in a foul frame of mind. I had no luggage, I had no clothes, I didn't want to speak to anybody, and above all I didn't want to be with anybody. My plans for a lovely Xmas weren't working out at all.

I was like a bear with a sore head and I knew I was taking it out on the woman I was with. This wasn't working, and that wasn't fair. So on Xmas Eve, I got her to drop me off at a hotel a couple of miles from her house, and I booked in there. I knew I needed to plan a way out, but to do that I needed my computer, and that was stuck in the luggage I hadn't got, which had gone missing somewhere between Amsterdam and Dallas. So I spent all Xmas Eve on the phone to the airline, chasing it down. In the end, some other airline - who'd got nothing to do with the one I flew with - rang up to say they had my bag. It was sitting in an office next door to the place I'd been ringing, and it had been there all along. Some bloke brought it over. And this being the US, he expects a tip.

A tip? Fuck off or you'll get my foot up your arse.

So on Xmas Day morning I'm sitting on my own in an empty Denny's across the road from the hotel, with a Corona and a club sandwich with fries. Am I depressed? No. I've got my computer. I finish my sandwich, head back to my room with my Corona, get all the writing paper out of the desk, lay it out on the bed, and make a list of every airport on the east coast. Then I make a list of every flight up and down the eastern seaboard, because – just to complicate things a little – there's a big storm coming in, and airports are going down like ninepins.

It takes me nine or ten hours work, and by the time I'm done I've not only worked out a flight plan, I've become a weather expert as well. I've been busy getting all the weather reports for all the airports, crossing off the flights that are being cancelled because the snow's coming in, and then crossing off the connections that means I can't get, and I've worked out a route. I can get a flight from Austin to the smaller airport in DC, then another flight from there to Allentown, Pennsylvania, which is 160 miles from Queens, which is where I want to go. And from Allentown, I've booked myself a hire car to drive myself into Queens.

That's the plan, anyway. I get to DC and the snow's coming down like you wouldn't believe. I'm looking out of the plane window at the snow building up on the wings, and the guys coming out to de-ice them. The snow's so heavy they have to do it all again the moment they've finished. It's touch and go, but we take off in a blizzard just before they close the airport down. At 1.30am, we land in Allentown. Wonder of wonders, there's still someone working in the office of the hire car company, so I'll be in Queens by morning. As I toddle up to the desk, I notice some other bloke walking away with a set of keys.

They've given him my car.

I'm about to give the bloke behind the desk an earful, when he pulls down the shutters, locks the door, and fucks off home for the night. I'm on my own in Allentown airport. There's only one thing to do. I put my bag under my head for a pillow, and sleep on the floor for a few hours till the office opens again and I can get my hire car. On Boxing Day morning, there I am, driving through Manhattan with snow piled up six feet deep around me, on my way to Queens to hang out with Danny, Antony, and Frank, the guys who I'd been drinking with when I first met Nikki.

I was pleased as punch with myself. Getting there had been a huge challenge, but I'd done it. I'd sat down with a list of all the airports and all the flights and the weather forecasts, and I'd worked my way through it. I knew all too well that if that had happened five years earlier, I'd have been stuffed, because - before I met Nikki - none of that would have been possible.

Nikki had shown me how to get used to the idea of plans when she badgered me into a two-year plan when she first got to Brum. She shown me how to change the way I lived my life, and in doing that she hadn't so much shaken things up as just put me in a bag and kicked the living crap out of me.

Naturally, she'd done it for my own good.

Now, even though I'd been dragged along kicking and screaming at the time, I knew I could deal with pretty much anything. And on my own, too. So I was understandably proud that I'd plotted a route across the US instead of just sitting in a bar.

At the same time, I knew that the whole reason I'd had to plot that route was because I'd had to leave Texas in the first place. I still wasn't much good at dealing with people, and sometimes – especially when I was stressed – I was a nightmare. If I was uncomfortable, I lashed out. If I was in a foul mood, I got locked-in and angry, and whoever was around me suffered. As I motored through Queens there was one question nagging away at me, and it wouldn't go away.

Why did I behave like such a cunt sometimes?

Maybe it was time to work out what was going on inside my head.

revelation

I knew I'd always been a bit weird.

On the one hand, there was my excessive shyness. Even as an adult, I won't go to the doctor's on a Monday morning because I know it'll be full of people, and that makes it too busy for me to deal with. As a teenager, I'd been even worse. I'd been so scared of girls that I made funny noises rather than talk to them. I'd been so scared of letting a mate see me play guitar that I made him stand outside my bedroom door to listen. How I ever managed to get on stage in front of hundreds of people with GBH, I'll never know.

On the other hand, if I do ever talk to someone, I expect them to be friends for life.

In 1981, when GBH played The Mayflower in Manchester supporting Discharge, I bumped into MJ, the singer from The Drones. I went *Do you remember me, then?* as though he was my best friend, and he looked at me blankly. So I reminded him how they'd played Brum on a Bank Holiday four years earlier and picked up two punks to help him find their way to the gig. There's an awkward pause, then he goes *Yeah! Right!* and I realise he doesn't remember it at all. Why should he? But I meet someone once and think they'll be my best friend forever. When I was nine I met Trevor Francis - the Blues player - in Baines's cake shop in Sheldon, and got his autograph. He'll have forgotten it the moment he walked out the door, but if I ever met him again, I'd expect him to remember it, and be hurt if he didn't.

I'm not daft. I know it's naive to think like that, but it's how I am. In Hawaii, it drove Nikki mad.

Not long before I moved there, I'd worked the Backstreet Boys at the NEC in Brum, and at the end of the show the main man walked past me and said *Thanks for your help.* Just that. Nothing more. In my book, that made us mates, and every time they came on TV I'd tell Nikki *That's my best mate, my man from the Backstreet Boys!* and she'd roll her eyes and tell me to shut up. One day we went out for a walk, down at Ka'ena Point, and when we got back to the car park, there he was.

Wow. What are the chances of that?

I want to go up and say *Hey! It's me!!* but he's having an argument with his girlfriend, which might mean that even if he does remember me, and even if we are best mates, this isn't quite the right time. *Nah, I'm sure it'll be fine.* I'm on my way across the car park to say *Hi!* and Nikki stops me. And even though I know she did the right thing – because I would have made a complete prat of myself – I still wish I had. We're at Ka'ena Point, 8500 miles from anywhere, and he's there too. I could have walked right up to him and said *NEC, mate? Remember me from the NEC?*

He'd have loved it, I know it.

Nikki couldn't grasp how I'd want to stride up to people I barely knew who I'd only met once, or stand on stage in front of hundreds of people, but be traumatised by setting foot in a crowded restaurant. We'd have rows because I'd look through the window of a restaurant and say it was too busy. She'd be straight in there, no problem, grabbing the last free table, settling herself in. It wouldn't matter to her in the slightest that it was next to the queue for the bar or the entrance to the kitchen, but it set my teeth right on edge to be so close to strangers. I wouldn't be able to eat because just sitting there was enough to make me break out in a cold sweat. I'd find it genuinely traumatic. She'd think I was ruining the evening for the sake of it.

What sent her over the edge were my obsessions.

I can get obsessed over the weirdest things. In Hawaii, I got obsessed about the mongoose. They were introduced to kill rats, I think, but seeing as one comes out by day, and the other one by night, it was a complete waste of time taking them over there at all. Except that it made me really happy to see them. I love mongoose. Unfortunately, that love grew into an obsession. Before long, I couldn't see a mongoose without shouting and pointing it out as we drove past.

Whaaaaa!!
What the fuck is it??!!
A mongoose!! Over there!!
Fuck's sake, Ross! I nearly crashed the fucking car!!

I wasn't much better when we were at home. If we were sitting round making leis out of Nikki's flowers and neither of us said anything for five minutes, I couldn't bear it. I'd have to say something. Something bizarre.

Look! Gecko!
Eek! I've been attacked by a mongoose!

I was like David Attenborough with Tourettes. It got right on her tits.

As I drove into Queens that Boxing Day morning, I thought back over how I'd behaved ever since I was a kid. It had always been odd. This episode in Texas was only the latest in a long line. Why did I find it so hard to be around people and so easy to upset them?

Suddenly I had a flashback to me and Nikki in the car in Hawaii. I yelled *Mongoose!* for the third or thirteenth or thirtieth time that day, and she screamed *Fuck's sake, it's like being with some autistic kid!*

A light bulb went on in my head, and everything fell into place.

While I was in Queens, I spent a lot of time online, finding out more. I found a blog by an autistic guy, and everything he said, I related to. It was as if I could have written the blog myself. When I got back to the UK, I went to the doctor. He sat me down and did some tests and told me

Yep, you're slap bang in the autistic spectrum.

If I was a kid they'd send me off to see a specialist, apparently, but - seeing as I've blundered through life without help, and made it to my fifties - I'm classified as *functional*, which means I'm on my own. If I've made it this far without treatment, the doctor says, then I'm too old for them to bother dealing with. It's not worth it. Why my age should make a difference, I don't know, but there you go.

Since the doctor told me that, I've been on a mission. My first ever mission was to get my green card. I did. I was able to put a big tick next to that. Now I want a tick to say *Yes, Ross, you're officially retarded.* I want to brandish that piece of paper. Like Neville Chamberlain promising peace in our time, I want peace of mind in my time. I'm obsessed about it. Of course I am. I wouldn't be me without an obsession. I want a piece of paper that makes this diagnosis official, so I can explain it to people, so they know what to expect.

You see, there are things you take for granted that I have to plan to get done. If I'm catching the bus to work, I'll wait across the road, far enough away from the bus stop to feel comfortable, near enough that I can get there if I need to.

When I see the bus coming, I check how many people are on it. If there's too many people, I'll wait. If there's a fair amount of space, I'll leg it across the road so I can get on.

In rush hour, a fair few buses can go past before I'll catch one. So if I've got to be at work for nine in the morning, I'll get to the bus stop for seven. That way I won't be late. Because even if there's space on the bus, I can only get on it if the coins I'm going to pay with are stacked up in order of size, largest at the bottom, smallest at the top, with the queen's head facing up on all of them. If they aren't stacked up properly, I can't get the bus, and we're back to square one.

All those circumstances have to line up just for me to catch a bus, which means my life is complicated enough already, without factoring anyone else – and all their expectations – into the equation. It's no wonder I never wanted to make plans. Dealing with everyday life took all my concentration. That's why I want that piece of paper, to recognise that, to make it official.

Maybe one day I'll decide that the doctor just confirming I'm retarded is enough.

But not yet. For now, I'm on a mission.

family

The thing about GBH is that Colin, Jock, and me may not be the best musicians in the world, or even the best at what we do, and it might just be that if you took us out of our little world and put us in another one, we wouldn't be any good. But put us together and let us do our thing, and we are. We're really fucking good. We're a team. And that's what a lot of the best bands are, they're teams. A football team may not be the best eleven players on the planet, but get the team spirit right, and practise and put the work in, and they can beat anyone.

One of our strengths is that whatever's happened, we've kept on going, and been there for each other every time the dust's settled. Whether it was Joe with the fight, Colin walking off tour, me not turning up for rehearsals, or leaving to go to Hawaii, or Jock going AWOL in LA - whatever's happened - we've shrugged your shoulders, got on with it, left room for them to come back and not really questioned it. That's got us through some really serious situations. I know it's a cliché to talk about punk rock family, but within GBH I think it's true.

I've done gigs where I've had to play lying down on the floor because I've been pissed or E-ing my tits off or whatever. I've still managed to play, but for the life of me I couldn't stand up. I've banged out the songs flat on my back with my feet up on the monitor, and when we've finished the set I've crawled off the stage. And never once did Colin or Jock go

You're a fucking disgrace, do that one more time and you're out.

280

My daughter had a go at me, but that's another story.

We bear the scars of being on the road, but – generally – we've only ourselves to blame. I broke my hand hitting a door. Scott got pissed and broke his collarbone a week before a tour of Japan. He had to have a plate fitted to hold the bone together, but he still came with us, and still drummed even though doing it was agony – you could see the collarbone moving and the plate lifting off underneath it – and he was just about passing out with the pain. But then Scott's done gigs where he's so pissed he doesn't know which way is up.

He even lost us a gig at a big festival in Eindhoven – and cost us a lot of money and let the promoter down – because he was out getting wankered and we missed the plane. That was a bit bad, even for us, and we had to give him his final warning. He's used it up a good few times since, mind, and he's still in the band, because – whatever his personal demons are – he's a real good mate, and we love him. Same as we love Jock, who likes to have a drink and crawl in to bed with the proprietors of wherever it is we're staying. I can't think how many times I've found him curled up in bed between two other people who go *Well he just came in and made himself comfortable…*

So we stick together through a lot of things, but we do let each other know when we've been idiots. We were doing a gig in Newcastle once, and Colin was hanging upside-down off the truss at front of stage. You always get your money's worth with Colin as a front man, but on this night he's made the mistake of calling Alan Shearer *Mary Poppins*, so some outraged Geordie pulls him off the truss for his pains. Colin hits the floor, dislocates his shoulder and breaks his collarbone, and then to add insult to already substantial injury the guy hits him and blacks his eye. Colin stumbles away, and we finish the set. There were only a couple of songs left, as I remember, so it was no big deal. A few hours later Colin comes back from A&E, all bandaged up. He got no sympathy from us. *What d'you expect, you muppet. You shouldn't call Alan Shearer 'Mary fuckin Poppins' in Newcastle!*

He's stopped drinking now. For over a year. Ever since the Moscow incident.

It was our first ever show there, 1000 people were crammed into the venue, and there was one toilet somewhere in the building. We hadn't a hope of finding it, because we couldn't even leave the dressing room. The place was too full. So we spent all day working our way through the rider - which was vodka and beer - and pissing in the bin. By the time we went on stage, we were wasted. Colin started by lifting his t-shirt up and playing with imaginary tassles on his nipples, and things went downhill from there. None of us were at our best. I think the audience were fine with it, but then they were in a venue with one toilet, so it's safe to say their expectations were pretty low.

Colin wasn't happy. Two weeks later we did a gig in Northern Ireland and he spent all day drinking wine. He remembers doing the gig and then the rest of the day is a complete blank. The next thing he knew he was standing in his own hallway back in Brum with his wife staring at him, with no idea how he got there. That shook him up every bit as much as Moscow. After that, he gave up the booze.

He's Dr Pepper all the way now, and - to be honest - our shows have got a lot less shambolic. Over the years, there's probably been some gigs when people were just watching the four of us stumbling around on stage, being drunk. Probably? Definitely. But not any more. Colin's as sharp as ever on stage now, and I'm proud of him for going sober. We all are. But, whatever happens, at the end of the day we tolerate each other's bullshit and fuck-ups, and we cut each other slack. Because we're family.

Jock's daughter Bridget was part of that family too. She was living in Texas with her mom, and - from the mid-2000s onwards - whenever we toured the States, Bridget would come along with us and do the merch, staying at her post even if there was a riot going on round her. If she wasn't busy selling t-shirts, she was drinking me and Jock under the table, and if she wasn't doing that, then her and Jock would terrorise the rest of us. On one tour they decided it would be great fun to both buy walkie-talkies. For the whole tour, that's how they talked to each other. They'd use them in the van

Jock to Bridget. Over.
Go Jock. Over.
You OK back there? Over.
Fine, dad. Over and out.

After six hours in the van, we'd get to a rest stop to stretch our legs and have a smoke and and go to the toilet, and I'd be having a piss and hear Jock in the bog, talking to Bridget over the walkie-talkies.

I'm having a piss. Over.
Me too, dad. Over.
Fancy a burger? Over.

Mad stuff. She was a little hellraiser, and we all loved her. She toured with us in 2010, and visited Brum the next March. I saw her in the Wagon and Horses, at the bar with Jock. It was the last time I saw her. On August 7th, she was in Texas partying, and me and Jock were working up in

Blackpool, crewing at Rebellion. Next day I was on my way home, and for some reason I decided to give Jock a ring. He sounded distant, low, wrong.

Ross, Bridget's gone.

She'd drowned in the pool at the party. No-one knew quite what had happened, and none of us could believe it was true. Jock flew over to Texas for the funeral. I was already booked on a flight back to LA. I got there, picked up a hire car, drove down to San Diego and picked up Nikki, then back to LA to collect Toscan - our US roadie - and his girlfriend, who'd decided they wanted to come along too. The four of us packed in to a tiny little Ford Focus and drove to Texas. It took us twenty-two hours, and we missed the funeral, but that wasn't the point. The point was that we were doing something for Bridget, showing how much she meant to us.

Jock was resilient. What he was like in private, I can't say. He was - and is - a bit more sombre. He knows that we're there for him, but we haven't sat down and had a big profound talk and a hug. That's not what he wants. We let him deal with this the way he needs to, because we're mates. That's what mates do.

And on that 1500 mile road trip from LA down to Texas, it felt like Bridget was with us every inch of the way. She was a special little friend and she's sorely, sorely missed.

She was family, and we loved her very much.

feral and free

I think one of GBH's main achievements is that we just kept going, and rode our luck. We started out all those years ago, and we were brash and naive, and didn't have any idea we'd be at it this long. At the time, there weren't that many bands that sounded like us, which put us - by accident rather than design - ahead of the curve. We certainly never set out to copy anybody. A lot of people copy us, which is flattering, but we were blazing our own trail. That gave us time to improve as musicians, which was good, because the first couple of albums - even though people love them - I can't really listen to. As we got better, we created something new. I'd take a riff into rehearsals and it might have elements of Blondie, Slade, and T-Rex, all put together, and you wouldn't know I'd used any of it because the end product sounded nothing like those bands.

We were still wet behind our little punk ears when we got our first lucky break supporting Discharge and then another signing to Clay. That opened the doors to our peak years, to tracks in the *Top 40*, sell-out shows, and MTV, and also to dodgy management who milked us dry. We were too busy having fun to notice. And when the roof fell in, and the money ran out, and it could all easily have come to an end, we hung on in there. Yes, we became a bit insular, but we closed ranks on each other, like family do, and looked after each other while we licked our wounds.

Now, Colin takes care of the business side of things to make sure we get what we're due. He's very protective of that. I'm too flaky, I live day to day, there's no point asking me to organise things three months ahead, or sort out a tour itinerary for a country I don't even live in. There really isn't. We all know that.

And we have agents who make our bookings. We did try - briefly - to do it ourselves, but it's way too much. There's bands that do go DIY, bless 'em, but it sounds like a nightmare. So we've The Agency, who look after us in North America, and Wilma Productions in the Basque Country in Spain, who do the same for Europe and South America. They're not just our agents, they're personal friends, and they do their level best to help us make a living.

We've been making music and gigging for thirty-odd years. That's quite an achievement. I know some people think it means we must be rolling in money. We're not. Anyone who thinks it does knows fuck all squared, to be honest. We make a bit of money out of our music, but we do it largely for love, because we enjoy what we do and we're good at it. We still live hand-to-mouth. There's no luxury pad in the Bahamas. My aspirations are to own a static caravan in the countryside somewhere. And to move back to Hawaii. I'm nowhere near that yet.

I mean we might get a windfall if one of our tracks gets used for an advert or a commercial, but that's about it - unless someone huge decides they're going to do a cover of one of our songs. Up to now no-one has, so it looks like we'll have to get on with writing the new album, something to follow *Perfume and Piss,* and sit down with Tim and Lars and talk about recording it.

That's in the pipeline.

Personally, I've finally found a way of living I'm comfortable with, which means I'm pretty much feral. All my possessions fit in a suitcase, everything musical is in the studio in Brum or a lock-up in LA. I can go anywhere I want, when I want. I love that sense of freedom. If GBH have got nothing going on, I'll disappear into the countryside with a tent, or fly over to the States and hang out there. I'm responsible for no-one but myself, and it suits me.

I've never been good with people, but somehow - despite myself - I'm lucky enough to have friends. And two wonderful daughters. Which is incredible, because I have been paternally defunct. I haven't got a paternal bone in my body. I have very little interaction with them, so whatever they've done with their lives is down to them and their mothers. Charlotte's a probation officer working in London. Samantha, my other daughter, lives with her lovely mom Sally and is at university. I know I've not been much cop as a dad in the past, and I'm still not much cop as a dad even now. But I'm proud of them both and I love them both dearly.

Charlotte asked me to be there when she graduated in Nottingham. She wanted me to wear a suit. And I wouldn't. She said *If you loved me you would*. I hate that emotional blackmail, so I told her *If you loved me you wouldn't ask because you know what I'm like*. In the end, we compromised. I wore jeans, a shirt, and my leather jacket, and looked half presentable. God knows what she expects when she gets married.

And Nikki and I have found a way of getting on, better than we ever did. Partly that's because all the attrition is over, but spending so much time thousands of miles away from each other doesn't hurt either. We can't live together, but if she and her mom are in Europe, they'll drop by, and if I'm in the States I'll visit her in San Diego, pick up the van, and toddle off up the Pacific Highway to LA.

Juan, who's our merch guy now, lives in South LA, and he's got a nice little compound at the back of his house where I can park the van. I reverse the beast in there, and stop over. I do a bit of crew work if it's on offer, and I do any work I can with the cargo van. I've had a tasty little number delivering bouncy castles to parties – a white guy covered in tattoos putting up bouncy castles in a predominantly black neighbourhood which twenty years earlier was the scene of the LA riots – and I've worked in a team of latinos stripping out houses and sharing their food, the only white guy for miles, having the time of my life.

When I'm not working, I'm at Juan's drinking Mexican beer, eating Mexican food, and being introduced to latino punk music, because Juan plays bass for Los Crudos, who are a famous latino punk band. He's got me into the whole latino punk culture, which is a world I never knew existed. There's all these bands no-one's ever heard of who've been doing garage or punk for years, and – me being me – finding out about it has become my new obsession.

At least it makes a change from mongoose.

Life in South LA is interesting. I've watched a kid on a skateboard being chased by someone in a Merc who's trying to run him over because a drug deal's gone wrong. Across the road there's another dealer in a wheelchair, shot because another drug deal went pear-shaped. Not that it's stopped him banging it out. I did, though. Not that I meant to. But when I turned up at Juan's place in the van, which is a big white pick-up, he did no business for a week. Everyone saw the van and thought the feds were staking him out. Then he came round for a barbecue and met me and put two and two together and and put the word out, and business picked up again. It's still not without its dangers though – he's had a gang strip him naked and leave him outside his flat tied up in his wheelchair with not a stitch on him – but that hasn't put him off any more than being shot did. He's resilient. It's South LA. You have to be.

Sometimes I'll head to north LA and hang out with Toscan, and clog up his furniture, or I'll spend a few weeks driving my best friend Amy to her different tattoo conventions, or I'll fly back to the UK for some gigs with GBH or a bit of crewing there. Every August I'll work Rebellion festival in Blackpool, which is a huge festival embracing everything to do with punk. There's reggae, ska, some off the wall type shit, poetry, spoken word, an acoustic stage, something for everyone. People I know from the States will turn up with a band, and there I am, loading their gear in, which always shocks them. But I look after them, and they're happy to see me, and there's a few beers later.

Whatever I do, and wherever I am, I wake up in the morning, lie there in bed and imagine myself with a big P for punk rock over my head. I'm part of the punk rock family. Sometimes people try and tell me what is and isn't punk, or that GBH do or don't fit in, but they're generally no older than my socks, and they know about as much. I've lived my life doing what I want the way I want to ever since I got expelled from school. Ever since 1977.

That's punk rock.

My life's been an adventure. There's been some hard times, and I came too close to taking a header off the balcony, and I'm still a work in progress, but now I've got to a place where I like the way it is, where it's finally coming together. My mom and dad taught me it's how you behave and how you treat people that counts, and I do my best to live by that. Being in the band has taken me all round the world, allowed me to do things and meet people I'd never have had the chance to otherwise, and it's given me two lifelong friends in Jock and Colin.

The three of us can sit somewhere and not say a word to each other. I can go round Colin's and just sit there for an hour and neither of us will need to say a word. I can go out for a drink with Jock and we'll get a pint and sit there and say nothing, and it's fine. And there's very very few people I feel that comfortable with, where I know them that well I can be in their company and be silent, and not start freaking out. If we've got something to say we say it, we have a laugh and a joke, but we don't have to talk to each other. After all, we've been in a van with each other for thirty-two fucking years, we've said just about everything. Even Scott, who we call the new boy, has been with us nineteen years. He's been our drummer for longer than everyone else put together, but he's the new boy and he always will be.

You'd think we might be sick of the sight of each other, but we're not. I look forward to seeing them, and that's the god's honest truth. When I got up on stage for that first gig with GBH all those years ago, it wasn't the big mistake I feared. It probably saved my life.

It gave me a space where I could learn how to deal with the world. Where it didn't matter if I fucked things up because I was with mates who'd forgive me and stick with me.

It gave me family. Punk rock family.

And nothing's more precious than that.

Ignite Books is a small, independent publisher. This book is the latest in our series which we hope puts fresh, thought-provoking, entertaining writing before a new audience. We have a lot of fun doing this, but we also survive on a shoestring budget and a lot of graft. So, if you've enjoyed this book, please tell your friends about us.

You can also find us on facebook, so drop by and say hallo. And to learn more about what we do, or shop for our other publications, just visit our website at ignitebooks.co.uk

Thank you.